Tourism in Developing Countries

Martin Oppermann
and Kye-Sung Chon

INTERNATIONAL THOMSON BUSINESS PRESS

I(T)P® An International Thomson Publishing Company

London • Bonn • Boston • Johannesburg • Madrid • Melbourne • Mexico City • New York • Paris
Singapore • Tokyo • Toronto • Albany, NY • Belmont, CA • Cincinnati, OH • Detroit, MI

Tourism in Developing Countries

Copyright © 1997 M. Oppermann and K-S. Chon

First published by International Thomson Business Press

I(T)P ®   A division of International Thomson Publishing Inc.
The ITP logo is a trademark under licence.

British Library Cataloguing-in-Publication Data
A catalogue record for this book is available from the British Library

First edition 1997

Typeset by Columns Design Ltd, Reading
Printed in the UK by the Alden Press, Oxford

ISBN 0-4151-3939-2

International Thomson Business Press
Berkshire House
168–173 High Holborn
London WC1V 7AA
UK

International Thomson Business Press
20 Park Plaza
13th Floor
Boston MA 02116
USA

http:// www.itbp.com

Tourism in Developing Countries

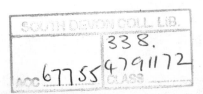

Series in Tourism and Hospitality Management

Series Editors:

Professor Roy C. Wood
The Scottish Hotel School, University of Strathclyde, UK

Stephen J. Page
Massey University, New Zealand

Series Consultant:

Professor C.L. Jenkins
The Scottish Hotel School, University of Strathclyde, UK

Textbooks in this series:

**Behavioural Studies in
Hospitality Management**
R. Carmouche and N. Kelly
ISBN 0 412 60850 2, 232 pages

**Managing Human Resources in the
European Tourism and Hospitality Industry
A strategic approach**
T. Baum
ISBN 0 412 55630 8, 280 pages

Interpersonal Skills for Hospitality Management
M.A. Clark
ISBN 0 412 57330 X, 232 pages

Hospitality and Tourism Law
M. Poustie, N. Geddes, W. Stewart and J. Ross
ISBN 0 412 62080 4, 320 pages

Business Accounting for Hospitality and Tourism
H. Atkinson, A. Berry and R. Jarvis
ISBN 0 412 48080 8, 432 pages

Economics for Hospitality Management
P. Cullen
ISBN 0 412 608540 6, 224 pages

Tourism in the Pacific
C. Michael Hall and Stephen J. Page
ISBN 0 412 12500 6, 304 pages

Managing Wine and Wine Sales
J. E. Fattorini
ISBN 0 412 72190 2, 200 pages

**Marketing Tourism, Hospitality and Leisure
in Europe**
S. Horner and J. Swarbrooke
ISBN 0 412 62170 3, 736 pages

Managing Packaged Tourism
E. Laws
ISBN 0 412 11347 4, ca. 224 pages

**Researching and Writing Dissertations
in Hospitality and Tourism**
M. Clark, M. Riley, E. Wilkie and
R. C. Wood
ISBN 1 861 52046 8, ca. 192 pages

The Business of Rural Tourism
D. Getz and S. Page
ISBN 0 415 13511 7, 192 pages

**Human Resources for Hospitality
Services**
A. Goldsmith, D. Nickson, D. Sloan
and R. C. Wood
ISBN 1 861 52095 6, ca. 224 pages

Hospitality Accounting, 5th edn
R. Kotas and M. Conlan
ISBN 1 861 52086 7, ca. 352 pages

Tourism Marketing
L. Lumsdon
ISBN 1 861 52045 X, ca. 304 pages

Tourism in Scotland
R. Maclellan and R. Smith, eds
ISBN 1 861 52089 1, ca. 304 pages

Tourism in Developing Countries
M. Opperman
ISBN 0 415, 13939 2, ca. 192 pages

Corporate Strategies in Tourism
J. Tribe
ISBN 0 415 14204 0, ca. 240 pages

Working in Hotels and Catering, 2nd edn
R. C. Wood
ISBN 0 415 13881 7, ca. 224 pages

Tourism: An Introduction
R. Youell
ISBN 0 415 13185, 5, ca. 304 pages

Books in this series are available on free inspection for lecturers considering the texts for course adoption. Details of these and any other International Thomson Business Press titles are available by writing to the publishers (Berkshire House, 168–173 High Holborn, London WC1V 7AA) or by telephoning the Promotions Department on 0171 497 1422.

Contents

Series editors' foreword   vii

Acknowledgements   ix

1 Introduction   **1**
   Development and developing countries   3
   Tourism development – a historical brief   7
   Research on tourism in developing countries   12
   Outline of this book   13
   Questions   15
   Further reading   15

2 Tourism and development   **16**
   Reasons for involvement in tourism   16
   Government and tourism   17
   International influence: tour operators and wholesalers   23
   International influence: boycotts and embargoes   26
   Summary   27
   Questions   27
   Further reading   27
   Case 1: The tourism industry in Vietnam   29

3 National tourism development   **35**
   Models to explain tourism development   35
   Measures of national tourism development   46
   Concentration or dispersal?   49
   Questions   51
   Further reading   51
   Case 2: Spatio–temporal tourism development in Mauritius   52

4 Tourism destination development   **56**
   Hill resorts   58
   Seaside resort development   59
   Urban tourism development   62
   The informal and formal sectors in tourism resorts   65
   Destination evaluation   66
   Trip Index   67
   Summary   69

Questions   70
Further reading   70
Case 3: Urban hotel location and evolution in Kuala Lumpur,
Malaysia   71

5 Demand for tourism   **79**
Motivations and attractions   79
Destination choice   83
Travel volume   88
Measures of demand patterns   93
Changing tourist types   97
Data problems   100
Questions   101
Further reading   101
Case 4: German outbound travel patterns   102

6 Tourism impacts   **106**
Resource evaluation   106
Economic effects   109
Socio-cultural effects   117
Physical effects   120
Summary   124
Questions   124
Further reading   125

7 Tourism marketing   **126**
Environmental factors influencing the growth of tourism   126
The role of NCOs   129
Marketing in the private sector: the hotel/resort industry   132
Infrastructure of the travel industry   133
Organization and deployment of the sales and marketing
department   136
Market mix and yield management   137
Questions   138
Further reading   138
Case 5: Marketing international tourism in Thailand   140

8 The future of tourism in developing countries   **146**
Changing travel behaviour   147
Health and safety   148
Quality versus quantity   151
Final reflections   155
Questions   156
Further reading   156

Bibliography   157

Index   174

Series editors' foreword

The International Thomson Business Press Series in Tourism and Hospitality Management is dedicated to the publication of high quality textbooks and other volumes that will be of benefit to those engaged in tourism, hotel and hospitality education, especially at degree and postgraduate level. The series has two principal strands: core textbooks on key areas of the curriculum; and the *Topics in Tourism Hospitality* series which includes highly focused and shorter texts on particular themes and issues. All the authors in the series are experts in their own fields, actively engaged in teaching, research and consultancy in tourism and hospitality. Each book comprises an authoritative blend of subject-relevant theoretical considerations and practical applications. Furthermore, a unique quality of the series is that it is student oriented, offering accessible texts that take account of the realities of administration, management and operations in tourism and hospitality contexts, being constructively critical without losing sight of the overall goal of providing clear accounts of essential concepts, issues and techniques.

The series is committed to quality, accessibility, relevance and originality in its approach. Quality is ensured as a result of a vigorous refereeing process, unusual in the publication of textbooks. Accessibility is achieved through the use of innovative textual design techniques, and the use of discussion points, case studies and exercises within books, all geared to encouraging a comprehensive understanding of the material contained therein. Relevance and originality together result from the experience of authors as key authorities in their fields.

The tourism and hospitality industries are diverse and dynamic industries and it is the intention of the editors to reflect this diversity and dynamism by publishing quality texts that enhance topical subjects without losing sight of enduring themes. The Series Editors and Advisor are grateful to Steven Reed of International Thomson Business Press for his commitment, expertise and support of this philosophy.

Stephen J. Page
Massey University – Albany
Auckland
New Zealand

Roy C. Wood
The Scottish Hotel School
University of Strathclyde

Acknowledgements

The authors would like to thank the following for permission to use figures and/or tables in the text: the Fördervereinr Wissenschaftliche Geographie for Figure 2.1 out of *Erdkunde*; Routledge for Figures 2.2, 4.2 and Tables 2.2, 5.2 and 6.6; the Koninklijk Nederlands Aardijkskundig Genootschap for Figure 3.2 from the *Tijdschrift voor Economische en Sociale Geografie*. We are indebted to Elsevier Sciences for their generous permission to use Figures 3.3, 3.4, 3.5, 3.6, 4.5, 4.7, 4.8 and Tables 3.1 and 6.1. The Centre des Hautes Etudes Touristiques granted permission for Figures 3.1 and 4.3. The Canadian Association of Geographers kindly consented to use of Figure 4.1. The *Journal of Cultural Geography* gave permission for Figure 4.4 and the American Geographical Society for Figure 4.6. The *Journal of Tourism Studies* granted permission to reproduce Figure 4.9 and Tables 5.9 and 5.10. The *Journal of Travel Research* provided permission for Figure 5.2. We are indebted to the *Tourism Recreation Research* for the generous permission to use Figures 4.10, 4.11, 4.12, 4.13 and 5.3. The Tourism Council of the South Pacific permitted the use of Table 5.3 and Henry Stewart Publications granted permission to reproduce Tables 5.12, 5.13 and 5.14. If any unknowing use has been made of copyright material, could the owners please contact the authors via the publishers as every effort has been made to trace owners and to obtain permission.

Figures

1.1	Origin regions of tourists to Latin America and the Caribbean	10
2.1	Transnational distribution and linkage structure of the tour operator TUI	25
2.2	Tourism between quasi-states	26
3.1	Tourist space dynamics	37
3.2	Plantation model of tourism	38
3.3	Enclave model of tourism in developing countries	41
3.4	Structural model of tourism in developing countries	42
3.5	Generalized distribution of tourist industry expenditure	43
3.6	Tourist space in developing countries	45
3.7	Hotel accommodation supply in Mauritius, early 1970s	53
3.8	Hotel accommodation supply in Mauritius, 1995	54
4.1	Tourist area cycle of evolution	57
4.2	Hypothetical cycle of tourist areas	58
4.3	Spatio–temporal development of international seaside resorts	60
4.4	Morphologic evolution of Gulf of Mexico seaside resorts	61
4.5	Seaside resort development	62
4.6	Model of urban tourism space	63
4.7	Formal and informal sector development in resort areas	66
4.8	Evolution of formal and informal sectors in resort areas	67
4.9	Trip index of Malaysian tourist destinations	68
4.10	Hotel location and distribution in Kuala Lumpur, Pre-Independence	73
4.11	Hotel location and distribution in Kuala Lumpur, 1970	74
4.12	Hotel location and distribution in Kuala Lumpur, 1980	75
4.13	Hotel location and distribution in Kuala Lumpur, 1995	77
5.1	Destination perception and decision making process	84
5.2	Tourist flow patterns	88
5.3	Tourist arrivals in ASEAN	92
5.4	Intranational flows of package tourists in Malaysia	93
5.5	Intranational flows of individual tourists in Malaysia	94
8.1	Distribution of cholera	151

Tables

1.1	Growth of world tourist arrivals	8
1.2	Tourist arrivals by world region	9
1.3	Tourist arrivals to developing countries	9
1.4	Interregional tourist flows	9
1.5	Developing countries' top destinations	11
2.1	Selected indicators of developing countries	17
2.2	Public–private ownership and direction	19
3.1	Characteristics of the formal and informal tourism sectors	44
3.2	Temporal change in Defert's Index by Malaysian states	47
3.3	Tourism intensities and densities in selected Latin American and Caribbean countries	49
3.4	Tourism development in Mauritius	55
4.1	Destination classification by percentage of tourists in the three Trip Index categories	68
4.2	Resort typology of Malaysian destinations	69
5.1	Travel motives of German pleasure travellers	80
5.2	Tourism policy priorities: the market – domestic or international	81
5.3	Multi-country itineraries of tourists to Western Samoa	87
5.4	World's top 20 tourism spenders	89
5.5	Tunisia's varying importance of origin countries using different measures	90
5.6	Tourist arrivals in selected South American countries	91
5.7	Market dependency	95
5.8	Country Potential Generation Index	96
5.9	The parameters of the Travel Dispersal Index	96
5.10	Characteristics of tourists to Malaysia by Travel Dispersal Index category	97
5.11	Family life cycle categories	99
5.12	Importance of German outbound travel in selected developing countries	102
5.13	German holiday destination choice	103
5.14	Familiarity with travel destinations	104
5.15	Previous travel experience with travel destinations	105
6.1	Composite ideograph of tourist attraction typology	108
6.2	Travel account of selected countries	110
6.3	Direct and indirect employment effects	112

6.4   Income multiplier effects   115
6.5   Sectoral distribution of tourist expenditure   117
6.6   Major impacts of tourism on the natural environment   121
7.1   Perceptual differences of South Korea between pre- and
       post- visit American tourists   131
8.1   Outbound versus inbound travel   149
8.2   International conference destinations   153

Introduction 1

For more than 40 years, tourism has been considered as an economic panacea for developing countries. Often dubbed as the white industry, it is thought to be a vital development agent and an ideal economic alternative to more traditional primary and secondary sectors. International tourism in particular from the developed to the developing countries is seen as generating crucially needed foreign exchange earnings, infusing badly needed capital into the economy of developing countries. The successful example of Spain, which managed to use tourism in its development process as an income generator, reinforced the notion that countries with 'sand, sun and sea' resources, which most developing countries incidentally have, can overcome other infrastructural, locational, and economic disadvantages and sell the tourist product. Stagnating and highly unreliable commodity prices as well as import barriers for manufactured goods in many developed nations only serve to focus the economic options on tertiary activities, with tourism undoubtedly being the most important one. For a lack of alternative development options and in view of the ever growing number of outbound tourists, most developing countries have opted for participation in the international tourism industry (Agel 1993). Especially for small developing countries with few primary resources and a small industrial base, and particularly for small microstates, tourism often constitutes the only viable economic activity within their economic means and their resource base (Lee 1987; Wilkinson 1989).

Rapid population growth, high unemployment, increasing social and regional disparities, high trade deficits, monostructured economies, and a generally high dependency on the industrialized countries force developing countries to utilize all of their available resources to survive. Among these resources are their climate, which promises a lot of sun for sun-seekers from the developed countries, exotic landscapes, people and cultures, and a usually very favourable exchange rate. In addition, the major attractions for mass tourism, sand, sun and sea, are available to all but a few of the developing countries. While some countries like Tunisia, Morocco, Mexico, and many Caribbean countries have gambled early on tourism, others like Vietnam, Laos and Bhutan have only recently joined the ranks of developing countries that are trying to benefit from international tourism. Employment and income generation, increase in foreign exchange and tax earnings, reduction of rural–urban migration, and balancing the trade account are the most often conceived goals of tourism development (Agel 1993). Yet to date, tourism often has not endowed developing countries with the envisaged economic benefits. Furthermore, a considerable number of socio-cultural and physical impacts have emerged that seriously deflect from the potential benefits that tourism can bring to developing countries when planned and managed appropriately.

A general lack of systematic treatments of tourism in developing countries can be observed. Specific issues are raised and discussed within the context of individual case studies but not in a comparative perspective of several developing countries. D. Pearce (1993) bemoans the lack of comparative studies in general: 'Studies have not built upon each other and no cohesive body of work using a comparative perspective is to be found' (1993, p. 20). Furthermore, most works concentrate on a narrow aspect of tourism and neglect other issues outside that domain. As in tourism studies in general, theoretical approaches are rare and a systematic testing of advanced theories almost non-existent. The prevalence of descriptive case studies has resulted in a vast accumulation of research work on developing countries with little applicability from one country or even destination to the next. Pearce notes that 'a lot of this [tourism] literature is seen to be fragmented and lacks a firm sense of direction' (1993, p. 1).

A bias towards studying international tourism can also be discerned. This is in line with the traditional viewpoint that tourism in developing countries consists of tourist flows from the developed to the developing countries (e.g. Tlusty 1980). Yet this perspective ignores the often larger domestic flows within developing countries, which are often not even measured, and the emergence of developing countries as major source countries (Butler and Mao 1995). In fact, in many developing countries domestic tourism is the primary demand generator and neighbouring developing countries often constitute the largest source of foreign tourist arrivals. In South America, for example, on average 69 per cent of all tourist arrivals are from within the region (Oppermann 1995c). In Central America intraregional arrivals often account for more than 50 per cent of all arrivals (Oppermann 1997). Similarly in South East Asia, neighbouring countries provide for 45 per cent of all arrivals (Chon and Oppermann 1996).

This book attempts to provide a systematic overview of tourism's potentials and pitfalls in developing countries. By treating the topic in a systematic and oriented perspective rather than taking a country by country approach, similarities and differences among developing countries are highlighted. Selected country case studies will focus on specific issues. The book brings together the fragmented literature on tourism in developing countries which consists mostly of a multitude of case studies.

This chapter introduces the readers to the complex topic of tourism in developing countries and the issues of what constitutes development and what are developing countries are discussed. This includes a reflection on the various measures of development as well as definitions of developing countries. The latter has regained renewed debate after the drastic alteration of the political landscape in the aftermath of the dissolution of the Second (Socialist) World.

The importance of tourism in developing countries is addressed in the third section (page 7). It provides a historical perspective of tourism development in developing countries and places these countries within the larger context of world tourism.

Tourism development in developing countries can be differentiated into at least four different phases which are closely interlinked with research into this topic. Tourism research in developing countries extends back more than 50 years and is almost as 'old' as tourism research in developed countries. The final section (page 13) provides an overview of the rest of the book.

DEVELOPMENT AND DEVELOPING COUNTRIES

Pearce (1989) notes that development can denote both a stage and a process of change. Yet both meanings require a measurement and, therefore, parameters to measure and an orientation of the development axis. Traditionally, in the context of nations and societies, development is commonly associated with economic situation and the most frequently used indicators have been gross national product (GNP) or gross domestic product (GDP) per capita. These measures have been heavily criticized, however, because of their limited value for international comparisons. Often expressed in US$ per capita or as per capita income, the values differ substantially between separate organizations like the World Bank and the United Nations. In addition, many people in developing countries derive a large part of their income from sources outside the registered economic activities. The informal sector in the form of subsistence production of food or the economy of the urban poor is sometimes more important than the formal sector. According to Nuscheler (1991), the informal sector employs some 60 per cent of the urban workforce and generates about 20 per cent of the national income in developing countries.

Furthermore, the expressed amounts in US$ per capita do not reveal the actual buying power of the local currency. Based on a survey by a UN research team (international comparison project), Nuscheler (1991) mentions that purchasing power parity (PPP) is two to three times higher than the per capita income would suggest. The per capita incomes also neglect the often wide disparities within developing countries between regions, social strata, urban and rural areas, men and women, etc. It also ignores the ecological, social and cultural effects of 'development' by simply viewing the monetary value of, for example, a logged forest. Moreover, it places more merit on high value items such as television than on conceivably more functional items such as writing tables or pads (Nuscheler 1991).

While GDP and per capita income still remain widely in use, other measures that integrate social aspects have been proposed. The United Nations Development Programme uses the Human Development Index (HDI) which integrates life expectancy, literacy rate and purchasing power parities (Trabold-Nübler 1991). The HDI has not remained without reproach for a variety of reasons. But it would appear that any index that integrates more than just monetary variables is a more plausible reflection of existing differences among countries.

The World Bank, in its 1991 World Development Report, suggested that 'development is the most important challenge facing the human race' (World Bank 1991, p. 1).

> The challenge of development, in the broadest sense, is to improve the quality of life. Especially in the world's poorest countries, a better quality of life generally calls for higher incomes – but it involves much more. It encompasses, as ends in themselves, better education, higher standards of health and nutrition, less poverty, a cleaner environment, more equality of opportunity, greater individual freedom, and a richer cultural life.
>
> (World Bank 1991, p. 4)

Definitions

Third World, less developed countries, developing countries, the South – they are all attempts at grouping a large number of countries into one category, often knowing that the reality is quite different. In essence, they all include the same countries with a few deviations depending on who is conducting the classification. In this book the expression developing countries will be used throughout because it is used by most United Nations organizations and, besides some other classifications, by the World Tourism Organization. While the term Third World remains widely in use, for example in publications, such as *Third World Quarterly*, *Tiers Monde*, and *Dritte Welt*, and some authors argue for its continued existence (e.g. Nuscheler 1991; Nohlen and Nuscheler 1993), it would appear obsolete with the dissolving of the Second (Socialist) World (Berger 1994; Boeckh 1993; Menzel 1991). The term less developed countries (LDC) is not used because of the common terminology problems with the term least developed countries, which is also abbreviated to LDC by international organizations although usually referred to as LLDC in the academic literature. The least developed countries are also alluded to as the Fourth World and they include 42 countries. They are distinguished from the rest of the developing countries by:

- a per capita income of less than US$355;
- a share of industrial production of less than 10 per cent;
- a literacy rate lower than 20 per cent among the population aged 15 years and above.

Countries should fulfil at least two of these three criteria and be close to the third. However, while commonly considered as the poor among the developing countries, Nuscheler (1991) advises that in India alone, which is not among these countries, more people live below these poverty levels than in all the least developed countries combined. More recently it has been suggested that the definition of least developed countries should include measures which reflect that they are 'suffering from long-term handicaps to development, in particular, low levels of human resources development and/or severe structural weaknesses' (Simonis 1991, p. 231). The proposed measures were per capita GDP and two composite indices: 'Augmented Physical Quality of Life Index' (comprising life expectancy, calorie supply, school enrolment ratio, and adult literacy rate) and 'Economic Diversification

Index' (comprising share of manufacturing in GDP, share of employment in industry, electricity consumption, and export concentration ratio). It is a reflection of the increasing recognition that development is a complex issue that cannot and should not be reduced to one economic measure alone.

The World Bank is doing just that despite their recognition that improvement in quality of life involves much more than higher incomes (World Bank 1991; see above quote). It distinguishes countries by one parameter, their per capita income. It has established three categories, low-income countries (LIC), middle-income countries (MIC), and high-income countries (HIC). It further differentiates the middle-income category into a lower and upper middle income. Using 1992 GNP data, low-income countries were those with a per capita income of US$675 or less, the lower middle was US$676–2695, upper middle was US$2696–8355, and finally the high income countries are those with US$8356 or more (World Bank 1994). Many of the oil-rich countries in the Middle East and elsewhere are among the HICs, simply because of their oil and their small population base. But as Nuscheler (1991) already pointed out, these countries often use their money for unproductive purposes and lack human capital.

Another group of countries that are often distinguished are the newly industrializing economies (NICs) or 'take-off-countries'. These are countries that often show more similarities with the developed world than with the other developing countries and the point at which to include some of them among the developing countries is increasingly hard to define. Again international organizations do not agree as to which countries should be classified as NICs. For example, while the World Bank and IWF include India, UNCTAD does not. Outstanding among the NICs are the four 'Asian tiger' countries (Hong Kong, Singapore, South Korea and Taiwan) whose per capita income is already higher than that of several European Union countries (e.g. Greece, Ireland and Portugal). However, since the 'Asian tigers' are commonly still classified among the NICs and, therefore, among the developing countries in general, they will be included as such in this book.

Whatever term is being used to group this wide range of countries, it appears fragile. The different development paths of the developing countries over the last few decades have increased rather than reduced the dissimilarities among these countries (Körner 1994; Nohlen and Nuscheler 1993). Körner intimates that the central problem of developing countries, whatever their level of development, 'is the compulsion to develop resources under strong, often rapidly increasing population pressure' (1994, p. 93). With respect to tourism, however, the developing countries share another common structure. Apart from Mexico, they are mid to long-haul destinations from the major tourist source countries in North America and Europe, mostly only or predominantly accessed by aeroplane. And, as will be shown in a later chapter, this often determines the form and type of tourism development as well as its spatial distribution.

Who is a tourist?

There are many different opinions on who should be counted as a tourist. Is everybody away from home a tourist? What is home for migrant workers?

Does one need to travel a certain distance before one graduates to a tourist? What may be an appropriate distance in large countries like Brazil, Canada, Russia or China may mean several border crossings in Europe. Is travel purpose a deciding criterion and only people on strictly pleasure trips are tourists? It is futile to ponder all the ramifications of the diverse definitions and the interested reader is referred to works by Arndt (1978/79), Smith (1995) and Przeclawski (1993) who discuss definitions of tourism and tourists at length. In the international context, the World Tourism Organization's (WTO) definition of tourists and excursionists is widely recognized despite some recurring data problems. The WTO defines as an international tourist anybody who visits another country for more than 24 hours, but less than one year, irrespective of travel purpose. Travellers remaining for less than 24 hours are defined as excursionists.

Yet there remain several data issues unresolved, especially if one attempts international comparisons or longitudinal studies. Some of the greatest obstacles one faces in analysing tourism on a supranational scale are data availability and compatibility. Even on a national level, most researchers will become frustrated at one point or other because of changes in data gathering practices, unexplained changes in the definition of tourists, non-compatibility of data from different sources, etc. In the Mexican case, for example, one can find tourist arrivals ranging from 6.4 million to 16.6 million for the year 1991 (Cockerell 1993; WTO 1994a). Some are actually visitor arrivals, others are tourist arrivals and yet others are classified as air arrivals. Who is a tourist? And should land arrivals simply be discounted? And what data to use when none is available for a longer time period? These are but three simple yet critical questions. Even relying on the same source, one may come across different figures. For example, in a special publication the WTO mentions 84 million arrivals to the Americas in 1990 (WTO 1991). This stands in contrast to 93.8 million in their annual publication (WTO 1994a).

The aforementioned problems tend to multiply when one moves from a national to a regional level since one now deals with different countries, different tourism and statistics departments, different objectives, and many more potential areas of divergence. Hence, data availability varies from country to country and a comparative study can only use, more often than not, the smallest common denominator or the simplest form of tourism data. This is usually total tourist arrivals because even in the breakdown of arrivals into different countries or regions of origin, the individual countries vary. For example, El Salvador provides a very detailed differentiation of its arrivals for 1992 (i.e. 77 tourists from Paraguay). Mexico, on the other hand, lists only its major segments, namely Canada, the United States and groups all other Latin American countries into one category of 'other C/S American countries' (WTO 1994a).

A yet larger obstacle is presented to researchers when they attempt to do a longitudinal analysis instead of the common cross-sectional study. Definition and counting practices change; detailed breakdowns of tourist arrivals may be available in recent but not in earlier years. El Salvador, for example, provides detailed data for 1991 and 1992 but not for the earlier years. Another good example of definition changes is the annual publication of tourism statistics by the World Tourism Organization. Mexico used to be included in Central America but moved to the North America section in the early 1990s. Hence, a less observant researcher may be amazed at the sudden drastic decrease of tourist arrivals to Central America and a strong growth in North America.

TOURISM DEVELOPMENT – A HISTORICAL BRIEF

Tourism in and to developing countries is almost as old as modern tourism and even in ancient times business travellers, explorers and researchers travelled within and to developing countries. Modern tourism is commonly associated with the name of Thomas Cook and his organized tours in the middle of the nineteenth century. In 1856, he initiated his first international tour through Europe. Shortly afterwards, Stangen and Cook opened their respective travel agencies in Berlin (1863) and London (1864) and soon started to offer tours to destinations and regions of today's developing world. Cook offered tours through Egypt and the Middle East from the 1870s while the Stangen agency organized its first tour of Cairo, Jerusalem, Smyrna and Istanbul in 1864 (Günter 1982). In 1878, Stangen inaugurated an 'around-the-world' trip and thus launched organized long-haul travel (Oppermann 1995b). Another infallible sign was the publication of tour guides on then already famous tourist destinations such as Bali and Egypt. Featuring a mild winter climate and many famous cultural sites, Egypt emerged as a tourist destination in the nineteenth century. It was mostly visited by wealthy people from the United Kingdom (Vorlaufer 1984), not unlike the development on the Mediterranean coast in southern France.

As early as 1914, the first official travel guide on Bali was published (Zimmermann 1990) and an average number of about 3000 tourists visited Bali annually before World War II (Oppermann 1992c), not at least due to the fact that tour operators offered it in their catalogues (Helbig 1949).

In Morocco, tourism dates back at least into the early 1920s and likely much earlier. In 1922, a Morocco Tourism Federation was established which brought 12 regional tourism bureaus under one umbrella (Mazières and Gattfossé 1937). Madras (1946) reported on a travel and tourism company that existed in 1922 and was very much involved in deluxe hotel developments at the time. Since 1920, tour operators offered sightseeing tours through Algeria and Morocco (Popp 1991) and in 1936, Morocco recorded almost 300 000 border crossings of people coming to Morocco. How many of these were tourists or excursionists remains inconclusive (Mazières and Gattfossé 1937). Considering that in 1962 about 150 000 tourist arrivals were recorded (Berriane 1978), Morocco seemed to be quite fashionable in the 1930s. Casablanca was a major stop for the transatlantic ship traffic and passengers had a day or two to explore Casablanca, Rabat or Marrakech (Mazières and Gattfossé 1937). Most arrivals, however, came by land from Algeria. Air traffic played a very minor role with just a couple thousand air passengers annually.

Collin-Delavaud (1990) refers to tourism development in Uruguay going back to 1890. Notable in that case is that the majority of this demand was domestic tourism generated by the Uruguayan elite.

In 1920, the West Indies already registered almost 80 000 visitors and this figure grew to almost 200 000 by 1938 (Blume 1963). This tropical island world was and is to a large extent a cruiseship destination which, coupled with its proximity to the United States, facilitated an early tourism development not dependent on technological developments in the airline industry. One of the foremost Caribbean destinations in the late nineteenth and early twentieth century was Cuba. Tourist resorts were developed, first for domestic and, after the war with America, for North American tourists (Bleasdale and Tapsell 1994).

Ungefehr (1988) mentions that tourist arrivals in the Bahamas grew between 1873 and 1937 from just 500 to 41 000. She also reports that hotels in the Bahamas date back at least to 1861. At around the same time, Nassau was already a stop for a passenger boats between New York and Cuba. In 1929, Pan American Airways started regular flight services between Miami and Nassau. World War II brought a temporary halt to tourism development and only in 1950 were pre-war tourist arrival figures attained.

These examples illustrate that tourism in developing countries is not an occurrence of the post-World War II era; it only increased tremendously in the last 30 to 40 years. As Tables 1.1 and 1.2 show, the colossal growth in tourist arrivals was a world phenomenon. However, growth was nowhere more dramatic than in the East Asia/Pacific region. Tourist arrivals rose from a mere 190 000 in 1950 to almost 70 million by 1993. It is noticeable that Europe and the Americas remain the world's major tourist destination regions. And almost 60 per cent of the latter's arrivals are registered in the United States and Canada alone. Hence, Europe and North America account for about 70 per cent of the world's tourist arrivals. The share of the developing countries is about 24 per cent (Table 1.3 overleaf) and it has not changed much over the last few decades if one relies on Tlusty's (1980) figure of 19 per cent in 1963 and 21 per cent in 1973. Thus, as other commentators have already remarked, international tourism largely remains an inter-developed

Table 1.1 Growth of world tourist arrivals, 1950–1994

Year	World tourist arrivals (in thousands)	World tourism receipts (in US$ millions)
1950	25 282	2 100
1960	69 320	6 867
1965	112 863	11 604
1970	165 787	17 900
1975	222 290	40 702
1980	284 282	103 535
1985	327 570	115 970
1990	455 812	261 014
1991	463 141	267 519
1992	502 938	305 021
1993	512 523	303 977
1994	531 388	335 780

Source: extracted from WTO 1995

Table 1.2 Tourist arrivals by world region, 1950–1993 (in thousands)

Region	1950	1960	1970	1980	1990	1993
Africa	524	750	2 407	7 337	14 975	17 875
Americas	7 485	16 705	42 273	61 387	93 845	106 525
East Asia/Pacific	190	704	5 331	20 961	52 263	68 548
Europe[a]	16 839	60 351	113 000	189 830	286 651	296 535
Middle East	197	630	1 864	5 992	7 444	7 200
South Asia	47	180	912	2 280	3 179	3 459

[a] Europe includes Cyprus, Israel and Turkey
Source: derived from WTO 1994a

Table 1.3 Tourist arrivals to developing countries

Year	World	Developing countries	Percentage
1963	7 820	1 468	18.8
1973	27 580	5 737	20.8
1978	63 500	11 500	18.1
1988	399 739	97 999	24.5
1990	455 812	115 924	25.4
1992	502 938	120 949	24.0
1993	512 523	126 083	24.6

Sources: Tlusty 1980; WTO 1994a, 1995

countries activity and developing countries receive only a small portion of the world share (Agel 1993; Harrison 1992; Thiessen 1993; Vorlaufer 1984). Nonetheless, international tourism contributes on average about two per cent to the GNP, constitutes 10 per cent of all export receipts and 40 per cent of the service industry in developing countries (WTO 1994a).

Perhaps more revealing is an analysis of the inter-regional tourist flows (Table 1.4). A cross-tabulation of the 1992 data indicates that most tourist arrivals are intraregional and not inter-regional flows from one region to another. Some 88 per cent of all tourist arrivals in Europe originated from other European countries. In the Americas this figure was 78 per cent, in East Asia/Pacific it was 71 per cent. Only in South Asia and the Middle East were more tourists counted from outside the region than from within. Oppermann (1997) illustrates the regional bias of tourist arrivals in the Latin American and Caribbean contexts (Figure 1.1).

Table 1.4 Inter-regional tourist flows, 1992

Origin region	Destination region					
	Africa	Americas	East Asia/Pacific	Europe	Middle East	South Asia
Africa	9 295	233	319	5 398	947	87
Americas	524	79 271	6 088	19 212	403	324
East Asia/ Pacific	267	6 786	43 270	7 575	527	475
Europe	6 393	14 442	9 821	255 683	2 489	1 461
Middle East	936	172	276	1 741	3 340	176
South Asia	51	202	1 514	493	211	985

Source: calculated from WTO 1994a

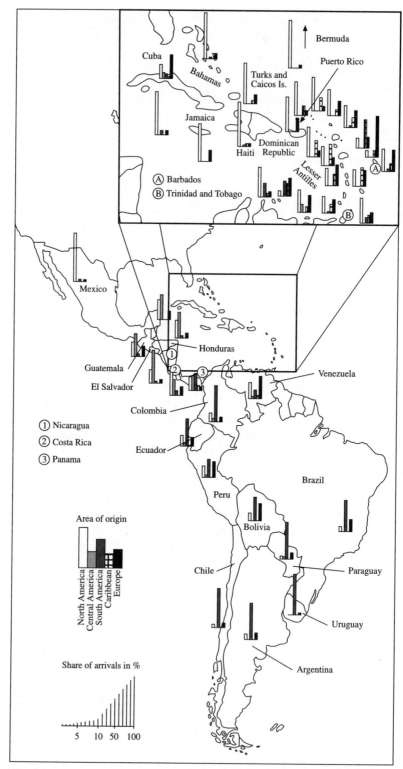

Figure 1.1 Origin regions of tourists to Latin America and the Caribbean. *Source:* data from WTO 1994a.

There are also vast differences among developing countries with respect to the size and importance of the tourism industry (Table 1.5). Clearly, Mexico and China are in their own league. The majority of the developing countries receive fewer than one million visitors each year, among them most Caribbean and African countries. The top ten developing countries accounted for more than 64 per cent of all tourist arrivals and the top 25 countries for 88 per cent. Considering that there are more than 150 developing countries and territories, it denotes a strong concentration of international tourism in a few countries.

Nonetheless, even the top ranked Mexico and China are just among the world's top ten destination with respect to tourist arrivals; Hong Kong and Turkey make it into the top 20 whereas the South East Asian tourist tigers Malaysia, Singapore and Thailand are ranked 20th, 21st, and 22nd respectively. A comparison with the world rankings in 1980 indicates that many of the top developing countries have been very competitive in attracting more visitors. Most were able to improve their ranking, some even significantly. Turkey, for example, jumped from 44th to 17th place. Several of the Caribbean and Latin American countries lost in standing. Oppermann (1997) called the 1980s a lost decade for tourism development in much of that region.

Table 1.5 Developing countries' top destinations

Rank	Country	Arrivals 1992	World rank 1992	World rank 1980	% share of arrivals to developing countries
1	China	18 982	7	15	15.1
2	Mexico	16 534	10	8	13.1
3	Hong Kong	8 938	16	24	7.1
4	Malaysia	6 504	18	21	5.2
5	Turkey	5 904	19	43	4.7
6	Singapore	5 804	20	19	4.6
7	Thailand	5 761	21	22	4.6
8	Morocco	4 027	23	28	3.2
9	Macau	3 850	24	25	3.1
10	Tunisia	3 656	27	27	2.9
11	Argentina	3 532	28	35	2.8
12	Indonesia	3 403	29	50	2.7
13	Korea, Rep. of	3 331	31	40	2.6
14	Puerto Rico	2 854	35	26	2.3
15	Egypt	2 291	38	31	1.8
16	Uruguay	2 003	39	37	1.6
17	Taiwan	1 850	41	29	1.5
18	Cyprus	1 841	42	55	1.5
19	India	1 765	43	33	1.4
20	Dominican Republic	1 691	44	54	1.3
21	Brazil	1 650	46	30	1.3
22	Bahamas	1 489	48	34	1.2
23	Bahrain	1 450	49	58	1.2
24	Chile	1 412	50	52	1.1
25	Philippines	1 246	51	39	1.0

Source: extracted from WTO 1995

RESEARCH ON TOURISM IN DEVELOPING COUNTRIES

Tourism research in developing countries dates back more than 50 years into the 1930s. Mazières and Gattfossé (1937) published an article on tourism in Morocco and discussed various forms of tourism in Morocco at the time, ranging from sightseeing in the major cultural and historical cities to convention tourism. It was followed in 1946 by an article on hotel developments in Morocco (Madras 1946). This was only slightly later than tourism research articles in developed countries which date back to 1930 in North America (Mitchell and Smith 1985) and to 1924 in Europe (Oppermann 1992b).

Not unlike the sporadic emergence of tourism studies in developed countries until the early 1950s, tourism research in developing countries was infrequent, and only the 1960s witnessed a more consistent interest in this field. Since then, however, an ever increasing number of research articles and monographs have been published. Theuns (1991) brought together a large number of these studies in a bibliography on tourism in developing countries. More recently, Thiessen (1993) and DSE (1993) provided overviews and bibliographies of the German language literature on tourism in developing countries. It is impossible to even cover a large number of the thousands of tourism publications on tourism in developing countries in this brief overview. In the period from 1950 to 1984 alone, more than 2000 articles, book chapters, and monographs are recorded that dealt with tourism in developing countries (Theuns 1991). Considering the addition of many new tourism journals and the expanding number of tourism books and conferences, this number has likely more than doubled since. Theuns (1991) showed how the average annual output increased from just three in the 1950s, to 26 in the 1960s, and to more than 130 in the 1970s. Hence, the following brief overview of major themes provides only examples of topics and references. The interested reader is directed towards the already mentioned bibliographies, to the tourism journals which regularly feature articles on tourism in developing countries, and to abstracts dealing with tourism such as the *CAB Tourism, Leisure, and Recreation Abstract* (London, UK) or the *Research and Tourist Database* maintained by the Centre des Hautes Etudes Touristiques (Aix-en-Provence, France).

Until about 1960, few people travelled to developing countries and few studies dealt with this topic. Nevertheless, some destinations in developing countries had already gained early fame, such as Bali, Indonesia or Acapulco, Mexico (Gerstenhauer 1956; Oppermann 1992c). Most of the very early studies were descriptive in nature and focused on individual resorts or destinations. Agel (1993) suggests that the period since 1960 can be divided into three phases of tourism research. The first period, from the late 1950s to 1970, corresponded with an expansion of tourism in developing countries facilitated by the increasing usage of wide-bodied aircraft. It was a time of euphoria and most studies were largely oriented towards the economic fortunes that tourism can bestow to developing countries (e.g. Anschütz 1965; Frentrup 1969; Lefort 1959; Sands 1966). Most of the research work was very uncritical in nature, praising the value and potential of tourism as a generator of foreign exchange earnings and a tool for economic development (e.g. Huckendubler 1970; Jones 1970; Mings 1969; Pollard 1970).

Agel (1993) calls the years from 1970 to 1985 the 'disenchantment period'. Controversial studies appeared that questioned the validity of the multiplier effects and the economic benefits in general (e.g. Benzing 1973; Bryden and Faber 1971; Levitt and Gulati 1970). As a whole, this period witnessed the advent of critical tourism studies dealing with a wide range of social, cultural and physical effects of tourism (e.g. Bryden 1973; de Kadt 1979; Eriksen 1973; Gormsen 1983; Jafari 1974; Labeau 1970; Lundberg 1974; McKean 1973; Myers 1974; Nettekoven 1969; Salem 1970). The 1970s also marked the introduction of the dependency paradigm into tourism studies in opposition to the prevalent development paradigm in the 1960s. It was a critical reaction to the unfulfilment of the great hopes that were placed on tourism as a panacea for economic development in developing countries and especially to the overtly positive development paradigm (e.g. Britton 1980, 1982). However, the supporters of the development paradigm remained in force and studies praising the value of tourism appeared consistently (e.g. Alleyne 1974; Leemann 1975; Loki 1974; Vorlaufer 1979).

Since about 1985, Agel (1993) notes a third phase, the 'differentiation period'. It is a time of more pragmatic approaches and a move away from the extreme positions. Alternative tourism forms that are environmentally, socially and culturally adjusted are promoted as a way to a planned and better tourism. Alternative tourism has come in many different names, for example as soft, responsible, integrated, nature and green tourism. And the latest, mostly environmentally oriented form is ecotourism. However, as Butler (1990) pointed out, alternative tourism is beset by many problems, the largest of which is the ever increasing number of tourists. Hence, any intentionally small-scale tourism development is eventually bound to be overrun by tourists if not protected by financial barriers. Another sign for the increasing recognition that not all tourism forms and tourists are the same is the introduction of the sectoral paradigm into tourism studies (Wahnschafft 1982; Oppermann 1993). Thus, in the mid-1990s, tourism research in developing countries appears to have moved towards individual evaluation of tourism effects on the economy, culture, society and environment. Few studies merge these perspectives in a holistic fashion to arrive at a comprehensive evaluation of tourism potentials and pitfalls. Furthermore, despite the accumulation of research on tourism in developing countries, conceptual advancements of many aspects of tourism remain sparse. Too much work is unnecessarily replicated and too few models are advanced and rigorously tested.

OUTLINE OF THIS BOOK

Research on the topic of tourism in developing countries dates back to the early beginnings of tourism research in general. Despite this 60 year tradition, little theoretical progress has been made. Most studies are not theoretically oriented and hardly any work builds upon previous ones. In essence, the vast majority of publications in this area of tourism research are anthologies of individual efforts, not unlike the criticism made by Pearce (1995b) of tourism research in general. One may view it as an abundance of studies that exist, with few interrelations, on a horizontal plane of our understanding of tourism. A few works, however, did make some in-roads in a vertical direction, advancing new theories and notions that have advanced our understanding of tourism in developing countries.

This first introductory chapter provided a brief overview of tourism in developing countries and its importance in these countries. It reviewed some of the main themes of tourism research and touched upon the concepts of developing countries and development and particularly development in developing countries.

Chapter 2 addresses the question of why developing countries want tourism, what are the expected benefits, and how do developing countries go about developing this industry. It also raises the question why some countries seem to excel whereas others fail. Chapter 3 examines tourism development on a national level. It deepens the issue of development theories already touched upon in Chapter 1 by emphasizing these concepts with respect to spatio–temporal tourism development processes in developing countries. Furthermore, by analysing development patterns in some countries it will show how and when tourism development usually occurs and how the symptoms might be used to improve the planning process. Chapter 4 moves the discussion from a national to a destination or resort level. It addresses the concept of the destination area life cycle and its strategic planning implications. It also highlights the fact that individual destinations within a developing country may be at completely different development stages that require entirely different approaches towards planning, marketing and management.

While Chapters 3 and 4 look mainly at the supply side perspective, Chapter 5 focuses on the demand perspective, the tourists themselves. It discusses the emergence and changing demand patterns for tourism in developing countries. It highlights the significance of domestic tourism and intraregional tourism for many countries which stands in stark contrast to the popular belief that the majority of tourists to developing countries come from the industrialized countries in Europe, North America, Australia/New Zealand and Japan. It also examines tourists' motivations and destination decision processes. Chapter 6 examines the effects of tourism on the physical environment and the social and cultural structure of both host and guest countries.

Chapter 7 scrutinizes the portrayed and perceived images of developing countries and the importance of such images and perceptions in the making and breaking of tourism destinations. The future of tourism is the topic of Chapter 8. It touches on the potentials and problems of the tourism industry that face developing countries at the turn of the millennium. Emerging concern over health issues, ecotourism, convention tourism and changing patterns of tourism demand are in the spotlight of this brief glimpse at the near future as it appears today.

QUESTIONS

1. What are commonly used indicators to define development and/or developing countries?
2. What was an important advancement in the development of tourism in developing countries?
3. Discuss the major problems associated with tourism data analysis in an international comparative perspective.
4. Name the major periods of tourism research and deliberate on the main themes of each period.

FURTHER READING

De Kadt, E. (ed.) (1979) *Tourism – Passport to Development? Perspectives on the Social and Cultural Effects of Tourism in Developing Countries.* Oxford University Press, New York.

> This collection of tourism chapters is a classic in the socio-cultural literature on tourism. It brings together systematic topics and destination case studies.

Harrison, D. (ed.) (1992) *Tourism and the Less Developed Countries.* Belhaven Press, London.

> This recent book starts out with two good chapters on systematic perspectives only to be followed by a collection of individual case studies that are not interlinked. Thus, this edited book loses its thread after the first two chapters.

Then there are several good reference and textbooks on developing countries in general.

Nohlen, D. and F. Nuscheler (eds) (1993) *Handbuch der Dritten Welt* [Handbook of the Third World] (3rd ed.; 8 volumes). J.H.W. Dietz Nachfahren, Bonn.

> This collection (8 volumes with about 4000 pages) is essential reading for anybody interested in developing countries. It provides a systematic treatment of development problems in its first volume. Volumes 2–8 are region specific and discuss all the developing countries, one by one, with respect to their individual problems and potentials. Tourism is addressed in most country sections although it is unfortunately not included in the systematic section in Volume One.

Simpson, E.S. (1994) *The Developing World: An Introduction* (2nd ed.). Longman, Harlow.

> Provides a valuable overview of the pertinent issues in developing countries in its first part. This is followed by more detailed case studies although the length imposes a barrier to the level of detail included.

2 Tourism and development

Why are developing countries around the world looking to tourism as a means for development? One reason was already alluded to in Naylon's (1967) discussion of the value of tourism to Spain, which at the time was also considered a developing country.

> Tourism is perhaps the only sector of economic activity in which the principles of free trade still apply. More important, it is now possible for underdeveloped countries to improve their economies, not by increasing exports via low-cost production, but by [tourism].
>
> (Naylon 1967, p. 23)

Furthermore, Naylon suggested that tourism was fundamental to Spain's rapid economic growth and, echoing Christaller's (1955) notion of tourism's tendency towards the periphery, that the very reason which prevented Spain 'from participating in the benefits of the Industrial Revolution, are now the attractions producing this influx of wealth to finance new development' (1967, p. 23). He was referring to Spain's location at the European periphery and its climate. It is this very successful example of Spain that developing countries aspire to repeat.

The advantage of tourism for the poorest among the developing countries has also been reiterated by Cater (1987, p. 202): 'It remains a fact, however, that the development of tourism has been regarded as a panacea for the economic malaise of many of the least developed countries (LDCs), faced with a narrow resource base and serious balance of payments difficulties.' However, as Hoffmann (1971) already mentioned, foreign exchange earnings are only the means for a higher purpose. They can contribute to economic development through reducing trade account deficits and, therefore, providing a favourable economic climate in the developing countries themselves.

REASONS FOR INVOLVEMENT IN TOURISM

While balance of payments and other potential economic benefits are usually provided as the main motivators for developing countries to become involved in tourism (e.g. Hall 1994; Jenkins 1991; Ungefehr 1988; Wood 1979), they may be considered the result of deeper structures. Population pressure and fast urbanization, high unemployment, monostructured economies and export products, decimal agricultural productivity, minor industrialization, low per capita income, insufficient infrastructure and low literacy rates are just a few characteristics that most developing countries share (Thiessen

1993). Declining terms of trade for most of their exports encouraged a search for other products or industries. With the strong growth in demand for world travel, tourism appeared as a strong candidate (Wood 1979) and still does in the 1990s. Furthermore, UN resolutions have glorified tourism as 'a basic and desirable human activity deserving the praise and encouragement of all peoples and Governments' (Burkart and Medlik 1974, p. 57).

Table 2.1 illustrates some of the common problems that face developing countries. For a comparison, data on the high-income countries are also provided. In addition many developing countries are small in area and population base, often in an island situation. Many commentators have remarked on the specific problems of such microstates and how tourism is in many cases conceivably their only hope of economic development (e.g. Lee 1987; Wilkinson 1987, 1989).

Faced with these structural deficits and disadvantages, developing countries conceive one easy way out: tourism. They recognize that they possess something which they otherwise consider as useless or even as a nuisance, namely a hot sun, blue skies, white beaches and an exotic culture. And it is these resources which are so immensely attractive to people in the developed countries and who are ready and willing to pay hard currency for them (Hoffmann 1971). 'However, with the perception of tourism as a "smokeless industry" and a panacea for economic malaise and unemployment, the full range of impacts of tourism development has often failed to be appreciated by either government or the private sector' (Hall 1992, p. 13).

GOVERNMENT AND TOURISM

Governments' involvement in tourism comes in many different forms and levels. Those in some developing countries take a very passive stand or even negative position, others are actively involved in fostering tourism growth:

Table 2.1 Selected indicators of developing countries, 1992

	GNP 1992[a]	Inflation[b] (%)	Life expectancy[c]	Population growth[d] (%)	Urban population growth[e] (%)	Adult literacy (%)
Low- and middle-income	1 040	75.7	64	1.6	3.7	36
Sub-Saharan Africa	530	15.6	52	2.8	5.0	50
East Asia and Pacific	760	6.7	68	1.2	4.2	24
South Asia	310	8.5	60	1.9	3.5	55
Europe and Central Asia	2 080	47.5	70	0.5	n/a	n/a
Middle East and North Africa	1 950	10.1	64	2.5	4.4	45
Latin America and Caribbean	2 690	229.5	68	1.6	2.9	15
High-income countries	22 160	4.3	77	0.5	0.8	<5

[a] GNP per capita;
[b] annual rate of inflation 1980–92;
[c] life expectancy at birth 1992;
[d] average annual population growth 1992–2000;
[e] average annual growth rate 1980–92;
The classification used is based on the World Bank classification of countries.
Source: data extracted from World Bank 1994.

national tourism organizations (NTOs), tourism development plans, national airlines, investment incentives or disincentives, general legislatory regulations, visa and tax regulations and financing of hotel and tourism infrastructure are just a few approaches that governments may use in furthering, guiding or impeding tourism development. Jenkins (1994, p. 3) notes that 'in the initial stages of tourism development, the government might be the only body which has resources to invest in the sector.' As a consequence, governments often emerge as tourism entrepreneurs for lack of private investors with capital, experience and willingness to invest in tourism (Jenkins 1994; Wolfson 1967).

Richter (1993) provides an overview of some public–private ownership issues, using South East Asian countries as examples (Table 2.2). She shows how, often independent of the political structure of the country, tourism is strongly influenced by government interests and actions.

Tourism organizations

In most instances when developing countries want to encourage tourism, a national tourism organization (NTO) is founded. Depending on the role tourism holds in the economy and how much emphasis is placed on this industry, a tourism ministry may even be established. In fact, many developing countries do have such a tourism ministry which stands in stark contrast to the developed countries where tourism is often not considered a serious industry and unworthy of having a major position in politics.

NTOs are usually charged with marketing the country overseas and, occasionally, domestically. Hence, their interest generally focuses on the international tourists rather than domestic tourists and data is often collected only on the former. For marketing purposes, offices are set up abroad in the country's primary tourist generating markets. The amount of money the government allocates influences the number of offices and the intensity and level of promotion campaigns. In turn, the performance of NTOs is often measured by the number of international tourist arrivals, or better the increase therein. Hence, the sheer number of tourist arrivals is commonly more important than the type of visitor; the issue of quality versus quantity (see Chapter 6) is rarely raised.

Tourism plans

Another responsibility of NTOs is usually to draw up a tourism development plan. Quite often these plans are developed by international consultancy firms who have limited insights into the actual problems of the countries concerned. In addition, these development plans are frequently generated without due respect to other industry sectors and development intentions (Wall and Dibnah 1992). Quite often such hastily composed development plans are filed, shelved and forgotten or classified and never publicly released. In Malaysia, for example, two successive national tourism master plans in the late 1980s and early 1990s have never been made public, despite having cost several million dollars each.

Table 2.2 Public–private ownership and direction

Public	Myanmar	Philippines	Singapore	Thailand	Vietnam
Airlines	Government-owned; poor safety record	Government-owned; is for sale	Government-owned	Government-owned; in the process of being sold	Government-owned; second under consideration
Hotels and inns		Government owns many resorts and hotels; trying to sell		A few establishments are government-owned	Government ownership of some large old hotels and 'mini' hotels
Buses	Government-owned; poorly maintained and downright dangerous				
Trains		National railways			
National agencies for tourism development and promotion	Myanmar Hotel and Tourism Services	Department of Tourism	Tourism Promotion Board	Tourism Authority	Overseas Finance and Trade Corporation
Regional/local public agencies with tourism tasks		Most cities have tourism programmes		n/a	Saigon Tourist is the tourist authority for the South
Regulatory climate of public bodies	Liberal investments and tax holidays to attract foreign exchange	Less central control than during Marcos era. Prostitution is widespread though illegal	Some controls on zoning to preserve the last of the ethnic historical buildings and some parks	Room and restaurant taxes are high, but licensing nil. Prostitution is widespread though illegal	85% of foreign investment in the South
Laissez-faire regulatory environment	Alcohol only permitted in clubs for foreigners	Licensing exists but is not onerous	No	$100 exit tax in 1982 Relatively unregulated	Government requires hotels to join hotel association, but control is relatively slight
Mostly private promotion		Yes	Yes	Yes	Yes. Golf courses and foreign-owned hotels are being built
Mostly private control		Yes. 43.9% of hotels are owned by multinational chains	Yes	Yes	Government liberalized to allow much private enterprise in tourist infrastructure

Source: extracted from Richter 1993 (pp. 182–3)

Many development plans would specify areas where tourism development is particularly encouraged (i.e. tourist zones) often in an attempt for regional development and dispersal away from the main urbanizations. As Oppermann (1992b) commented, these attempts have had limited success not at least due to the fact that such regions are often centred on the international airports and, therefore, the main urban and economic centres of the country. Some countries have worked together with the World Tourism Organization and international tourism experts on their tourism development plans (WTO 1994b). The most recent National Development Plan in the Philippines is an example of such an international cooperation. However, even in that case some commentators have critically remarked that the three identified tourist development regions are unlikely to contribute towards regional development as they are centred on the existing main gateways and economic centres (Chon and Oppermann 1996; Oppermann 1994/95).

Nonetheless, tourism master plans are recommended because they force the government to focus on tourism and on the objectives of their tourism strategy. As a consequence, after a number of years, they allow an evaluation of progress towards the objectives specified. Unfortunately, few official attempts are ever made. Wall and Dibnah mention that 'there has been no official attempt to date to evaluate the economic, environmental and social consequences of the Nusa Dua resort' (1992, p. 124), a planned resort within the Bali Tourism Study. Further, they suggest that such an evaluation would be important within the future of overall tourism planning in Bali and Indonesia.

> It would be appropriate to assess the strengths and weaknesses of the Nusa Dua development in order to learn from the experience, prior to the initiation of additional resort developments in Bali and elsewhere in Indonesia.
>
> (Wall and Dibnah 1992, p. 124)

Government investment policies

Governments of developing countries can directly influence tourism development through their fiscal and investment policies. Four different approaches can be distinguished which, if pursued, will facilitate tourism development:

- investment into the general infrastructure of a destination or region;
- investment into tourism infrastructure;
- investment incentives for companies; and
- influencing exchange rates.

Investments into the general infrastructure are among the most popular side-effects of tourism development as long as they do not only benefit the tourists. Road construction or upgrading, provision of electricity and fresh water, waste disposal and sewage treatment, airport construction or expansion, and establishment of city parks are a few examples of such investments. They are also costly and often not considered in the economic balance of tourism's financial contribution (Ruf 1978; Wood 1979). However, they are imperative when developing countries vie for international tourists and particularly mass tourists. Nonetheless, the provision of infrastructure solely or primarily for tourists' use may result in serious antagonism in the host population as Aziz (1995) illustrates for the case of Egypt.

A more direct boost to tourism development are government ventures into the tourism industry itself. In many cases, developing countries are compelled to do so in the early stages of tourism development (Jenkins 1994; Jenkins and Henry 1982; Wolfson 1967) and when they want to bring tourism to previously undeveloped areas (Sezer and Harrison 1994). Such ventures could take the form of constructing hotels or guesthouses. When Malaysia aimed at the development of tourism on the east coast of the peninsula, the federal and state governments financed the construction of several resort hotels which were then operated by international hotel resort management companies such as Hyatt and Club Méditerranée. Furthermore, it constructed and operated several motels and a visitor centre. Naylon (1967) mentions that, since 1942, the Spanish government offered to hotel developers the advancement of 70 per cent of costs. In addition, the tourism ministry opened and operated several dozen small hotels. Other forms of investment are construction and operation of tourist information centres, operation of travel agencies and/or tour operators and tourist attraction development.

Direct government investments are commonly undertaken to lead the private sector in a certain direction and it is hoped that private entrepreneurs will eventually follow suit. In the above Malaysian example, this intention succeeded with increased private investments following some ten years after the original government involvement. Eventually, the government was able to disinvest its ownership and the area is now even considered a 'gold coast'.

In some instances, governments opt not to become financially involved in the tourism industry but rather give companies additional investment incentives. These can be income tax or service tax reductions. Sometimes these reductions are higher for 'pioneer' or peripheral areas where the government would like to see more tourism development occurring and lower for investments in the major urban and economic centres (Oppermann 1992b). Wood (1979) mentions that several South East and North Asian countries used long term loans at low interest rates, tax exemptions or reductions, duty-free import of equipment, and admission of foreign workers as government incentives for hotel investors. In a more recent study, Schlentrich and Ng (1994) indicate that restrictions on ownership in South East Asia is partially offset by development incentives, tax abatements and development subsidies. In Turkey, soft loans, allocation of public land to investors, tax exemptions, preferential tariff rates for electricity, water and gas, foreign worker allowance and investment allowances were but a few incentives offered by the government to lure foreign investors (Sezer and Harrison 1994). Nowadays, Cuba offers incentives such as repatriation of profits, extensive tax holidays and up to 100 per cent foreign ownership (Bleasdale and Tapsell 1994). Ahmed (1991) reports that entrepreneurs in India willing to invest in tourism are given tax reductions, low interest loans and reduced import duty rates.

The fourth area of government influence is the exchange rate. It is commonly accepted that a favourable exchange rate will bring more tourists to a destination (EIU Travel & Tourism Analyst 1995). Through their fiscal policies, governments can directly influence the exchange rate although they should be aware of the side effects. While the country becomes more attractive for tourists and exports overseas become more competitive, imported goods will rise in value pushing up the bill for the country's imports. Frequent adjustments to exchange rates also reduce the confidence in the currency. As a result, foreign investors may be less inclined to invest and local people may prefer to hold their earnings in other currencies or invest elsewhere. The latter is a frequent occurrence in South America where the runaway inflation has thoroughly destabilized the currencies, resulting in a drain of money overseas.

Airlines and visa regulations

Earlier it was mentioned that most developing countries share one common characteristic with respect to tourism: most of their tourist arrivals arrive on aeroplanes. Thus, flight capacities and connectivity are among the influencing variables in tourism. A country with no direct and/or nonstop flight connections to the major tourist source countries is less likely to be visited than a country with many such links. Singapore realized the importance of an international airport very early and has systematically worked on making Singapore the regional hub in South East Asia. It has consistently upgraded and expanded its facilities to accommodate the ever growing number of airlines and planes and the changing technological requirements of modern airports.

An issue often raised in this context is the question of whether a developing country should insist on reciprocal landing rights or not, provided is has its own airline. Some countries will allow non-reciprocal rights in order to allow for an unhindered development of airline connection for the benefit of tourism development. Others insist on bilateral agreements in order to shelter their own airline and to improve its cost-effectiveness.

Many developing countries have established their own airlines and some of these are now ranked among the world's finest. To own an airline is more than just a political statement. It is an important step in the country's development because it reduces the country's dependency on foreign airlines and other countries and their flight capacity decisions. It usually allows a country to establish flight connections with those countries and destinations it considers important. Malaysia Airlines was the first airline to establish direct flights from South East Asia to South Africa and on to South America. This innovative routeing was an immediate hit and was imitated by other airlines. Aerolinas Argentinas has a regular flight service to New Zealand and Australia, a connection not offered by any other airline. And many south Pacific islands are almost dependent on their own airlines as hardly any other airline provides services to them. Kissling and Pearce (1990) observe that tourist volume and composition crucially depend on the nature and capacity of air services between the origins and destinations in the south Pacific region. 'Who controls aviation bears considerable influence upon the potential of tourism regionally. ... Scheduled airline services provide the web of opportunity for visitors to the islands to reach their chosen destination (Kissling and Pearce 1990, p. 10). Hall (1994) reports how Vanuatu's loss of two convenient airline connections to New Caledonia and New Zealand resulted in a decline of 50 per cent from the respective markets.

One problem that national airlines often cause is the concentration of tourism development. From an airline perspective, the hub and spoke system is the most economic one although it is not the most attractive one from a consumer perspective (Page 1994). Hence, most airlines in developing countries adopt such an approach and, through government regulation, ensure that no other airline is allowed to fly to the regional centres. As a result, most international tourists are forced to arrive in the primary airport cities which are generally the capital city and other large cities. It focuses tourism activity on these centres as tourists are often not willing to endure yet another flight or a several hours' bus ride to different destinations. In Tunisia, the development of international airports outside Tunis in Sousse/Monastir and on Djerba Island facilitated the spread of tourism development to these areas, effectively reducing Tunis' former primacy in the tourism industry. Thailand followed a similar path with the opening of Phuket as an international airport. More recently, the Philippines appear to be moving in the same direction after abolishing the monopoly of Philippine Airlines and giving foreign airlines landing rights in Cebu and Davao. As a result, some 6 per cent of all air passengers entered the Philippines via these two airports despite having just 3 per cent of the total international flight capacity.

Another point that hinders tourism development, sometimes purposely done, are visa regulations. Relaxed visa requirements or even the renunciation of such can be a great facilitator in tourism development. It makes travelling to the country easier and is likely to encourage more cross-border traffic. On the other hand, if a country wants to discourage or limit tourism it can create visa hurdles for any potential tourists. Myanmar used this approach by limiting the length of stay to two weeks or sometimes even just one week.

Sensitive border areas are sometimes off limits for tourists. Shackley (1995) reports how only recently an area was opened to tourism in India. Tourists had to obtain a special visitor permit and even then had to travel in groups accompanied by an official representative not unlike the situation in some Eastern European countries not too long ago.

INTERNATIONAL INFLUENCE: TOUR OPERATORS AND WHOLESALERS

Few developing countries are involved in running their own travel agencies or tour operations. In contrast to aviation, this is an area often left to the free market enterprise and, because of their location close to the source markets, usually to foreign or multinational companies. Britton (1991) argued that airlines and tour wholesalers are the two key players in the tourism industry.

> The competitive advantage of the tour wholesalers lies in their doubly strategic position between all principal suppliers and between suppliers and consumers. Their power derives from the enormous volumes they can command, their pivotal familiarity with diverse market segments, and the capacity to shift tourist flows from one destination to another.
>
> (Britton 1991, p. 457)

Especially their power to shift tourist flows from one developing country to another, often facilitated by the ubiquitous product being sold (sand, sun and sea), provides them with substantial bargaining power over hotels and smaller airlines. Many tour wholesalers invest into other sectors in the industry in an attempt to increase their profits from vertical integration as well as horizontal integration. Tour wholesalers are particularly interested in three sectors: airlines, hotels and tourism service companies at the destination. In view of current overcapacities, flight capacity is easily available and tour wholesalers tend to invest in the other two sectors (Vorlaufer 1993).

Germany's largest tour wholesaler and travel agency chain TUI (about 30 per cent market share), for example, is the owner or major stakeholder in several hotel chains (e.g. Robinson Club, Iberotel) and tour operators in the primary destinations areas (e.g. in Kenya, Turkey and Morocco). As a result, they have almost 100 hotels with about 50 000 beds at their immediate disposal. Many developing countries do not even have such a hotel capacity. In 1991/92, these 94 hotels counted almost 10 million guest nights which is about twice as many as Kenya registered in total (Vorlaufer 1993).

From a developing country's perspective there are advantages and disadvantages to the investment of foreign tour wholesalers and airlines in their country. On one hand, it is likely to increase the outflow of profit and, therefore, is liable to reduce the multiplier effect (see Chapter 6). On the other hand, if a company owns hotels in the destination area they are prone to keep on sending tourists there in an effort to maximize occupancy rates and their profit. Hence, they are less likely to switch destination countries at will.

For tour wholesalers, vertical integration is an effective way to improve on their takings from each customer. The split of the customer's expenditure is, in Germany for example, 35–40 per cent to both the hotel and the airline, 10 per cent to the tour operator, 12 per cent to the travel agency, and 3 per cent to the destination agency (ground operator). Thus, if a tour wholesaler owns and operates hotels and destination agencies besides the travel agency at home, the takings increase to about 60 per cent of the tourists' expenditures (Vorlaufer 1993).

An excellent example of the international orientation of a large tour operator is given in Vorlaufer's (1993) figure of TUI's tourist flows (Figure 2.1). It shows the strong focus of German package tours to the Mediterranean countries and particularly Spain. But it also illustrates that other developing countries are also offered and integrated in the distribution network.

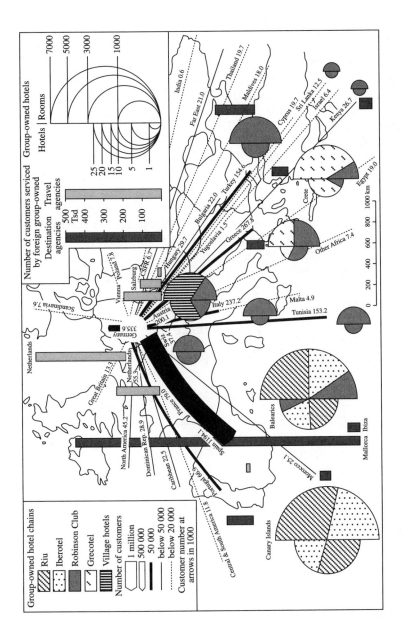

Figure 2.1 Transnational distribution and linkage structure of the tour operator TUI.
Source: Vorlaufer 1993.

INTERNATIONAL INFLUENCE: BOYCOTTS AND EMBARGOES

A less common factor to be considered is the influence and impact of foreign governments and their policies. Yet in some cases these policies can seriously affect tourism development in a developing countries, especially when adverse decisions are reached in major source markets. But boycotts and embargoes came in many different forms and varieties and are often more subtle than that. A number of countries (i.e. United States, Japan) have established advisory lists regarding safety concerns in many different countries. To be negatively mentioned in such a list is likely to keep the less adventurous tourists away and redirect their travel to other destinations. Gayle relates that 'Jamaica's efforts to expand tourism from the United States were partially undercut ... when the US State Department issued a travel advisory warning American citizens to limit exposure to possible robbery or assault ...' (1993, p. 47).

Butler and Mao (1995) address the issue of tourist flows between quasi-states (Figure 2.2). These are countries or territories that share a common history and are politically separated. Some of Butler and Mao's examples are obvious cases of strict travel restrictions or embargoes, sometimes in both directions and in other cases in only one direction. The authors also note that quasi-state tourism itself is a dynamic process: flows can become more or less intense depending on whether the countries are on a political convergence or divergence course. Germany is a good example of the former,

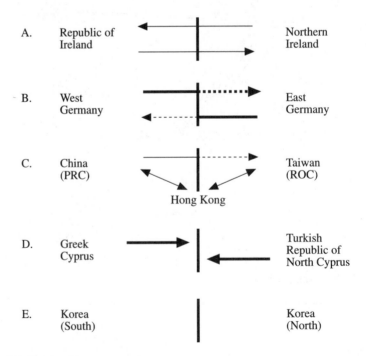

Figure 2.2 Tourism between quasi-states.
Source: Butler and Mao 1995.

where two previously separated entities became unified again and the quasi-state tourism status ended. Yugoslavia and the former Soviet Union are examples of the latter: several countries emerge from one former entity resulting in international tourist flows between these newly formed countries. In some instances tourism statistics are 'politically' adjusted, such as in the Chinese case. Visitors from Hong Kong, Macau and Taiwan to China are not considered as international tourists but listed under a separate category.

SUMMARY

This chapter discussed why governments are interested in tourism and tourism development and provided an overview of the main tools available to governments in initiating, supporting or restricting tourism. The case study on Vietnam at the end of this chapter indicates the value that tourism can have in economic development and also how much emphasis governments place on tourism. Cuba is also an excellent example of the influence of foreign countries on development in general and tourism in particular.

However, tourism is not always an effective development agent, especially when fundamental requirements are left unfulfilled. Adu-Febiri (1994), for example, lists eight problem areas which have hindered tourism development in Ghana, many of them the fault of the government, such as ineffective tourism development planning at national and regional levels, burdensome immigration requirements and lack of tourist information

In summary, it appears that tourism, when planned and managed properly, can act as a valuable agent in the economic development of developing countries. However, if tourism development is left to itself and governments provide unequivocal or contradictory standpoints, tourism development is unlikely to be very strong, either in the form of foreign investments or in tourism demand.

QUESTIONS

1. Discuss the most important government options to regulate and further tourism development.
2. Why should governments draw up a tourism development master plan?
3. Examine the common structural deficiencies of developing countries.
4. Debate the advantages and disadvantages of national airlines.

FURTHER READING

Pearce, D.G. (1989) *Tourism Development* (2nd. ed.). Longman, London.

This book provides a good overview of development theories and their applications in tourism as well specific issues and concerns of tourism development.

World Tourism Organization (1995) *National and regional tourism planning: Methodologies and Case Studies*. Routledge, London.

This is a collection of national and regional development plans in developing countries. It discusses the specific problems involved and provides an overview of development approaches.

The tourism industry in Vietnam

After the victory of the communist forces of North Vietnam in 1975, Vietnam was cut off until recent years from the flow of tourism from the non-communist world. As a member of the communist trading bloc Comecon, it was involved in limited trade with its main supporter, the former USSR, as well as other Eastern European countries. Consequently, most of its tourism flows were from and to those countries.

Since 1988, US$1.96 billion has been invested in 104 hotel development projects making tourism one of the country's most important industries. Tourism earnings were estimated at US$400 million in 1994, contributing 10.2 per cent of the total gross national product.

After the reunification of the country, a process of national cohesion took place under the auspices of the central planning authority from Hanoi. The psychological toll of the civil war and limited foreign involvement meant that the government became more isolated and shunned any form of foreign involvement in its internal affairs. However, enormous strains were placed on the fragile Vietnamese economy by the occupation of Cambodia and by the short war with China in 1979. The 'boat people' became a new symbol of Vietnam as its economic refugees fled to other countries in the region.

Further, during the early 1980s, the underlying flaws of a centrally planned economic system became apparent. Given the economic and military pressures from its neighbours, and coupled with the booming 'dragon' economies in the rest of South East Asia, the Vietnamese government saw the need to adapt the economy for survival. Consequently, during the Sixth Party Conference in 1986, the 'doi moi' (renovation) decree was passed in the new provision of the Investment Code. This decree sought to modify the previously centrally planned economy of Vietnam and to adopt a free enterprise system. Slowly, central control was being dismantled as restrictions on private companies were lifted, and foreign investment and ownership encouraged. As a result, foreign investors, including hotel developers and tourism businesses, flocked to Vietnam to take advantage of the numerous opportunities presented.

The opening of the economy resulted in its significant growth. With an abundant supply of cheap labour, attractive landscapes, untouched forests, emerald-green rice fields and unspoiled beaches in a central Asian location, Vietnam has been heralded as *the* investment opportunity of the 1990s. The country was referred to in the international investment community as an untapped tourist destination with significant growth potential.

Lifting of the US trade embargo against Vietnam in 1994 was a significant step forward for the development of tourism in the country. Following the fall of the South Vietnamese government, the US government placed and enforced an economic embargo on Vietnam. The US government extended its 1964 trade embargo on North Vietnam to cover the entire country in 1975. Before the lifting of the embargo, the World Bank and the International Monetary Fund (IMF) withheld loans to the Vietnamese government.

CHALLENGES FACING THE DEVELOPMENT OF THE VIETNAMESE TOURISM INDUSTRY

Attempting to understand the recent developments of the tourism industry in Vietnam has been made difficult by the multiplicity of organizations involved and the lack of historically reliable and timely statistics. There is a general lack of visitor arrivals data and no reliable sources of information on tourism available for planning and promotion. As international agencies such as the World Tourism Organization (WTO) and financial institutions become more involved, the tourism situation will improve. Vietnam's recent entry to the Association of Southeast Asian Nations (ASEAN) and expected admittance to the ASEAN Tourism Association should improve the quality of tourism statistics in the future.

Following the 'doi moi' decree, the WTO received funding from the United Nations Development Program (UNDP) to prepare a master plan for Vietnam. The WTO report noted that 'Vietnam has been totally absent from international tourist markets ... leaving aside the close-circuit tourist trade with the countries of Eastern Europe ... other countries in the region, especially Thailand and Indonesia, have, however, developed such strategies with notable success ... Asia and South East Asia in particular is regarded as the region likely to experience the highest growth rate of tourism in the next fifteen years.' However, the WTO reported that Vietnam is not yet ready for a large influx of tourists since it lacks an adequate infrastructure, rooms that meet international standards, a skilled staff and an appropriate tourism organization.

As visitors were once again allowed into Vietnam after 1986, tourism grew as international business travellers entered the country searching for investment opportunities. The year 1990 was designated as the 'Visit Vietnam Year', but little success was reported in association with the campaign. The campaign failed largely due to a shortage of airline seats, hotel rooms and other tourist services. Strict visa restrictions and difficulty in obtaining the visa were partially responsible for the low level of success for the campaign. A tourist visa officially costs only US$25 but goes for as much as US$140 in some countries. The normal wait for a visa is five to seven days. Nevertheless, the campaign was a major step in promoting Vietnam as a tourist destination. Tourist arrivals increased by 63 per cent from 300 000 visitors in 1991 to 550 000 in 1992, and further to 1.3 million visitors in 1995. The growth of the national tourism organization under the name of the Vietnam National Tourism Administration (VNTA) in stature and responsibility as a body of independent ministry also contributed to the increase of tourism over the years.

It is estimated that leisure travellers currently make up about 25 per cent of total arrivals. A report on Vietnam by *Asia Travel Trade* stated that, 'although attractions abound, for the time being at least, most travel agents … expect the bulk of their bookings to come from the business community' (McKinnon 1993). It is also expected that more leisure tourists will discover Vietnam once new airline routes open up, thereby increasing the pressure on the hotel industry to add more rooms. With many hotels recording high occupancy rates in the high 80s, the supply of rooms will increase.

Regardless of the accuracy of these figures, significant growth is projected for the tourism industry in the next few years. In addition, the Vietnamese government has also encouraged domestic investment to provide the necessary facilities for domestic tourism as well as the Viet Kieu (overseas Vietnamese).

One of the biggest challenges facing the tourism industry is ensuring an adequate supply of rooms to meet the demands of business travellers in the short term. Until 1993, less than 11 000 hotel rooms were available in Vietnam. When excluding Ho Chi Minh City (formerly Saigon) and Hanoi, there were virtually no international class hotels in other areas. Over the years of 1993 through 1996, the situation favourably changed with the entry of multinational chain hotels throughout Vietnam. French chains such as Hotel Metropole and Sofitel, Hong Kong based Omni Hotels and New World Hotels, as well as US based Hyatt International and Marriott were among the new hotel companies which opened properties in Vietnam.

THE PROBLEMS OF INVESTING IN VIETNAMESE FINANCING

Since the country is facing a shortage of capital, foreign investors have been the primary source of capital to fund the hotel projects. Securing the necessary capital for investments in Vietnam from foreign banks is difficult. The investment environment in Vietnam is too risky on any given terms. Many banks are reluctant to finance Vietnamese projects, citing inadequate loan security and political and economic risk. Foreign banks generally demand that borrowers provide offshore security. For example, New World Hotels has been trying to arrange financing for its $62.5 million hotel in Ho Chi Minh City which was scheduled to open in late 1994. The hotel was licensed in 1989 and began construction two years later, after the company decided to start the project with internal financing. Banks generally are reluctant to lend more than $10 million for a single project (Hiebert 1992).

The financial and banking system in Vietnam is also very primitive. To make matters worse, the government has borrowed heavily to finance its budget deficits. Difficulties in obtaining credit and the country's economic instability have also contributed to numerous business closures (Gerlach 1991). Under the current conditions, French and Asian banks are the most open-minded about Vietnam, with a number of them helping to finance several of the current hotel projects.

The legal system

The investment laws in Vietnam guarantee investors the right to remit their profits and dividends abroad. It also protects foreign-owned assets from nationalization (Dove 1992). Despite safeguards to secure the interests of foreign investors, Vietnam's legal system is still very weak. While capital transfers are permitted, the exchange of local dong into hard currencies such as US dollars is restricted. The investment regulations also require foreign companies to hire workers through state agencies.

Although the Vietnamese government has been adopting market-oriented policies since the late 1980s, foreign investment projects are mired up in red tape. The bureaucratic rules and administrative procedures have created mistrust in the government and have lead to a misuse of power, confusion and delays in completing projects. Bureaucracy is rampant and decisions on projects are slow and painful. The bureaucracy has been described as heavy, overlapping, costly and ineffective. Experts on Vietnam emphasize that survival and prosperity will depend on persistence and patience. Some foreign investors have even been asked for as much as 10 per cent of a contract's value before a business licence is granted. For example, a Singapore-based property developer was asked to pay local building contractors in full even before the foundations were laid for a hotel and leisure complex in Ho Chi Minh City (Hiebert 1992).

Land, lease and ownership

Since the Vietnamese government launched its tourism blueprint in 1988, approval has been given to some 45 hotels, offering more than 7000 rooms. However, less than half of the rooms have been built. Many developers have got no further than finding a name and a possible site. The biggest problem facing hotel investors in Vietnam is the issue of land ownership. Vietnam's constitution currently does not allow private land ownership because the government owns all the land. The government does allow leasing, provided it is for a stable and long-term use. However, it does not specify the duration of such use or permit the use of land as collateral. On the other hand, buildings on the land can be owned, and the government agency which usually has control over the land will get involved in the joint venture. For example, in the case of a recent hotel development site with Groupe Accor, the partner turned out to be the Vietnamese army.

The first real wave of hotel projects such as the Century, Embassy, Metropole and Norfolk hotels were generally renovations of existing properties. These hotel projects offered minimum investment risk and required less involvement with government rules surrounding land ownership, which was preferable to investors. Furthermore, encouraged by the government, investors could easily set up as joint ventures, with the Vietnamese contributing the initial building and land.

The second wave of new hotel developments has largely been bogged down in the problems of land ownership, financing and construction. Vietnam's first foreign hotel investment, the Saigon Floating Hotel which opened in 1989, was faced with land ownership problems. However, Southern Pacific Hotels' unique approach allowed the company to circumvent the problem by bringing a complete barge structure up from Australia's Great Barrier Reef and anchoring it in the Saigon River. As Reggie Shui of Groupe Accor put it, 'You can set up anything you want there but Vietnam is still outlaw land ... there's no specific and concrete laws and regulations for the hotel industry' (Boyd 1993).

Bankers and investors have stalled many of the hotel projects due to the lack of security in the investment. This situation is not likely to change soon unless more pressure is applied on the government. As John Brisden, chief representative of the Standard Chartered Bank in Ho Chi Minh City, noted: 'Certainly from a lender's point of view, we don't see too much to encourage us, which is giving any early expectation of being able to lend against leasehold land ... We're all very conscious of what happened in China in the 1970s. There's no great rush to repeat the experience' (Sherry 1993). Other deterrents to property investment have been the relatively high land prices, the massive amounts of red tape and corruption affecting the construction industry (Sherry 1993).

Construction problems

A further problem affecting hotel developers has been the inability to obtain construction materials. Between 1975 and the start of the building boom in 1990, there was little building in Vietnam and consequently little need for materials. This shortage of the required construction materials has now become a severe problem facing hotel developers looking to invest in new hotel projects. As such, many executives are resigned to staying at low standard minihotels or guesthouses. The expansion of aviation links with the rest of the world is also exacerbating the problem.

Staffing

The World Tourism Organization (WTO) in its 1991 report identified the lack of skilled staff as a constraint for the Vietnamese hotel and tourism industry. The WTO found that with the current population of 70 million growing 2.5 per cent annually and expected to reach 90 million by the year 2000, 20 per cent of the active population was unemployed and some 40 per cent underemployed. There were no hotel training programmes at either the vocational or managerial level. With employment in the hotel and tourism sector expected to grow at an annual rate of 17 per cent between 1990 and 2005, approximately 25 000 new jobs have to be created to meet the projected demand. The WTO report suggested that integrated training programmes would be the most appropriate method of quickly training the large number of workers needed for the hotel and tourism industry. The WTO also recommended that during negotiations with foreign investors, the Vietnamese should require that a training commitment be included in investment and operational programs (Wain 1993).

Vietnam's key endowment is its large pool of youthful, disciplined and relatively well-educated workers. Half the 32 million labour force is under the age of 20 with a literacy rate estimated to be about 85 per cent. Nevertheless, the hiring and training of local staff presents a challenge to hoteliers. The employees know nothing about the hospitality business, but are eager to learn. Recruiting employees is a problem, because the bureaucracy in Vietnam dictates that official job pools have to be inspected before positions can be advertised. In addition, given the distinct shortage of qualified hotel personnel such as kitchen and front-line employees, retaining staff may be difficult because other hotels and new businesses have resorted to poaching employees.

Another problem affecting the emerging hotel industry in Vietnam has been the issue of labour laws. Several hotels have reported a range of problems from expatriates not having approved work permits, lack of established labour contracts that meet Vietnamese employment regulations to issues over unfair dismissal. The Vietnamese workforce is essentially fully unionized under the government trade union labour committees, which makes the management of labour extremely difficult and frustrating. As one hotel executive in Ho Chi Minh City noted in dealing with his workforce, 'It is very difficult to discipline people properly or improve productivity without running into one or another labour committee'.

Infrastructure

The destruction from the Vietnam War and the inability to obtain loans for 18 years has rendered Vietnam's infrastructure too inadequate to handle even a small number of tourists. With the US government dropping its objections to international investment in Vietnam, the international financial community has moved quickly to provide the much needed capital. Recognizing the infrastructure crisis facing the country, the World Bank has earmarked US$158.5 million to upgrade the main north–south highway. The Vietnamese government is seeking a massive infusion of US$20 billion in foreign investment by the end of the century. At a donor conference hosted by the World Bank in Paris in November 1993, major contributions for 72 economic and social infrastructure projects costing US$9.3 billion and technical assistance programmes worth US$220 million were sought. The aim was to attract US$7–8 billion in foreign aid and US$12–13 billion in foreign investment by the year 2000.

National tourism development

3

Many developing countries choose tourism not only for its economic benefits to the national economy but also for its supposed capacity as a regional development agent. Tourism is often thought to be particularly beneficial to peripheral regions which often have few other resources, a notion that can be traced to Christaller's (1955) seminal article which was later translated into English (Christaller 1964). Yet to what extent tourism actually contributes to the regional dispersion of economic development, and to what extent it is a better regional development agent than other industries or services, remains largely unexplored. This chapter addresses the issue of tourism development on a national level, purposely leaving destination or resort development aside for Chapter 4. It will look at the various spatio–temporal models of tourism development that have been proposed over the last few decades, distinguishing between three different streams of thought: models drawing on the diffusionist, dependency and sectoral paradigms.

MODELS TO EXPLAIN TOURISM DEVELOPMENT

Within the tourism literature generated there has been a development of 'models' designed to describe and explain the spatial organization of tourism activities in differing contexts. It is pertinent to examine the concept of a model, its application in tourism and the value in explaining tourism development in developing countries. Models were developed from the logical positivist tradition in geography in the 1960s (see Johnston 1991 for a discussion of logical positivism) with its concern for providing a more analytical research framework. That is to say, logical positivists sought to move the research frontiers in geography forward from a descriptive regional paradigm to one where explanation could be the ultimate goal.

A 'model' in geography still remains a contested concept, with Johnston (1991, p. 8) arguing that it is 'a theory, a law, a hypothesis or any other form of a structured idea' whereas Unwin (1992, p. 215) considers a model is 'a structure used to interpret the operation of a formal system; a structured representation of the real. Models are usually at different scales or levels from the reality they seek to represent'. Haggett (1985), however, provides the most meaningful explanation of why geographers use models, as they are designed to simulate reality by substituting similar and simpler forms of what they are studying. Models are built, acting as a source of working hypotheses for research and these models can then be modified or reformulated dependent upon the results.

If models are designed to explain the spatial structure and patterns of tourism, and as a basis to begin exploring the processes shaping the tourism phenomenon, one needs to consider the different routes to explanation. According to Harvey (1969), there are two principal routes to explanation. The first, known as the 'Baconian' or inductive route, derives generalizations out of observations. In other words, a pattern is observed and an explanation developed. Critics of this approach indicate that this route to explanation is too reliant upon the idiosyncrasies of the researcher and the unproven representativeness of the cases examined. Therefore the preferred route to explanation is one where researchers make observations of patterns in the world; they then develop experiments or tests to prove the validity of the explanations offered for the patterns observed. Thus, the explanation is usually only accepted once the observations and data from other cases have been tested successfully so that it is not a single–case explanation. This tends to offer a more robust explanation than the former method which is more widely used in tourism research by marketers and those solely relying on case studies as the basis for an understanding of reality.

The preferred approach, known as positivism, developed from a group of philosophers working in Vienna in the 1920s and 1930s who viewed an objective world in which order is waiting to be discovered. They argued that order (i.e. the spatial variations of phenomena) exists and cannot be contaminated by the observer. Hypotheses are derived and translated into speculative laws which then become accepted. If tests or research data do not match the predictions or deductions from other research studies, which are then thrown into doubt, the concept of negative feedback occurs and a new hypothesis is created. Once successful tests have occurred, a hypothesis may be given law–like status and fed into a body of theory (Johnston 1991). It is in this context that models are used to build up explanations of reality which have a robust and valid meaning in the wider academic community.

The diffusionist paradigm

The basic assumptions underlying the diffusionist paradigm is that development is inevitable, that is occurs in development stages, and that development is diffused from the development core towards peripheral areas at one point. As the previously mentioned early work by Christaller (1955) suggested, it was the first paradigm adapted into tourism studies. Butler's (1980) article on the 'Tourism Area Cycle of Evolution' certainly had the greatest impact on the tourism development literature. Drawing on the general product life cycle concept and work forwarded by other authors, it essentially stipulates that tourism destinations evolve through six different stages of development from inception to decline or rejuvenation. The scale of what constitutes a destination has been open to debate since Butler was not specific in this aspect. Consequently is has been applied to small resorts, cities, regions and islands (e.g. Din 1992; France 1991; Ioannides 1992; Weaver 1990). Since different parts of a country may be in different stages of tourism development (Oppermann 1993; Weaver 1990), however, Butler's model appears more appropriate for city level and will be discussed more in detail in Chapter 4.

In earlier works, other authors proposed a different number of stages. Thurot (1973) suggested three phases and Miossec (1976, 1977) proposed five. The latter is among the best graphic illustrations of what tourism development means (Figure 3.1). Miossec differentiates the development process not only into five stages but also provides an overview of the different stages with respect to resorts, transportation issues, tourist behaviour and the attitudes of the decision makers and the population in the host region. It illustrates how resorts develop from an original pioneer resort through multiplication and specialization towards a hierarchical structure which saturates the whole country. Along with the development comes an improvement in the tourist transportation infrastructure. Notable is the interconnectivity among the resorts and the development of excursion circuits. Concurrent with the development of the physical tourism infrastructure, a radical shift occurs both in tourist behaviour and knowledge and the attitudes of the host

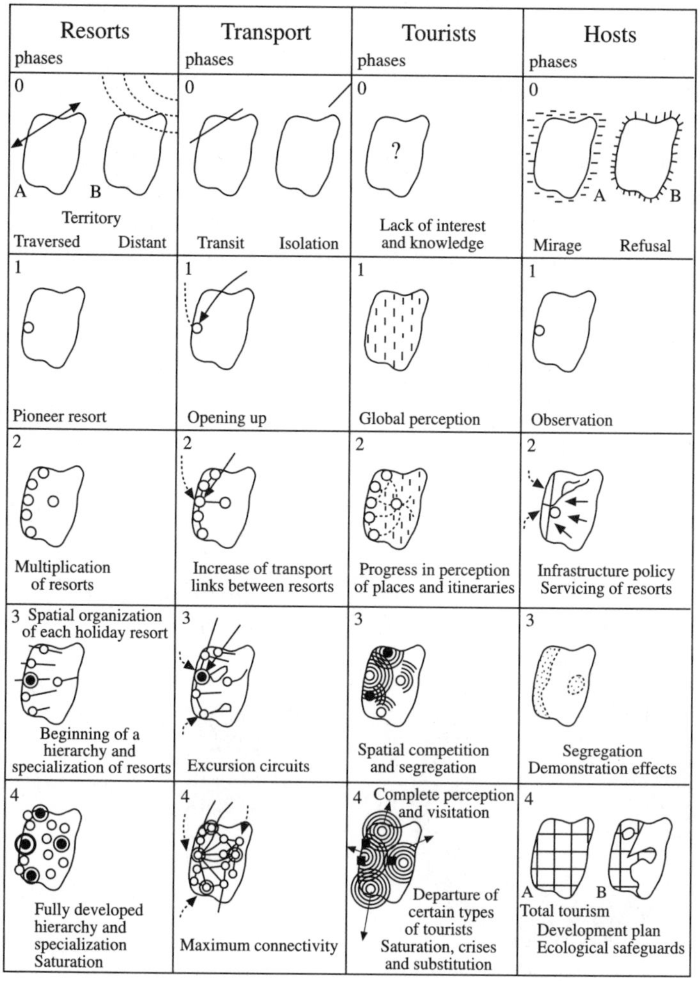

Resorts phases	Transport phases	Tourists phases	Hosts phases
0 A B Territory Traversed Distant	**0** Transit Isolation	**0** ? Lack of interest and knowledge	**0** A B Mirage Refusal
1 Pioneer resort	**1** Opening up	**1** Global perception	**1** Observation
2 Multiplication of resorts	**2** Increase of transport links between resorts	**2** Progress in perception of places and itineraries	**2** Infrastructure policy Servicing of resorts
3 Spatial organization of each holiday resort Beginning of a hierarchy and specialization of resorts	**3** Excursion circuits	**3** Spatial competition and segregation	**3** Segregation Demonstration effects
4 Fully developed hierarchy and specialization Saturation	**4** Maximum connectivity	**4** Complete perception and visitation Departure of certain types of tourists Saturation, crises and substitution	**4** A B Total tourism Development plan Ecological safeguards

Figure 3.1 Tourist space dynamics.
Source: Miossec 1976.

community. The former moves from a complete lack of interest and information on the country through an increasing awareness of its various parts and attractions to a complete disintegration of the perceived space into small regional or locational units. Pearce already critically remarked that tourism development generally occurs 'within an existing socioeconomic structure where some forms of urban hierarchy and transport network are already found' (1989, p. 18), and not in empty space. In addition, its application to developing countries is hindered by the fact that tourism in these countries 'often occurs in the form of isolated resorts, which do not form a highly interconnected hierarchical structure. Thus, the transportation linkages between resorts remain sparse' (Oppermann 1993, p. 537).

Weaver's (1988) plantation model of tourism development is explicitly based on developing countries and specifically the Caribbean islands. Although he places it in the dependency paradigm, his spatio–temporal model is essentially an evolutionary or development stage model. Weaver proposes three stages of tourism development, namely pre-tourism, transition and tourism dominant (Figure 3.2). He specificly recognizes that tourism development occurs within the given socioeconomic structure of developing countries. Furthermore, his model underlines the fact that the main town is commonly the primary development focus of tourism development, at least in the early stages. Overall, Weaver's model suggests that tourism in developing countries is not evenly distributed and that peripheral areas, which in the case of islands are the inland areas, are little or not at all integrated into the 'tourism space'. A comparison of Weaver's model with the situation in

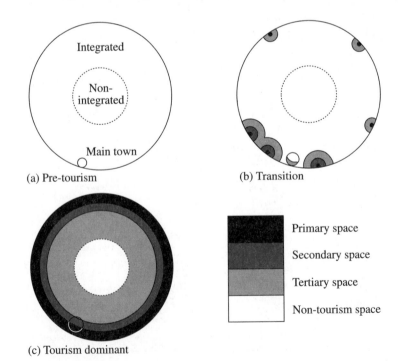

(a) Pre-tourism

(b) Transition

(c) Tourism dominant

Primary space

Secondary space

Tertiary space

Non-tourism space

Figure 3.2 Plantation model of tourism.
Source: Weaver 1988.

other islands outside the Caribbean suggests the high validity of his propositions. For example, in Mauritius very little accommodation is found inland
from the immediate coastal area and a similar situation can be noted for the
Canary and Balearic Islands, Fiji and Bali (see Case Study 2 on Mauritius at
the end of this chapter). However, Weaver's model also has some limitations
with respect to its applicability to other developing countries. It is obviously
limited to island nations. Its purposeful placement in the dependency paradigm precludes its application to countries without a plantation landscape or
colonial heritage.

The dependency paradigm

The dependency paradigm was a reaction to the diffusionist paradigm and it
found its way into tourism studies in the late 1970s and early 1980s (e.g.
Britton 1982; Hoivik and Heiberg 1980; Husbands 1981; Matthews 1977). It
essentially arose out of a dissatisfaction with the diffusion paradigm when,
after several decades, it increasingly became obvious that tourism did not act
as the development agent it was thought to be. Multiplier effects were considerably less than expected, the international orientation and organization of
mass tourism required high investment costs and led to a high dependency on
foreign capital, know-how, and management personnel (Bryden 1973;
Müller 1984; Oestreich 1977; Pavaskar 1982). Other studies indicated that
tourism is not a powerful regional development agent. Oppermann (1992b)
illustrates how tourism is least important in peripheral regions while the
economic and political centres have an above average share of the industry.
In addition, this distribution pattern remained fairly stable, a result supported
by many other studies in developing countries (Bernklau 1991; Berriane
1990; Jurczek 1985; Müller 1984; Radetzki-Stenner 1989; Vorlaufer 1980).
In particular the international orientation and organization of mass tourism
has drawn severe criticism by supporters of the dependency paradigm.

> The paradox arises therefore, where tourism is being used as a tool for
> the development of the periphery, but the entire organization and control
> of the industry reside in the core region. This provides an example of
> 'organizing the dependence on the core' in order to foster development
> of the periphery.
>
> (Husbands 1981, p. 42)

The required typical standardization of the tourist product for mass tourism
often resulted in the establishment of enclavic resorts and a general spatial
concentration of international tourism in developing countries (Arnold 1972;
Britton 1982; Jenkins 1982).

> In physical, commercial and socio-psychological terms, then, tourism in
> a peripheral economy can be conceptualized as an enclave industry.
> Tourist arrival points in the periphery are typically the primary urban
> centres of ex-colonies, now functioning as political and economic cen-
> tres of independent countries ... If on package tours, tourists will be
> transported from international transport terminals to hotels and resort
> enclaves. The transport, tour organization and accommodation phases of

their itinerary will be confined largely to formal sector tourism companies. Tourists will then travel between resort clusters and return to the
primary urban areas for departure.

(Britton 1982, p. 341)

Thus, according to the dependency theory, tourism is an industry like any
other, which is used by the developed countries to perpetuate the dependency
of the developing countries. Instead of reducing the existing socioeconomic
regional disparities within the developing countries, tourism reinforces them
through its enclavic structure and its orientation along traditional structures
(Oppermann 1993).

With respect to the temporal process, Britton (1982) suggests that tourism
development does not occur from evolutionary, organic processes within
peripheral areas but is very much dependent on demand processes in the
developed countries. Britton's (1982) enclave model of Third World tourism
(Figure 3.3) illustrates the dependency paradigm notion that tourism in
developing countries is spatially concentrated and organized in the metropolitan economy. It is, however, also a good representation of the two-tier
dependency: developing countries depend on metropolitan countries and,
within developing countries, peripheral, rural areas depend on the urban centres and particularly the capital city. Britton's (1982) structural model of
Third World tourism (Figure 3.4) presents the more system-oriented perspective and the influences and dependencies between metropolitan and peripheral economies on the one hand and between the capitalistic (dominant) and
marginal sectors within developing countries on the other.

Oppermann (1993) summarizes several critique points of the dependency
paradigm. The focus of the dependency paradigm on international mass
tourism results in the neglect of domestic tourism and budget or drifter
tourism, both of which display significantly different spatial organization
patterns. In addition, as Din (1990) already noted, not all accommodation or
transportation chains are in the hands of the developed countries. Many
developing countries have established their own airlines and several of them
are very successful. Similarly, some companies in the developing countries
have become very prosperous hotel chains that are not only offering accommodation facilities in developing countries but also have bought or developed properties in the industrialized countries. Finally, Oppermann suggests
that 'perhaps the most significant limitation of dependency theory is its fail-
ure to formulate alternative prescriptions for tourism development into
developing countries' (1993, p. 541).

One aspect commonly neglected in the discussion of the dependency paradigm is its domestic aspects. While most researchers automatically equate
the core–periphery power relation with industrialized–developing countries,
there exists another power relation within developing countries, namely
between the more developed urban areas and the rural and peripheral regions
within the country, as Britton already indicated in his model (Figure 3.4).
Urban based companies are usually the only ones that have enough financial
capital available and the political insight into where development will occur
and consequently are the only companies to invest in these regions. As a

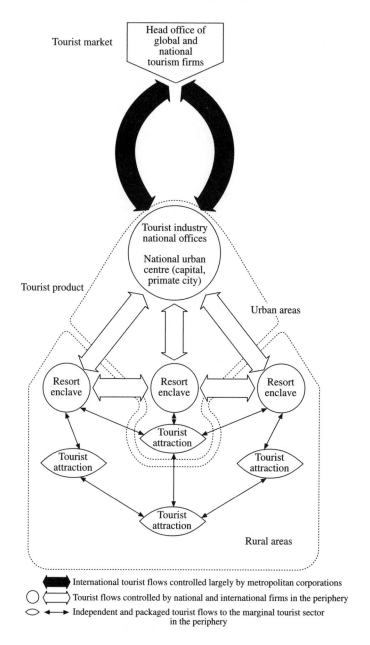

Figure 3.3 Enclave model of tourism in developing countries.
Source: Britton 1982.

result, a considerable percentage of spending in peripheral areas is drawn towards the metropolis (Jurczek 1985), reducing the local multiplier effect even further.

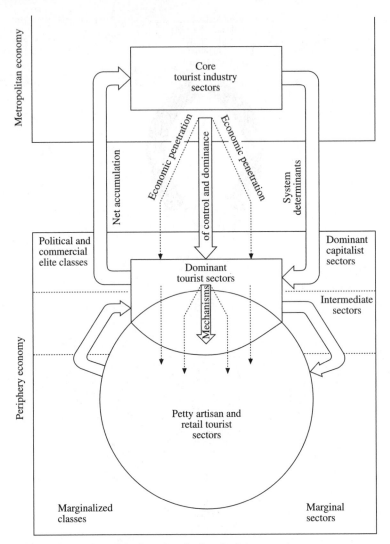

Figure 3.4 Structural model of tourism in developing countries.
Source: Britton 1982.

The sector paradigm

The general sector paradigm stipulates that the economy of developing countries is composed of two different sectors that co-exist side by side with few interlinkages. If applied to tourism, this paradigm states that different types of tourism co-exist in developing countries; different types of tourists are served by different tourism suppliers. Cohen (1972) was among the first to recognize the existence of two different groups of tourists, namely 'institutionalized' and 'non-institutionalized'. The latter have received very little attention although in recent years the number of studies recognizing and examining all forms of budget, backpacker or drifter tourism is on the rise (Loker-Murphy and Pearce 1995; Ross 1997; V. Smith 1990).

Only a limited number of tourism studies have explicitly adopted the sector paradigm in their analysis of tourism development (e.g. Kermath and Thomas 1992; Michaud 1991; Oppermann 1992b, 1993; Wahnschafft 1982). Britton (1982) touched on the existence of two different sectors in developing countries (Figure 3.4). He even forwarded a model suggesting that the marginal sector benefits the least from tourism (Figure 3.5). Implicit in his model is that tourists are from the industrialized countries and he did not give due consideration to domestic or inter-developing country tourist flows.

Among those researchers who adopted the sector paradigm, only Oppermann (1992b, 1993) explicitly addresses tourism development on a national level, forwarding a spatio–temporal development model of the tourism space. Based on previous studies he identifies several characteristics of the two tourism sectors (Table 3.1). Oppermann uses 15 characteristics to differentiate both sectors. The formal tourism sector in developing countries is typified by international standard hotels, airlines, bus operators and tour companies. This entails high capital investment costs, often accompanied by high foreign participation and ownership. Due to the size of the enterprise, the organization tends to be bureaucratic and regular wages are prevalent. The formal sector also entails high leakages in the form of profit transfers, large imports of food and general items to satisfy 'western' demands, and large imports for the construction of these hotels. Consequently, the formal sector is relatively little integrated into the local economy, considerably reducing its local multiplier potential. Governments of developing countries usually only consider the formal sector when addressing tourism development. Government aid is provided in form of large-scale infrastructure developments (for example for water and electricity supply). Since the prices of these hotels or tours are generally beyond the reach of the average citizen, formal sector enterprises largely depend on foreign tourism demand.

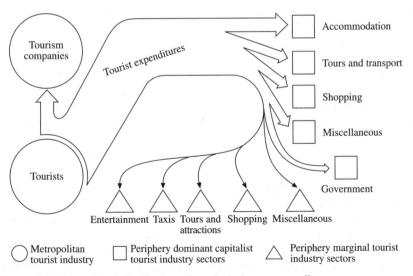

Figure 3.5 Generalized distribution of tourist industry expenditure.
Source: Britton 1982.

Table 3.1 Characteristics of the formal and informal tourism sectors

Characterictics	Formal sector	Informal sector
Capital	abundant	limited
Technology	capital-intensive	labour-intensive
Organization	bureaucratic	primitive
Ownership	companies	individual, family
Prices	generally fixed	negotiable
Inventories	large quantities and/or high quality	small quantities, poor quality
Fixed costs	substantial	negligible
Advertisement	necessary	almost none
Credit	institutional	non-institutional
Turnover	large	small
Profit margin	small per unit and investment costs	large per unit and investment costs
Education	skilled	unskilled
Regular wages	prevalent	less prevalent
Government aid	extensive	none or almost none
Dependence on foreign countries	high, externally orientated	small or none

Source: Oppermann 1993, p. 544

The informal sector commonly consists of hawkers or street vendors, simple accommodation forms, and minibus operations. The ownership of such businesses usually rests with an individual or a family. It is a labour-intensive operation with limited capital and very primitive organization forms. Their turnover is small; however, they can derive relatively high profits per unit. Regular wages are the exception. Owing to their price structure, many informal sector tourism enterprises have a relatively high domestic demand component, sometimes constituting more than 90 per cent of their total demand (Oppermann 1993).

Oppermann (1993) proposed a schematic model of the tourism space. He distinguished four different spaces, namely the non-tourist, the informal and the formal tourism space as well as a space where an overlap occurs between the informal and formal sector. Set into a spatio–temporal development context, Oppermann's model of the tourism space in developing countries vividly depicts the evolution of tourism in developing countries (Figure 3.6). To some extent, Oppermann's model integrates both aspects of the diffusionist and the dependency paradigm. Hence, it may be understood as a consequential development of both theoretical models and their spatio–temporal implications. It is an example of a consequential development of tourism theory which builds on previous work. The lack of such endeavours has been bemoaned widely (e.g. Pearce 1995a).

Oppermann's model recognizes that tourism development occurs not in empty space but within the preset parameters of the general socioeconomic structure of developing countries. Thus, tourism development occurs first and foremost in the capital and other large urban centres in the vicinity of the international gateways to developing countries, the international airports. Oppermann (1993, p. 551) suggested eleven statements for the description of tourism development:

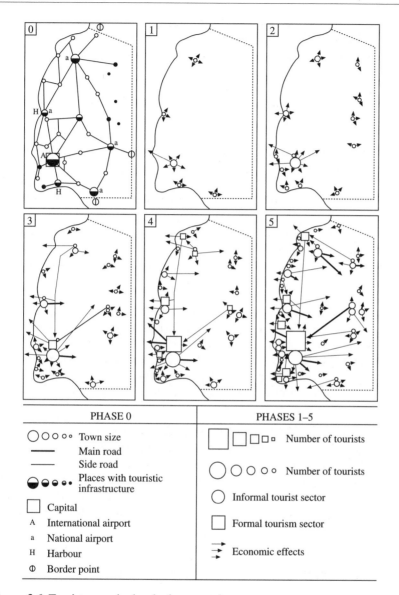

Figure 3.6 Tourist space in developing countries.
Source: Opperman 1993.

1. The capital city has a dominant role in the industry, especially during the early development phases of international mass tourism, owing to its 'pretouristic' structures.
2. The dominant function of the capital city is magnified when the only or main international airport is located close to it ('gateway effect').
3. The capital retains the dominant function over a long period. Only in later years does it lose its relative position, due to the increasing number of resorts in the country.

4. The informal sector has a 'discovery function'.
5. The formal sector penetrates the established informal resorts. In the later stages, formal tourism sector resorts are drafted on the drawing board in completely new destinations.
6. Not every resort develops through the same stages from discovery through the informal sector, over penetration of the formal sector to a world renowned international tourism resort.
7. The informal sector is characterized through its high integration into the local economic structure that results in a low leakage and, therefore, in a high multiplier effect on the local economy.
8. A high proportion of the formal sector expenditures are lost from the local economy due to high leakage towards the national capital and overseas.
9. The formal sector is typified in its spatial occurrence as very concentrated, close to international or at least domestic airports, the low absolute number of resorts and the low connectivity of these resorts with respect to tourism flows among them.
10. The informal tourism sector is spatially better distributed. Owing to the better acceptance of domestic transportation types, the members of this sector have a higher mobility and informal tourism sector resorts are, therefore, much better connected.
11. Domestic tourists participate in the formal or informal tourism sector depending on their financial ability. In developing countries, with a large middle and upper class, the volume of domestic tourism is likely to be larger.

The main weakness of Oppermann's model is that while the individual proposition is supported with evidence from a number of different developing countries, the model as such has never been tested with empirical data for any developing countries. However, it is a common deficit for much of the tourism literature that proposed models and theories remain largely isolated and few, if any, researchers make an effort to test and validate these models (e.g. Mitchell and Smith 1985; Pearce 1995a; S. Smith 1990).

MEASURES OF NATIONAL TOURISM DEVELOPMENT

When a developing country places emphasis on tourism as a regional development agent, it should also have appropriate measures in place to actually appraise tourism's impact and/or contribution towards the reduction of regional imbalances. A number of different indices or indicators have been suggested over the years.

Tourism intensity

One of the earliest indicators to estimate tourism's contribution to the regional economy is Defert's Index (Df). Although attributed to Defert (1954) and consequently called Defert's Index, its usage dates back into the 1930s (Poser 1939). It is a ratio of tourism supply to host population:

$$Df_i = (A_i/P_i) \times 100$$

where A_i = accommodation in area i as measured in rooms or beds;
P_i = host population in area i.

Obviously these two variables are usually readily available, which is a great advantage in developing countries where data sources are scarce and information is often classified. This simple index can give a fairly good estimate of tourism's importance in a specific region because the number of rooms or beds directly determine the number of people employed in this sector. For most international standard hotels, the ratio of rooms to employees ranges from 0.5 to 2.0 (Chapter 6), often depending on the availability and cost of labour. A high Defert Index, therefore, implies that a relatively high proportion of the local population works in the tourism industry. Hence, the higher the Defert Index, the more important is tourism's role in the local economy. Defert's Index is most useful in comparative studies of several different regions. Arguably it is particularly useful in developing countries, where most accommodation supply is in the form of hotels and where camping and campervans play a much less important role in the overall tourism accommodation supply than in industrialized countries.

Oppermann (1992a) applied Defert's Index in comparing the importance of tourism in different states of Malaysia and also how this changed over time. Tourism was more important in the urban centres and on the west coast of peninsular Malaysia than in the rural and eastern parts of the country. In addition, he showed that over a ten year period, during which tourism was primed as a regional development agent, the situation remained de facto the same (Table 3.2).

Table 3.2 Temporal change in Defert's Index by Malaysian states, 1979–1989

State	1979	1989
Kuala Lumpur	0.71	0.88
Penang	0.41	0.59
Selangor	0.04	0.08
Kedah	0.05	0.10
Perlis	0.04	0.09
Perak	0.10	0.14
Negeri Sembilan	0.16	0.13
Johor	0.13	0.20
Melaka	0.12	0.34
Pahang	0.41	0.44
Terengganu	0.12	0.17
Kelantan	0.05	0.08
Sabah	0.27	0.27
Sarawak	0.12	0.27
Malaysia	0.16	0.21

Source: Oppermann 1992b, p. 74

Tourism Intensity Index

A variation of Defert's Index is the Tourism Intensity Index (TII). Instead of using the accommodation supply in a ratio to the host population it utilizes tourist demand. This measure is considered a better approximation of tourism's actual impact since it accounts for differences in seasonality among regions. Two variations exist, namely either to use tourist arrivals or tourist nights as a measure of demand. The latter is preferable since it also accounts for differences in length of stay.

$$TII_i = (TN_i/P_i) \times 100$$

where TN_i = Tourist nights in area i;
           P_i = Host population in area i.

If using tourist arrivals, TN would need to be replaced by TA (tourist arrivals). The Tourism Intensity Index has been applied in developing countries for 30 years (Eriksen 1967; Kulinat 1991; Oppermann 1992c). In a comparative study of tourism in Latin America and the Caribbean, Oppermann (1997) contrasts 27 countries based on their TII as well as their tourism density (tourists/sq km). He shows that most Caribbean Islands had considerably higher TII values than Central and South American countries, despite the fact that the Caribbean Islands have on average a smaller number of tourist arrivals (Table 3.3).

Capital City Index

The capital city of developing countries is often the premier tourist destination, particularly in the early stages of tourism development. This has been recognized or is implicit in all spatio–temporal models and theories of tourism development (e.g. Miossec 1976; Oppermann 1993; Weaver 1988). Since the capital city is supposed to lose its predominant position at one stage, to measure the capital city's share in the total tourism industry appears as an obvious measure of the development process. Mergard (1986) proposed the Capital City Index (CCI). It is a ratio of the percentage of tourism accommodation in the capital and the latter's share of the country's population.

$$CCI = (A_c/A_n)/(P_c/P_n)$$

where A_c = Accommodation in capital city;
           A_n = Accommodation in the country;
           P_c = Population of capital city;
           P_n = Population of the whole country.

He then went on and compared several developing countries over a ten year period. In 1980, apart from a few countries in Latin America (Colombia, Jamaica and Mexico), all other countries had an index of greater than 1. This indicates that the capital offered, compared to its population, a more than average share of the country's accommodation. India (20.2) and the

Table 3.3 Tourism intensities and densities of selected Latin American and Caribbean countries in 1992

Region/country	Tourist arrivals (1000s)	Tourism density (tourists/sq km)	Tourism intensity (tourists/1000 pop.)
Central America			
Costa Rica	610	12	193
Mexico	17 271	9	193
Panama	291	4	115
El Salvador	314	15	57
Guatemala	541	5	56
South America			
Guayana	93	*	845
Uruguay	1 802	10	575
Chile	1 283	2	94
Argentina	3 031	1	92
Paraguay	334	1	74
Venezuela	434	*	21
Brazil	1 475	*	10
Peru	217	*	10
Caribbean			
Cayman Islands	242	931	12 100
Br. Virgin Is.	117	780	11 700
Aruba	542	2 808	9 033
Bermuda	375	7 075	6 250
Bahamas	1 399	100	5 181
US Virgin Is.	487	1 424	4 427
Barbados	385	893	1 425
St Lucia	177	287	1 264
Martinique	321	297	973
Puerto Rico	2 640	297	737
Dominica	47	63	671
Dominican Rep.	1 524	31	204
Cuba	410	4	38
Haiti	120	4	18

* = less than 1

Philippines (16.8) had the highest index. However, the comparative analysis of the situation in 1970 and 1980 suggests that the capital's dominant position appears to decrease over time. Unfortunately, Mergard's study has never been replicated and a longitudinal study of many countries over a long time period is required to establish certain parameter limits as indicators for the actual development stage of a given country.

CONCENTRATION OR DISPERSAL?

The physical infrastructure of tourism activity tends to be concentrated in certain places and along particular axis. In particular, tourism in developing countries appears to be very concentrated, with its full-service resorts and a focus on urban activities and/or beaches. Rural tourism, defined as tourism in a 'non-urban territory where human (land related economic) activity is going on, primarily agriculture; a permanent human presence seems a qualifying requirement' (Dernoi 1991, p. 4 as in Oppermann 1996a), and rural tourism activity hardly exists. At least very few international tourists visit these areas and domestic visiting friends and relatives (vfr) tourists usually do not require any commercial accommodation facilities. The concentration of international tourism in developing countries is a direct result of economies of scale since the absolute number of tourists in these countries is nowhere close that of the developed world (Vorlaufer 1993; Voss 1984).

Other commentators have emphasized the importance of the transportation network on the spatial organization of international tourism in developing countries (Franz 1985a; Lundgren 1972; Oppermann 1993). Airports as the international gateways of modern tourism are arguably the key factor (Oppermann 1992c, 1994/95; Ungefehr 1988; Voss 1984; Wilkinson 1989). Tourists are forced to arrive and depart from these locations, giving these gateway locations a tremendous advantage over others (Oppermann 1992b, 1994a; Pearce 1995a; Vorlaufer 1979). Opening airports for international air traffic routinely ensures fast growth of tourist arrivals in that particular location and/or region. Phuket (Thailand) is a classic case for such a development pattern (e.g. Uthoff 1991).

An exception to the airport rule are the Riau Islands (Indonesia). Over the last few years they have emerged as a major entry point for international tourists after they were declared an official entry point and and duty-free zone. Not surprisingly, the vast majority of arrivals are from neighbouring Singapore and arrive by sea across the only 20–30 kilometre wide straits.

The question 'should concentration or dispersal be the objective of tourism?', however, often does not arise for developing countries. A lack of financial resources forces many countries to concentrate tourism development in areas where the necessary infrastructures (i.e. airports, water supply) are already in place or can be provided at relatively low costs. Ungefehr (1988) shows how these limitations have forced the Bahamas to abandon original dispersal objectives in favour of continuing concentration in the primary islands. This problem is further compounded by an unwillingness on the side of domestic and international investors to develop 'new' sites (Oppermann and Brewer 1996). The lack of general infrastructure provision throughout a developing country is a major distinction between developing and developed countries with regard to tourism development (Voss 1984).

One country that has successfully attempted a diversion of tourism development away from the capital city is Thailand. In the 1970s, it adopted a regional development plan that sought tourism development in secondary urban centres around the country. While reducing development costs through usage of existing infrastructure in these urban centres, it provided enough impetus for tourism development outside Bangkok, which was already suffering under overdevelopment and rapid population growth (Lubeigt 1979; Uthoff 1991).

Yet whatever national tourism policy is adopted, it should be in accordance with general national development guidelines and adequate systems should be put into place that measure and evaluate progress being made.

Unfortunately, evaluation is seldom done despite the potential learning outcomes of such an exercise (Wall and Dibnah 1992).

QUESTIONS

1. Discuss and contrast the perspectives of the development and dependency paradigm on tourism in developing countries.
2. Why may the sector paradigm be considered as a symbiosis of both the development and the dependency paradigms?
3. What are the main spatial implications of Oppermann's tourism space model?
4. What measures can be used to measure spatial distribution of tourism?
5. Explain why the Capital City Index might be a valuable tool in establishing parameters of development stages.

FURTHER READING

Pearce, D.G. (1995) *Tourism Today: A Geographical Analysis* (2nd ed.). Longman, London.

> This book, now in its second edition, provides a very good overview and discussion of tourism development on all geographical levels. It covers the important theories and points the readers to areas that require further research.

Spatio–temporal tourism development in Mauritius

Mauritius – many immediately associate with this word two things: exoticness and the stamp. Whereas the stamp 'Blue Mauritius' has given the island world fame, it is the exoticness of this remote island that attracts the tourists. Mauritius is located approximately 850 kilometres east of Madagascar and about 20 degrees south of the equator. Shortly after its independence in 1968, tourism was propagated as the industry of the future and accordingly tourism development was supported (Marquardt 1976). This was at a time when tourism, as the 'white industry' was advocated around the world by the World Bank and other development institutions as the chance for developing countries. Today, tourism is an important part of Mauritius' economy and especially important as an earner of foreign exchange. About 14 per cent of the foreign exchange earnings are attributed to tourism and more than 10 per cent of the population is directly or indirectly employed by this sector. However, a large share of all tourism earnings are lost to leakage for imports and estimates of the leakage rate are as high as 80 per cent (EIU 1991b).

Tourism development

Weaver (1988) forwarded a 'plantation model of tourism development' based on the Caribbean experience. Since Mauritius shares many common traits with Caribbean islands, such as colonialization, high dependence on agriculture and agricultural exports, plantation economy and more recent emphasis on tourism, it seems appropriate to place the spatio–temporal development of tourism in Mauritius within the context of Weaver's model. Unfortunately, such attempts to test models in different settings are rarely undertaken.

Since no information is available on the tourists and their actual travel behaviour within Mauritius, the following analysis is based on whatever limited data is available on hotel accommodation supply. As discussed at length by other authors (e.g. Oppermann 1992a; Pearce 1995a), the usage of accommodation supply data has its own limitations as there is no information available as to occupancy of the rooms. Furthermore, smaller accommodation facilities and 'alternative' facilities such as campgrounds and the residences of friends/relatives are generally not included. Hence, there is an inherent bias towards the more upscale, larger and formal types of accommodation.

Weaver's model propagates that tourism development occurs mostly along the coastline and urban areas which, given the nature of most small islands, are usually located on the coast too. The inland areas are only slightly or not

at all integrated into the tourism space (Figure 3.2). Early tourism development tends to occur in the main town and slowly spreads to isolated resorts
which eventually form a coastal string of tourism development covering
most of the island's coastline. Hence, if that model also holds true for island
nations in other parts of the world, and especially Mauritius, one would
expect that tourism development first started in the main town, Port Louis,
followed by the emergence of tourism resorts along the coastline, until eventually almost the whole coast is 'covered' by tourism facilities whereas the
inland areas remain untouched by tourism development.

Two sets of data are available for Mauritius, covering a 20-year interval
between the early 1970s and 1995. Figure 3.7 illustrates the distribution of
tourist accommodation in the early 1970s. However, hotels in Port Louis
itself are not depicted. Nonetheless, the difference between the number of
hotels in Figure 3.7 and other data available (Table 3.4) suggests that at that
time at least 50 per cent of all hotels were located in Port Louis. Thus, this
number indicates the early emergence of tourism in the capital which is in
line with Weaver's model and other authors' suggestions (e.g. Oppermann
1993). Most of the hotels outside Port Louis are in a coastal location in line

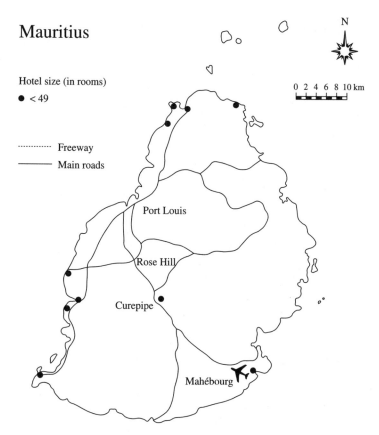

Figure 3.7 Hotel accommodation supply in Mauritius, early 1970s.
Source: Marquardt 1976.

with Weaver's proposition. Only one hotel was indicated as being inland and that was in Curepipe, another urban area. Obviously, tourism development in Mauritius in the early 1970s had already progressed from the pre-tourism to the transition stage in Weaver's model.

Figure 3.8 exhibits the location and size of hotels in 1995. It vividly demonstrates the dominance of coastal areas as locations for hotels. Only a small number of hotels are situated inland and again all of those hotels are to be found in the towns along the major route across the island between the airport and the main town. By 1995, tourism had definitely transformed the landscape along many stretches of the Mauritius coastline and only the south coast remained largely untouched. Yet it is quite obvious that tourism development had not occurred in inland areas and that a large part of the country could be classified as non-tourism space. While tourism may not have attained a dominant status in the overall economy, it certainly appears on its way to be the dominant landscaping industry along the coast.

This case study suggests that Weaver's model is also applicable in other parts of the world and not restricted to the island economies of the Caribbean. The slight difference with respect to the tourism development of

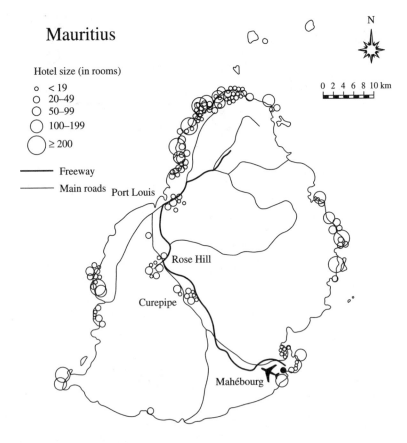

Figure 3.8 Hotel accommodation supply in Mauritius, 1995.
Source: Mauritius Government Tourist Office 1996.

inland town areas of Mauritius, which is not explained by Weaver's model, is
a result of the somewhat different infrastructure and urban development in
Mauritius. In contrast to most Caribbean islands where the airport is connected with the main town (also usually located on the other side of the
island) with a good road along the coast, in Mauritius the major road leads
straight across the island which in turn has given rise to the urban development in those inland areas. The lack of adequate roads has hindered a more
rapid development of coastal resorts along the east coast for a long time
although this seems to have changed in the late 1980s and 1990s as most
future hotel developments are forecast to be in that very area.

Table 3.4 Tourism development in Mauritius

Year	Tourist arrivals	Tourist nights	Hotels	Hotel rooms
1970	27 700	287 600	16	486
1975	74 600	746 900	34	1 499
1980	115 100	1 301 700	43	2 000
1985	148 900	1 700 000	55	2 630
1990	291 550	3 534 600	75	4 603
1991	298 510	3 635 800	89	5 087
1992	335 400	4 110 430	n/a	n/a
1993	376 630	4 610 440	n/a	n/a
1995	n/a	n/a	122	6 335

Sources: Archer 1985; EIU 1991b; MGTO 1996; WB 1992; WTO 1995.

4 Tourism destination development

The development of tourism resorts and destinations is among the most researched topics within tourism studies. The studies range from an analysis of historical tourist arrivals and tourism supply data (e.g. Franz 1985b; Oppermann, Din and Amri 1996) to resort typologies (e.g. Wong 1986) and to more theoretical generalizations of tourism resort development in the form of spatio–temporal models (e.g. Meyer-Arendt 1990; Smith 1991). As already mentioned in the previous chapter, Butler's (1980) notion of the evolution of tourist areas is probably among the most frequently cited and applied theories in tourism studies. It is an application of the life cycle concept to tourism areas and resorts. Weaver (1990) recognizes that tourism resorts may considerably differ in their development from the whole nation. Thus a different set of development policies may need to be applied to tourism resorts as compared to the whole country, and even among individual resorts consequential differences may occur. Consequently, a single national development strategy may be suitable for some but irrelevant and potentially damaging for the development of other tourism resorts. Agarwal (1994) extends Weaver's (1990) commentary further by suggesting that even 'a resort is made up of a mosaic of different elements (…), each of these exhibiting separate life cycles' (Agarwal 1994, p. 194). Bianchi (1994) notes that the generalization of the resort life cycle does not recognize the existence of different economic subsystems.

In his seminal paper, Butler (1980) outlined the evolution of tourism destinations from their beginning or inception stage through exploration, development, saturation, stagnation and eventual decline or rejuvenation (Figure 4.1). Interestingly enough, Defert (1954) had already proposed a very similar notion, namely that the age of tourism resorts connotes the degree of evolution.

> Moreover, it is not impossible for a tourist resort to be born, grow old and die. As human beings, each resort has a determined age, but it can take a new lease on life by adapting itself to tourist requirements.
>
> (Defert 1954, p. 119)

Thus Defert did not only recognize the evolutionary or life cycle nature of tourism resorts, but also, as did Butler, that resorts may escape the decline stage, even if temporarily, through reinvention and rejuvenation.

While Butler's model has not remained uncriticized and a number of different modifications have been suggested (e.g. Haywood 1985; Wall 1982), it remains popular for placing tourism destination development into a

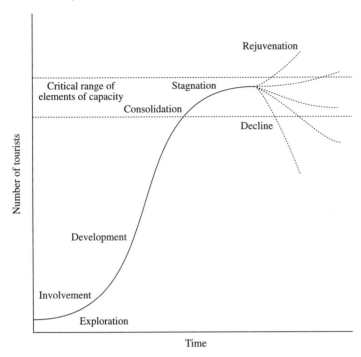

Figure 4.1 Tourist area cycle of evolution.
Source: Butler 1980.

theoretical framework (e.g. Din 1992; France 1991; Ioannides 1992; Weaver 1990). As Oppermann (1995a) suggests, its simplicity and intuitive appeal as well as its generality are major contributing factors to its popularity. The model is neither specific with respect to actual tourism numbers (y axis) nor to its time horizon (x axis). Hence, it may be applied for every and any situation, and tourism destinations can be categorized according to where they seem to appear on the destination life cycle curve. As Cooper and Jackson (1989) point out, the model is not a predictive tool, rather one of hindsight. Again, its main strength is that it provides tourism planners with the clear message that, if not managed properly, every destination may simply wander through a boom and bust cycle.

More recently, Butler (1993a) extended his model further and explicitly integrated the hypothetical development of variables such as facilities, contact between hosts and guests, change, control and tourist type (Figure 4.2). He also emphasizes that not all destinations may be able to rejuvenate themselves. And when such a rejuvenation does occur the destination's 'perpetual success cannot be guaranteed' (1993, p. 76). He also indicates that existing problems that contributed to the resort's decline do not disappear, especially those related to saturation and overuse.

Another popular article also addresses the issue of destination development. Plog (1974) details how destinations evolve through a product cycle. In contrast to Butler's (1980) model and Defert's (1954) propositions, however, Plog's curve is rather deterministic and does not provide an option of

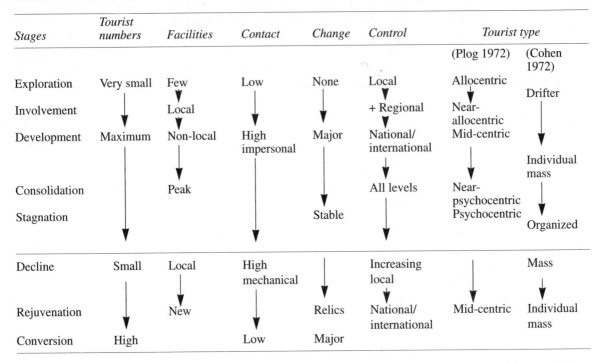

Stages	Tourist numbers	Facilities	Contact	Change	Control	Tourist type (Plog 1972)	(Cohen 1972)
Exploration	Very small	Few	Low	None	Local	Allocentric	
Involvement		Local			+ Regional	Near-allocentric	Drifter
Development	Maximum	Non-local	High impersonal	Major	National/international	Mid-centric	
Consolidation		Peak			All levels	Near-psychocentric	Individual mass
Stagnation				Stable		Psychocentric	Organized
Decline	Small	Local	High mechanical		Increasing local		Mass
Rejuvenation		New		Relics	National/international	Mid-centric	Individual mass
Conversion	High		Low	Major			

Figure 4.2 Hypothetical cycle of tourist areas.
Source: Butler 1993a.

rejuvenation. Plog's main contention is that as destinations develop their clientele changes from an allocentric to a near-allocentric, mid-centric, near psychocentric and finally psychocentric customer. In this progression, a destination reaches its maximum visitor number when it is in its mid-centric stage since the majority of the population belongs into this category. Based on his research, Plog also placed a number of destinations along this axis. In a further extension of his model, Plog (1991) provided a second set of the psychographic position of destinations, reflecting the situation almost 20 years later. As Oppermann and Chon (1995a) note, however, the actual development visitor numbers of some destinations do not correspond with their placement on the axis, which questions Plog's evaluation and perhaps the whole model. Unfortunately, others have not been able to test Plog's model since he never revealed his methodology (S. Smith 1990).

HILL RESORTS

Hill resorts are among the earliest tourism resort developments in a number of developing countries, especially in South and South East Asia. Commonly founded by the colonial powers, they were largely aimed at providing an amiable climate and retreat for the colonial administrators. The early history of these resorts is reflected in the fact that several early inquiries into tourism in developing countries were devoted to them (e.g. Senftleben 1973; Spencer and Thomas 1948; Withington 1961). Most of these studies were descriptive, however, and provide few insights in regard to hill-resorts' spatio–temporal development or even why a particular site was chosen. The changing tourist demand over the last 40 years toward a more beach-oriented tourism has meant that hardly any new hill resorts have been established. An exception is Genting Highlands in Malaysia (Reed 1979). However, this is an exception in many ways and its casino is the primary attraction rather than the cooler climate or the rural atmosphere. Hill resorts are seldom the primary destination of visiting international tourists; often they function as a stopover destination, constituting simply an additional attraction to be visited (Oppermann 1994b).

SEASIDE RESORT DEVELOPMENT

One of the earliest attempts at establishing a resort typology is Blume's (1963) discussion of tourism and tourism destination development in the Caribbean. He identified three different types of tourism destinations:

● cities in which tourism co-exists with other economic activities;
● tourism resorts with a predominance of tourism activity;
● hotel resorts outside urban areas in which tourism is the sole economic activity.

He then went on and gave several examples of destinations that belong to these three categories. He recognized that the third category was by far the most important one and that modern tourism in the Caribbean is characterized by this type of tourism resort.

Another author who examined seaside resorts was Franz (1985a). Based on his observations of 61 resorts in South East Asia he distinguished three types of resort settings:

● well established resort towns or cities;
● beach resorts in an 'isolated' location;
● resorts with small-scale accommodation of lower standards.

Focusing on the major resorts at the time, Franz (1985b) plotted the spatial distribution of hotel rooms over a period from 1967 to 1981 for Pattaya (Thailand), Batu Ferringhi (Malaysia) and Sanur (Bali). He vividly demonstrated the spatio–temporal evolvement of these resorts. His figures suggest that the development largely occurred along the beachfront with few, if any, extensions, into the hinterland which characterize many of the other seaside resort models. However, such extensions may have developed since then, as 1981 (his last date) was still relatively early in the overall development of these resorts.

Wong (1986) forwarded a classification scheme of beach resorts in Malaysia. He distinguished four different categories: planned resort complex; individual resort of international and of national standard and resorts providing basic accommodation. He suggests that the development of resorts adheres to a development sequence of local popularity, development for domestic tourists and upgrading to international standard. This corresponds with Butler's (1993a) intimation of a changing level of local to national/international control of the industry (Figure 4.2). Unfortunately, Wong did not provide any measure which might be used in establishing the resorts' development stage.

In the wake of Butler's (1980) model emerged a number of theoretical studies that addressed the issue of resort development from a more spatio–temporal perspective. These studies may be categorized into two groups: models of seaside resorts and urban resorts. Within the former, Gormsen (1981) contributed a model on European seaside resorts. Although not directly placed in a developing countries context, he suggested that tourism development occurs from the centre towards the periphery and that seaside resorts in northern Africa and other developing countries belong to the third and fourth periphery respectively based on a European perspective. From a North American perspective, Cuba, the Bahamas and Bermuda belong to the second periphery, Mexico and other Caribbean islands to the third, while more remote developing countries are part of the fourth periphery. Of greater interest in the destination development context is Gormsen's differentiation of accommodation development in the different peripheries. He argues that while guest houses and private rooms are an important aspect in the accommodation supply in the first and second periphery almost from the start, this type of accommodation was almost non-existent in the third and fourth periphery until 1980 (Figure 4.3). Using Gormsen's model of changing accommodation supply one could categorize individual seaside resorts into a specific stage of development according to its accommodation supply distribution. Yet this line of categorization and inquiry has not attracted any attention.

Drawing on a number of tourism seaside resorts in the Gulf of Mexico, Meyer-Arendt (1990) developed a model of the morphologic evolution of a

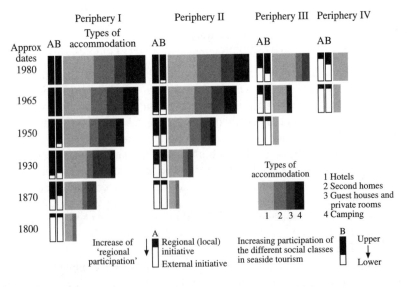

Figure 4.3 Spatio–temporal development of international seaside resorts.
Source: Gormsen 1981.

typical Gulf of Mexico seaside resort (Figure 4.4). It is an extension of ear-
lier works in other contexts and locations (e.g. Barrett 1958; Lavery 1971;
Pigram 1977; Stansfield 1971; Taylor 1975; Wolfe 1952) and, therefore, a
fine example of how theoretical advancement may be built on previous work.
Essentially, Meyer-Arendt's model suggests that the development occurs in a
T-shape pattern with the initial point of beach access becoming the locus of
tourist activities. The point evolves into the recreational business district
(RBD) and usually remains at the core of any further development. Summer
homes, condominiums and high-rise resort hotels develop outside the RBD
and give the seaside resort a compact, urban atmosphere.

The T-shape pattern also underlies Smith's (1992) beach resort model.
Besides the schematic model of beach resort development (Figure 4.5),
Smith also provided an extended model where in eight stages, a seaside
resort develops from no tourism to fully fledged urban tourism resort (Smith
1991). Notable in Smith's extended model is the emphasis on second homes
and low budget tourism in the early stages of development, although soon to
be replaced by hotels and high-budget tourists. Drawing on one Australian
and three South East Asian seaside resort examples, Smith's model seems to
mirror some of Wong's (1986) propositions. The value of this model may be
seen in its conceptual integration of many different aspects of tourism

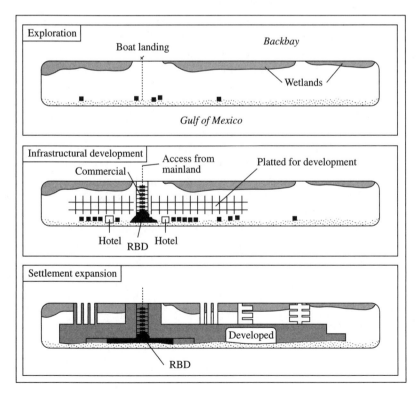

Figure 4.4 Morphologic evolution of Gulf of Mexico seaside resorts. RBD = recreational business district.
Source: Meyer-Arendt 1985.

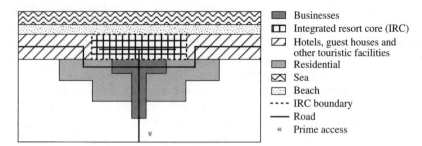

Figure 4.5 Seaside resort development.
Source: Smith 1992.

development, beyond the changes in morphology, such as environmental, planning, political and management aspects.

Another researcher who developed a model of tourist zones in developing countries is Vielhaber (1986). Basing his proposition on experiences in southern Thailand, Vielhaber suggests that tourism resorts develop independently from each other with no direct linkage. Seaside resorts are only directly connected to an urban area in the hinterland which grows as a consequence of tourism development. These urban areas are connected with each other through transportation networks.

Uthoff (1991) also based his model of beach resort development on examples in southern Thailand. He argues that tourism development in all the bays of Phuket island followed essentially the same pattern. In the very early stages, simple accommodation in the form of chalets is provided for young individual travellers whom Uthoff terms 'the pioneers of international tourism'. An almost parallel development is the construction of small single or double storey hotels also along the beachfront. Both developments are characterized by their favourable ratio between open and built-up land. In the second stage, additional hotels and general tourist infrastructure (i.e. souvenir shops, restaurants, shops) are added, resulting in an increasing density of development. Single storey buildings are replaced by multi-storey hotels as pressure on land increases. Additional residential areas are developed at the foot hills away from the tourist zone. Land use changes from agriculture towards residential or commercial. With increasing land pressure, landfills occur in the lagoons to provide additional space. A lack of available land in the bay area eventually forces the development of the hillsides along with an ever increasing pressure to construct multi-storey hotels with 20 to 40 floors. As a result, the originally rural character of the bay is lost and replaced by an urban outlook. The transformation of the landscape is complete and only the attractions of sun, sand and sea remain the same.

URBAN TOURISM DEVELOPMENT

Compared to seaside resorts, city tourism and urban models have attracted less attention. With respect to developing countries, Weaver (1993) suggests a model of urban tourism space (Figure 4.6). Drawing on small Caribbean islands, Weaver proposes five zones: specialized tourist zone, central business district (CBD), local neighbourhoods, resort strip and rural areas. It is mixture of a Thünen-Weber model and the T-shape pattern of the seaside resort models. Zones one to three and five form concentric rings around the main tourist foci of tourism in small Caribbean Islands, the cruiseship dock. These concentric rings denote a decreasing intensity of tourism penetration into the urban sphere not unlike the decreasing intensity of tourism development and usage as forwarded by Yokeno (1968) in his application of the Thünen-Weber analysis to tourism studies. The strip development along the coast is found in almost all seaside resort development models (e.g.

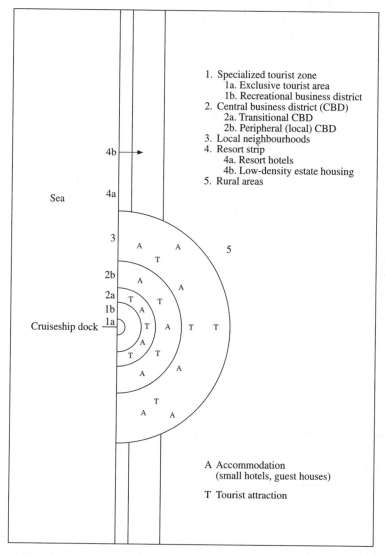

Figure 4.6 Model of urban tourism space.
Source: Weaver 1993.

Meyer-Arendt 1990; Smith 1991) and is a very typical component of tourism in developing countries (Oppermann and Sahr 1992). Nonetheless, Weaver's model of the urban tourism space is a very valuable addition to the literature of resort development in developing countries and it may be usefully applied to other parts of the world once a systematic analysis of the urban tourism space development is undertaken.

Based on urban models in industrialized countries (e.g. Ashworth 1989; Ritter 1986) and noted deviations to such developments in developing countries, Oppermann, Din and Amri (1996) developed a model of urban tourism development in developing countries. Based on their case study of Kuala Lumpur, they proposed seven types of hotel locations:

(a) *Railway station*
   Very early development which never gained much importance.
(b) *Old historic city/old CBD*
   Very early development which kept its momentum into the 1970s, but has almost stagnated since then with the emergence of new CBDs and the inherent loss of its central function. It is characterized by smaller hotels with a few large additions after national independence. Urban renewal and regeneration efforts, historic preservation and addition of tourist attractions (i.e. Central Market) may result in a future revival of this location as a hotel site.
(c) *Access road location*
   Originally mostly aimed at workers from the surrounding tin mines and less for long-haul travellers as in other cities. Extension of the old CBD and establishment of shopping complexes resulted in an increased attractiveness and eventually the construction of several large hotels forming a second core of hotel location in the wider Chow Kit area.
(d) *Ethnic neighbourhoods*
   Owing to the high number of immigrants of two major different ethnic origins with a strong male bias throughout most of the early twentieth century, brothels were widespread. These hotel locations still linger on but are a specific Kuala Lumpur phenomenon.
(e) *New CBD*
   The majority of Kuala Lumpur's up-market hotels are in an area that was once a prestigious residential suburb. As hotel construction boomed, and more businesses, offices and shopping centres were located there it developed into the new CBD and is Kuala Lumpur's foremost hotel location.
(f) *Extension of new CBD*
   Although the hotels at Jalan Ampang/Jalan Tun Razak are still a location in their own right, it appears to be only a question of time until they merge with the hotels in Kuala Lumpar's 'Golden Triangle'/new CBD.
(g) *Airport location*
   Several large hotels can be found in the vicinity of the international airport and on the feeder roads to Kuala Lumpur.

Oppermann *et al.* discerned that the most important hotel location in Kuala Lumpur, the 'Golden Triangle' or new CBD, is not included in Ashworth's (1989) typology. It is a location type commonly found in South East Asian countries, especially in the combination of large modern hotels and de luxe shopping centres with an abundance of designer names. In Singapore, for example, Orchard Road is a synonym for such a location type and similar developments can be observed in other cities as well (i.e. Jakarta, Kuching). Weaver (1993) also suggests that shopping is the main function of urban areas in Caribbean developing countries. It appears as if tourism as a 'modern' tertiary activity is an integral part of today's CBDs in at least some developing countries.

THE INFORMAL AND FORMAL SECTORS IN TOURISM RESORTS

All of the models of resort development addressed above disregard the existence of two different sectors in the tourism economy. Not unlike the discussion of spatio–temporal tourism development on a national level, most researchers place their models in the development or diffussionist paradigm. An exception is Kermath and Thomas' (1992) discussion of the spatial dynamics of Sosúa in the Dominican Republic and Wahnschafft's (1982) analysis of Pattaya, Thailand. The latter was among the first to introduce the sectoral paradigm into tourism studies but few followed. He discussed the development of both formal and informal tourism sectors in Pattaya in the context of government policies and intervention.

On a resort level, Kermath and Thomas' (1992) model of formal and informal sector development remains the only paradigm that discusses the almost parallel evolution of both sectors (Figure 4.7). They placed it directly into Butler's (1980) concept of resort evolution. They argue that the informal tourism sector emerges first, soon followed by the formal sector. Consequently, both sectors vie for space and tourists.

> As both sectors expand, competition for space and local tourist market develops. The result of this competition ranges from mutual co-existence to one-sector dominance ... Formal sector domination of the informal sector primarily is a response to biased policy and disincentives to informal sector growth.
>
> (Kermath and Thomas 1992, p. 178)

Thus, Kermath and Thomas support Wahnschafft's (1982) notion that the informal sector is purposely held back and negatively affected by government intervention. According to Kermath and Thomas' model, the final conclusion of the development process is either absorption of the informal into the formal sector or spatial relocation of the former. However, the authors have already suggested several exceptions to this rule, namely for places where tourism caters to local residents, market towns which drive on street vendors, and enclave development where the informal sector can be easily controlled because it emerged as a consequence of the formal resort establishment.

Developing Butler's (1980) model further and accommodating the existence of both sectors, Kermath and Thomas also suggested a modification to Butler's model (Figure 4.8). Essentially it is Butler's original model with two

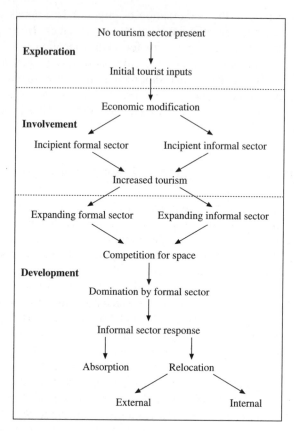

Figure 4.7 Formal and informal sector development in resort areas.
Source: Kermath and Thomas 1992.

curves, one for the informal and one for the formal sector. Another deviation is that it refers to the number of tourist-related establishments on the y-axis and not tourist numbers as in the original. It stipulates that the informal sector is arriving somewhat earlier and initially develops faster than the formal sector. However, at one stage there will be more formal sector enterprises, and along with the strong expansion of the formal sector comes a stagnation and decline in the informal sector. To what extent decline and rejuvenation occur in both sectors in cyclical or opposite terms remains ambiguous.

DESTINATION EVALUATION

As mentioned above, most resort evaluations and resort models are rather descriptive and, for a lack of hard indicators, not predictive. Hindsight often determines the development stage and serious attempts at establishing specific indicators and threshold limits are needed. One aspect often not addressed in the resort models is the type of destination. Apparently researchers have either assumed that the resort destination in question is the

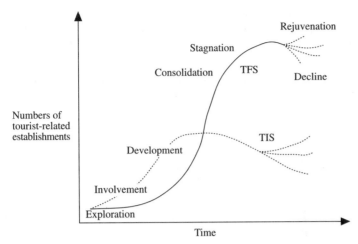

Figure 4.8 Evolution of formal and informal sectors in resort areas (compare Figure 4.1) TFS = tourism, formal sector; TIS = tourism, informal secor.
Source: Kermath and Thomas 1992.

only destination of its visitors or thought it of little relevance. Yet implicit in the term tourism is the touring aspect; many tourists visit more than one destination although most of the 'sand, sun and sea' package tours to developing countries are of the single destination type (Oppermann 1995d). Pearce and Elliott (1983) recognized that not all destinations on the itinerary of tourists are of the same importance and they proposed the Trip Index.

TRIP INDEX

The Trip Index (TI) is a ratio of the nights a tourist spends at a certain destination to the whole length of the trip (Pearce and Elliott 1983):

$$TI = (Dn/Tn) \times 100$$

where   Dn = Nights at destination;
            Tn = Total nights on trip.

The TI values range from greater than 0 to a maximum of 100. A value of 100 would imply that the tourists spend their entire trip at one destination. This is often the case in developing countries, resulting in true tourist enclaves where tourists do not get to see anything else of the country they are visiting but the tourist resort. The calculation of TI values for all tourists or a representative sample can yield very valuable insights into the tourists' intra-national travel behaviour and the relative function of each destination. Places with an average TI value of 10 or less may be considered as stopover destinations while all those with a TI value of higher than 50 would be principal destinations.

Despite its relative simplicity, the Trip Index is still rarely applied in developing countries. Oppermann (1992b) applied the Trip Index in the

Malaysian context. He reveals that the Club Méditerranée with a TI value of 100 is indeed a tourist enclave, not connected to any other tourist destination. He also disclosed a very high TI value for the capital city Kuala Lumpur (67) and Penang (59), indicating that these two major cities and locations of international airports are not gateways to Malaysia but rather primary tourist destinations in their own right (Figure 4.9).

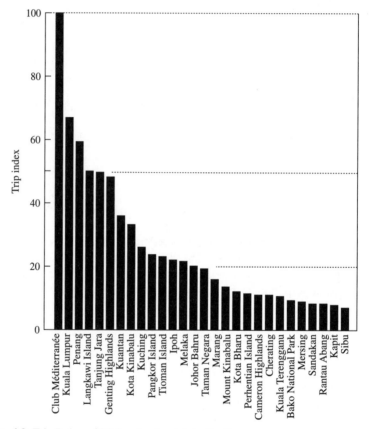

Figure 4.9 Trip Index of Malaysian tourist destinations.
Source: Oppermann 1992e.

Table 4.1 Destination classification by percentage of tourists in the three Trip Index Categories

	Trip index category		
Destination type	*1–20*	*21–50*	*51–100*
Principal destination	none	< 40	> 60
International gateway with principal destination function	0 < x < 20	20–40	> 50
Getaway resort	< 60	> 40	> 0
Regional gateway/ Major tourist attraction	40–80	10–40	possibly
Stopover destination	> 80	< 20	none

Source: Oppermann 1994b, p. 17

Taking the Trip Index one step further, Oppermann (1994b) used it to derive a destination typology (Table 4.1). He recognized that the calculation of a TI average may conceal differences between destinations owing to a different composition of their travellers. He defined five destination types: principal destination, international gateway with principal destination function, getaway resort, regional gateway/major tourist attraction, and stopover destination. While the class definitions partly overlap in one or two categories, overall all five destination types are mutually exclusive compositions of different TI values among their visitors. Oppermann then went on to classify Malaysian destinations along the proposed typology and suggested that the refined distinction among destination could improve marketing strategies (Table 4.2).

Table 4.2 Resort typology of Malaysian destinations

Aggregate trip index	Destination type	Examples (trip index values)
> 50	Principal destination International gateway	Club Méditerranée (100) Kuala Lumpur (67) Penang (59)
21–50	Getaway resort	Langkawi Island (50) Genting Highlands (48) Tioman Island (23) Pangkor Island (23)
	Regional gateway/ major tourist attraction	Kuantan (35) Kota Kinabalu (33) Taman Negara (28) Kuching (26) Ipoh (22) Melaka (22)
1–20	Stopover destination	Johor Bahru (20) Kota Bharu (12) Cameron Highlands (11) Cherating (11) Kuala Terengganu (10) Mersing (9) Rantau Abang (8)

Source: Oppermann 1994b, p. 18

SUMMARY

This chapter examined tourism resorts and their evolution over time. A large number of studies have addressed this topic and it apparently has attracted the largest number of theories and models, especially for seaside resorts. Yet little progress has been made with respect to establishing measures of such development which could be used in tourism planning. While the resort life cycle is a useful conceptual tool, it is not prescriptive and judgements of where a destination is on the life cycle curve at any one time are almost impossible to make. Gormsen's (1981) notion of a changing accommodation composition may be a valuable avenue towards establishing development indicators. Perhaps as useful could be the issue of ownership which Butler (1993a) includes in his updated model. Without providing tourism planners with a practical guide of where a destination currently stands in the destination life cycle, any further models of resort development appear as academic egoism rather than applicable research.

QUESTIONS

1. What is the tourism destination life cycle and what are its advantages and disadvantages?
2. Discuss the reasons for the apparent evolution of a T-shape pattern in seaside resorts.
3. What is a main feature of urban tourism development in developing countries?
4. Consider the usefulness of the trip index as a method of classifying destinations.

FURTHER READING

Page, S. (1995) *Urban Tourism*. Routledge, London.

Most comprehensive textbook on the topic of urban tourism although with very few examples from developing countries.

Vetter, F. (ed.) (1986) *Grossstadttourismus*. Reimer Verlag, Berlin.

Although a bit dated, this collection of several dozen articles covers a wide range of issues in urban tourism development. It also includes the largest number of papers on urban tourism in developing countries.

Urban hotel location and evolution in Kuala Lumpur, Malaysia

Capital cities and large urban areas are commonly the major tourist destinations in developing countries, especially during the early stages of tourism development (Oppermann 1993a). National capitals like Kuala Lumpur are also bearers of national symbols, parliament, company and government headquarters as well as a cosmopolitan community significantly coloured by the presence of a sizeable diplomatic community. They are the gateways to their countries due to the prevalence of air transportation and a large proportion of the total hotel capacity is found there (Oppermann 1993).

A brief history of Kuala Lumpur

Kuala Lumpur's rise to today's position as the predominant urban and economic centre of Malaysia can be considered coincidental. It was only one of many trading towns founded in the progress of tin extraction during the nineteenth century. As with many other towns founded on mineral extraction alone, it may have become a ghost town if not for the state capital status which was transferred from Kelang to Kuala Lumpur in 1880. From this moment, Kuala Lumpur was put on a growth path and its destiny was predetermined. In 1896 it became the capital of the Federated Malay States and remained the centre of colonial administration until independence in 1957. In turn, the administrative status brought more and more people, more investors and especially more infrastructure to Kuala Lumpur than to its rival towns at the time. The rail connection with Port Kelang in 1886 gave Kuala Lumpur a crucial economic link to the outside world and facilitated an easier transfer of goods. Through the first half of the twentieth century Kuala Lumpur was expanding gradually and its economy was based on tin extraction, rubber estates and trade. With independence in 1957, Kuala Lumpur became the capital of Malaya and occupied the same status after the formation of Malaysia in 1963. The establishment of free trade zones in the Klang valley and the subsequent location of manufacturing companies diversified the type of jobs offered. Restricted by its boundaries and the limited land area therein, Kuala Lumpur's economy is currently dominated by tertiary activities such as government services, corporate headquarters, trade, banking, finance and tourism while many manufacturing plants are situated in the greater Kuala Lumpur/Klang valley area.

Tourism development in Kuala Lumpur

Tourism development in Kuala Lumpur is more coincidental than well planned. There exists no explicit policy regarding tourism development in Kuala Lumpur except for the Kuala Lumpur Structure Plan from 1984 which called for the construction of more luxury hotels. Some commentators have even stated that Kuala Lumpur lacks urban related tourism attractions (e.g. JICA 1989). Yet one may consider Kuala Lumpur as a pace setter in tourism. New values based on the hotel or 'invented traditions' such as 'high tea', wedding, birthday and valentine dinners are foreign features in the new urban lifestyle which are promoted by the hotels. Thus, although the examination of hotel development reveals only one facet of the overall tourism development, it illustrates the pace of development and it may stand as a symbol for other associated changes.

Pre-tourism stage (1895–1957)

Kuala Lumpur's pre-tourism stage is defined by the opening of the first hotel in 1895 and Malaysia's independence in 1957. Although it was not a time without tourism, tourism played an insignificant role. In 1895, the FMS Hotel was opened and in 1907 the Empire Hotel was added, followed by the (railway) Station Hotel (1911), Eastern Hotel (1915) and Coliseum Hotel (1921). More important than these hotels catering to a more international clientele (i.e. colonial administrators) were those for locals. The highly biased sex ratio as a result of the largely immigrant Chinese and Indian population (there were about 40 females per 100 males in the 1920s and 1930s) resulted in widespread prostitution. In 1893 there were some 50 brothels housing about 1000 prostitutes including Chinese, Japanese, Indians and Malays. Recognizing this trend, the government allowed brothels which were mostly located in the respective ethnic neighbourhoods. These were the Chinatowns along Jalan Petaling/Jalan Sultan, Pudu Road and Batu Road (now called Jalan Tunku Abdul Rahman) and the more Indian dominated Brickfields area. Although prostitution laws were again tightened in the 1930s and after World War II, the emergent spatial pattern of hotels remained.

Unfortunately, historic data on hotel openings is limited especially as regards the small hotels which dominated the accommodation scene until 1957. Figure 4.10 shows a simplified version of hotel locations in Kuala Lumpur in the pre-tourism stage. Five distinct areas of hotel development may be identified: old Chinatown at the confluence of the Klang and Gombak rivers (historic centre), railway station, Pudu Road, Batu Road, and Brickfields. The old Chinatown, at the location of the original settlement, was the CBD of Kuala Lumpur until well into the 1970s. It was and is a Chinese dominated area with typical shophouses. Until the 1920s, it was the main location of brothels serving the needs of a heavily male biased population.

The Station Hotel (1911) and Hotel Majestic (1932) form the second category. Unlike in most European cities, the railway station never gained much

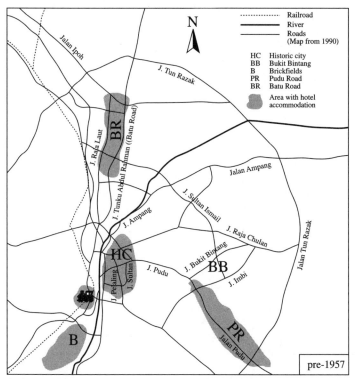

Figure 4.10 Hotel location and distribution in Kuala Lumpur, pre-independence.
Source: Oppermann, Din and Amri 1996

prominence as a hotel site despite the early construction of two, at the time, prominent hotels. One reason was the limited number of passengers arriving by train. The railway was mostly used for freight transportation, namely transfer of tin from the mines around Kuala Lumpur to Port Kelang.

Both Pudu and Batu Road can be considered as access road locations and areas where the CBD was slowly expanding. Both locations were the 'gateways' to Kuala Lumpur for the Chinese workers in the tin mines surrounding Kuala Lumpur and consequently the tourism sector consisted mostly of brothels and lodging houses.

Tourism inception (1957–70)

The year 1957 marked not only Malaya's independence but also a drastic change in hotel location pattern in the years to come. In the very same year, the first large hotel (less than 100 rooms), the Federal Hotel (120 rooms, later expanded to 450 rooms in 1969), was opened in Bukit Bintang. This was an area with Chinese shophouses in the vicinity of an exclusive residential neighbourhood. Only two years later followed the Hotel Merlin (700 rooms) and in 1963 the Equatorial Hotel (300 rooms), both located along Jalan Sultan Ismail in relative proximity to each other. These were the first hotels in an area that was to become the 'Golden Triangle'. Until 1970 it was zoned as a residential neighbourhood and was considered Kuala Lumpur's most

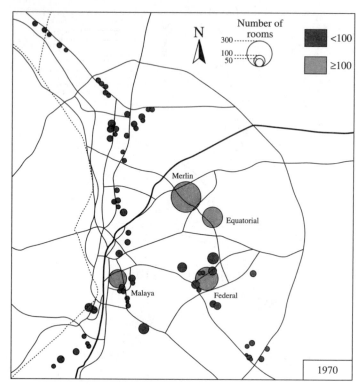

Figure 4.11 Hotel location and distribution in Kuala Lumpur, 1970.
Source: Oppermann, Din and Amri 1996.

prestigious residential suburb. Even today, there are pockets of bungalows in the area and some foreign embassies are still located there. Another large hotel, Hotel Malaysia, was built in the old Chinatown.

Hence, by 1970 (Figure 4.11), a different pattern had emerged with renewed emphasis on previous locations (Chinatown CBD) and the establishment of a completely new cluster of locations (Golden Triangle). The difference in size of some of the new hotel additions already signified the start of a new era and the location of two of the largest hotels at the time in a formerly residential, non-commercial neighbourhood, foreshadowed a changing urban development pattern. While all the other smaller hotels were of a somewhat lesser standard and were more geared to catering for domestic travellers, the new hotels were aimed at the small but growing number of international travellers and business visitors.

Tourism evolvement (1970–80)

The 1970s brought a rapid growth of tourist arrivals to Malaysia and Kuala Lumpur and necessitated the construction of more and more hotels. In 1972, the Hilton Hotel was opened at the site of the former French Embassy in the Golden Triangle and the Holiday Inn on the Park followed the next year in

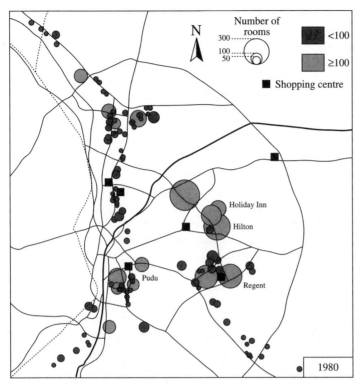

Figure 4.12 Hotel location and distribution in Kuala Lumpur, 1980.
Source: Oppermann, Din and Amri 1996.

the same general locality. The construction of yet another two large hotels in
the Golden Triangle indicated the rapid development of this area into a predominantly up-market hotel location. At the eastern end of Jalan Sultan
Ismail, the opening of the Regent Hotel added importance to the Bukit
Bintang area which had evolved into one of Kuala Lumpur's foremost hotel
locations by 1980 (Figure 4.12).

Several hotels were added in the old Chinatown area with the Pudu Raya
Hotel on top of the new bus station being the most notable. It demonstrates
the importance of the road system and public bus transportation vis-à-vis the
railroad where no new hotels were built at the railway station.

Another noticeable development was the construction of several large and
medium sized hotels in the Chow Kit area. Among them the Asia Hotel and
the Grand Central Hotel. By 1980 the old CBD had effectively expanded
along Jalan Raja Laut/Jalan Tunku Abdul Rahman (formerly Batu Road).
The loss of the old CBD's central function can be deduced from the construction of several shopping complexes outside the old CBD in the 1970s.
Among them were the Weld Supermarket and Sungai Wang Plaza in the
Golden Triangle and Bukit Bintang area respectively. Shopping centres were
established along Jalan Tunku Abdul Rahman (e.g. Pertama Kompleks,
Kompleks Campbell).

One of the very first shopping centres, Kompleks Ampang along Jalan Ampang, was again a sign of future development to come. Although fairly isolated at the time with only a few other shops and businesses located close to it, it was a location close to the prestigious neighbourhood along Jalan Ampang (extension of the Golden Triangle area) and the new suburbs being developed on the outskirts of Kuala Lumpur.

Tourism unfolding (1980–90)

The early 1980s experienced a slump in hotel construction, not least due to the rapid expansion during the late 1970s. In 1984 the Ming Court Hotel was opened along Jalan Ampang in proximity to the Ampang Shopping Centre mentioned earlier. Again it was a new development in an area without previous accommodation. It was not until 1988 that MiCasa Hotel Apartments were opened at the junction of Jalan Ampang and Jalan Tun Razak (circular road around most of Kuala Lumpur).

During the 1980s several developments occurred. First, both railway location hotels vanished from the supply scene. Second, the old Chinatown stagnated in its development with no new major hotel developments. Third, similarly Brickfields, Pudu Road and Jalan Ipoh areas remained stagnant. Fourth, the Golden Triangle and Bukit Bintang area merged (henceforth only referred to as the Golden Triangle) and, with the addition of new large hotels, became more compact and featured an unrivalled concentration of up-market hotel rooms. Fifth, the construction of the Pan Pacific Hotel in 1985 along with the World Trade Centre and a shopping centre (The Mall) next to the aforementioned Chow Kit area gave Kuala Lumpur a third development frontier. This development was complemented by the opening of the Holiday Inn City Centre, Grand Continental and the Plaza Hotel along Jalan Raja Laut.

Tourism comes of age (1990–5)

Figure 4.13 shows the hotel supply pattern in 1995. Very obvious is the intense concentration and continued growth of the Golden Triangle area with several new large hotels (i.e. Istana, Swiss Garden). The opening of several new shopping complexes in the same area (i.e. Lot 10, K.L. Plaza) at a time when one of the official tourism strategies was to compete with Singapore as a shopping paradise suggests the prominence of the Golden Triangle area in up-market, international tourism.

Another conspicuous development in the early 1990s was the rapid development of hotels and shopping complexes in the Jalan Ampang/Tun Razak area. The addition of about 1400 rooms in this locality along with two large shopping centres signifies a whole new hotel location.

Although not as conspicuous but nevertheless remarkable is the continued development of the Chow Kit area. The construction of the Mall Hotel on top of the identically named shopping complex is adding another large-scale hotel to the area. Perhaps more important is the planned addition of the Sheraton Hotel between the Chow Kit and the Golden Triangle area. It

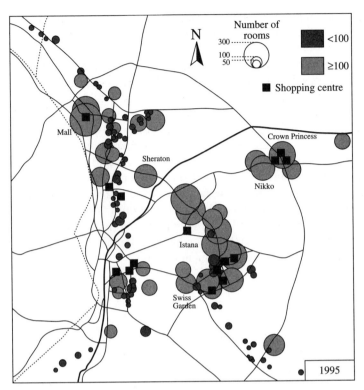

Figure 4.13 Hotel location and distribution in Kuala Lumpur, 1995.
Source: Oppermann, Din and Amri 1996.

suggests that in the future these two distinct hotel locations may merge along the axis of Jalan Sultan Ismail. The planned construction in the post-1995 era of another two very large hotels at the junction of Jalan Ampang/Jalan Sultan Ismail is another indicator for such a development.

The stagnation of some of the very early hotel locations (old Chinatown, Brickfields, Pudu Road) are signs for the changing emphasis on new hotel construction and the changing fortune of different areas. Although efforts are being made to renew the old Chinatown and preserve some of the cultural heritage, it has lost many of its CBD functions and the limited space in a densely developed area is a hindrance for large-scale projects. Nonetheless, the construction of a few new shopping centres and one large hotel may indicate some revival of the historic city. And the street market at Jalan Petaling remains one of Kuala Lumpur's major tourist attractions.

Conclusion

While railway station, historic city, access road and airport location are included in previous hotel location typologies, the most important hotel location in Kuala Lumpur, the Golden Triangle or new CBD, is not included in Ashworth's typology. It is a location type commonly found in South East Asian countries, especially in the combination of large modern hotels and deluxe shopping centres where designer names abound. In Singapore, for example, Orchard Road is a synonym for such a location type and similar developments can be observed in other cities as well (e.g. Jakarta, Kuching). Weaver (1993) suggested that shopping is also the main function of urban areas in Caribbean developing countries. It appears that tourism as a 'modern' tertiary activity is an integral part of today's CBDs in, at least some, developing countries.

In conclusion, the analysis of the spatio–temporal evolution of hotel location in Kuala Lumpur suggests that different factors may be at work in developing countries as compared to the developed world. It indicates that the transfer of urban tourism concepts from developed to developing countries may be inappropriate. More research on urban tourism is needed in both developed and developing countries, to further our understanding of this very much neglected field of tourism. The hope placed upon tourism as an agent in urban renewal and re-imaging requires a better comprehension of the underlying urban tourism development patterns.

Demand for tourism

5

Tourism is inextricably linked with tourism demand. It is people who travel from their usual place of residence to a different place or places and, after a limited time period, return to their usual or new place of residence. Hence, without tourists or tourist demand there would be no tourism. The reasons why people embark on a journey are varied and probably differ as much over time and between generations as between different countries. And many people have multiple reasons for travel. For example, they may combine a visit to friends or relatives with a visit to some tourist sites. Or a conference participant may stay one or more additional nights to visit museums, go shopping, or just take a break from the everyday routine. Even among people travelling together, such as a family on their holiday vacation, travel motives are likely to differ. While the parents may prefer to visit cultural sites, the children would perhaps rather spend the whole day on the beach or in a theme park. Even the travel destination chosen is likely to be a reflection of the varying interests within the family in order to accommodate these.

On a generic level, the most commonly identified travel purposes to differentiate the tourist demand are 'pleasure', 'business', and 'visiting friends and relatives (vfr)'. Within these three categories many different subsets exist and, as indicated above, these categories are not mutually exclusive. Even the inclusion of business and vfr travel has drawn critique with the opposing faction arguing that only pleasure travel is real tourism. Arndt (1978) provides an excellent overview of some early definitions of tourism as they were published in a number of articles and textbooks between 1911 and 1955. More recently Przeclawski (1993) and Smith (1995) provided some discussion on definitions of tourists and tourism. In Germany, for example, annual surveys of outbound travel by German residents only include 'pleasure' travel (FUR 1994; StfT 1993).

MOTIVATIONS AND ATTRACTIONS

A look into the history of tourism immediately reveals that at different times in the past a number of different motives were prevalent. 'Escaping from unfavourable seasonal climates', 'exploration', 'travel for business', the 'Grand Tour', 'health motives', 'adventure', and 'pilgrimages' all were and still are primary travel motives for travelling in industrialized and developing countries. In a review of several travel motivation studies, Pearce suggests that 'the fundamental motivation for tourist travel is a need, real or perceived, to break from routine and that for many this can be best achieved by a physical change of place' (1989 p. 118).

A study in Germany showed that 'escape from everyday life' was the highest ranked travel motive (Table 5.1). Other highly ranked travel motives were 'relaxation', 'gain new experiences', 'time for each other', and 'gather new energy'.

In the context of international travel from developed to developing countries, the three 'Ss' (sun, sand and sea) are usually touted as the primary purpose of pleasure travel. And, certainly, many developing countries do have plenty of these. Some authors have extended the three to four 'Ss' in order to include 'sex' (e.g. Hobson and Dietrich 1994). Tourism for sexual purposes has made some destinations notorious and a look into destination brochures suggests that most countries use this 'attraction' in an at least a subliminal way. Three 'S' tourism probably best represents and symbolizes today's mass tourism to developing countries. In a way, it is a replication of tourist travel to Spain, Italy, Florida and California where sun, sand and sea constitute a major if not the primary tourist attraction.

However, sun, sand and sea are not the only reason for pleasure travel to developing countries. A completely different travel motivation is 'educational travel' to historic and cultural attractions. The Egyptian pyramids, Borobudur in Indonesia and Macchu Picchu in Peru epitomize this type of attraction. Naturally, for others a look at today's culture and lifestyle in developing countries is of interest. From a tour operator perspective, strictly educational tours are often a small but lucrative niche and statistics suggest that this segment may grow in importance in the years to come (StfT 1993). In a sense, it is a modern day version of the 'Grand Tour'. Again, the differentiation of package tour operators into educational and general mass

Table 5.1 Travel motives of German pleasure travellers, 1992

Motive	Percentage	Motive	Percentage
Relaxation/recuperation		**Adventure/sport**	
Relaxation	76.5	Escape everyday life	77.0
Gather new energy	57.2	Have fun	48.5
Freedom/do what I want	47.1	Experience a lot/variety	46.4
Enjoyment/to indulge	46.5	Be active in sports	14.2
To exercise	43.9		
To do nothing	39.2	**Social contacts**	
Get a suntan	12.6	Time for each other	57.2
		Sociability	49.7
		Meet new people	41.7
		Contacts with locals	39.2
Education/exploration		Be together with children	28.9
Gain new experiences	50.5	Meet friends/relatives	28.3
See new countries/cultures	37.0		
Touring	34.7		
Broaden one's mind	31.1	**Nature**	
Renew memories	28.1	Experience nature	60.9
Exploration/encounter something unusual	14.5	Clean environment/escape pollution	53.7
		Sun, escape bad weather	41.6

Source: extracted from StfT 1993

tourism operators is difficult (Oppermann 1995b). General package tours often also include visits to the major cultural and historical attractions; however, such visits are commonly only interlaced with the primary activities of general sightseeing and sun, sand and sea themes.

Another major motivation to travel to developing countries is 'health'. Many people and especially mature travellers attempt to escape the colder weather in the northern hemisphere during the winter and travel, sometimes for several months, to destinations offering a milder climate. The Canary Islands, Morocco and Tunisia are primary examples for such travel from Europe, as are Mexico and several Caribbean Islands for North America.

The major reasons for inter-developing countries travel are not quite as clear but are likely to follow similar lines. What may be of relative greater importance is business and vfr travel. Among Singapore travellers to Malaysia, for example, vfr visitors account for almost 30 per cent of all tourists (MTPB 1992).

Domestic tourism demand

Domestic tourism demand in developing countries is among the most ignored topics in tourism research. The causes for this general negligence are threefold: a focus by tourism organizations in developing countries on the international inbound tourists (Table 5.2); consequently, an almost universal dearth of data on domestic travel; and an international bias by tourism researchers who mainly reside in industrialized countries. Thus, to examine domestic tourism demand and travel patterns usually requires primary data collection which international tourism researchers can often not obtain a permit for. Moreover, researchers from industrial countries are often deficient in the local language(s), and data collection in developing countries requires more financial and time resources than can be mustered. Research undertaken domestically is often regulated by the government and researchers are commonly not allowed to publish their results.

Nonetheless, the available literature suggests that domestic travel in developing countries is often of equal if not greater importance than international tourism (e.g. Gunawan 1996; Kulinat 1991; Oppermann 1992a; Teuscher and Lang 1982). Kulinat (1991) also suggests that domestic travel is less seasonal than international travel and, therefore, contributes to a higher occupancy throughout the year.

Domestic tourism contains a considerable proportion of vfr travel. In the process of rapid urbanization, a high proportion of city people have rural roots and return to their family and village whenever time and money permit. This high proportion of vfr traffic is yet another reason for our lack of understanding of domestic travel in developing countries. On the one hand, as Morrison and O'Leary (1995) described, vfr tourism is desperately seeking respect: little research has been undertaken on vfr travel in general. On the other hand, because these travellers stay with their friends or relatives and usually do not require formal tourism accommodation, their nights are not registered and difficult to trace.

Besides vfr, domestic demand usually entails a considerable portion of

Table 5.2 Tourism policy priorities: the market – domestic or international

	Brunei	Cambodia	Indonesia	Laos	Malaysia
Focus of tourism infrastructure development		International luxury and business tourists	International luxury tourists		International luxury tourists; increasingly more domestic tourists
Focus of tourism promotion		International	Luxury tourists; business travellers; domestic tours	Promotion is nil but international tourists are the ones sought	International luxury tourist, business travellers, Muslims
Collection of tourism statistics		International	International	International	International

	Myanmar	Philippines	Singapore	Thailand	Vietnam
Focus of tourism infrastructure development	International moderate to luxury tourists	International luxury tourists	International luxury tourists	Domestic or international tourists	International moderate to luxury tourists
Focus of tourism promotion	Promotion is nil but international	International luxury tourists; business travellers; balikbayans	Business and convention travellers	Business and luxury escapist travellers; some domestic promotion	Students/FIT; former Vietnam War participants; international
Collection of tourism statistics	International	International and balikbayans	International	International; but domestic statistics developing	International

Source: extracted from Richter 1993

business travel. In some developing countries, religious travel is quite pronounced and dates back a considerable time (Rinschede 1992).

In recent years, a trend towards imitation of western travel behaviour can be noted. More and more residents of developing countries flock to the sea during their holidays (Kulinat 1991). In Turkey, Höhfeld (1989) notes a shift towards establishing summer cottages at the sea instead of the more traditional inland and mountainous areas. For example, in the case of the beach resort, Pagandaran, Indonesia, domestic demand outnumbers international demand by more than nine to one (Pratiwi and Wilkinson 1994). It is also noticeable that many tourism resorts are trying to attract domestic travellers, specifically targeting the middle to upper class in their promotion endeavours.

DESTINATION CHOICE

With the continuous addition of new tourism resorts and opening up of new destinations, the destination choice is becoming more and more complex. A number of destination choice models have been forwarded over the years which recognize the importance of alternative destinations (e.g. Crompton 1992; Mansfeld 1992; Um and Crompton 1990; Woodside and Lysonski 1989). While theoretically all destinations may be included in the destination choice, people are often unaware of many of these (Figure 5.1). Starting from a set of all potential destinations, people narrow down the number of destinations they actively consider. This appears to be a process of several stages, from the initial awareness set of destinations, to the evoked (shortlisted) set, and then to the selection of the final destination. According to several empirical studies, the evoked set includes no more than four destinations (Um and Crompton 1990; Woodside and Sherrell 1977). After the final decision and the actual travel to the destination, the tourists undertake a post-purchase choice evaluation. This choice evaluation impacts future destination choices as a possible dissonance between expectations and experiences can have a negative impact on the person's attitudes towards that particular destination (Chon 1991, 1992). However, since at least neighbouring destinations share some characteristics, a negative dissonance may also affect other countries. For example, a tourist on a first time vacation to a developing country who gets very sick for a variety of reasons including climate and food safety aspects may easily decide to never travel to that particular country or any other developing country again. Unfortunately, in-depth studies of destination choice for developing countries or even for residents in these countries appear to be still lacking.

Approaching the destination process choice from a slightly different angle, Mansfeld (1990, p. 387) argues that the final destination choice is influenced by constraints. He lists seven of these filtering effects, namely availability of free time, disposable money and paid holidays, accessibility of transport systems, family obligations, workplace obligations and values and norms of tourism behaviour prevailing among one's 'reference group'.

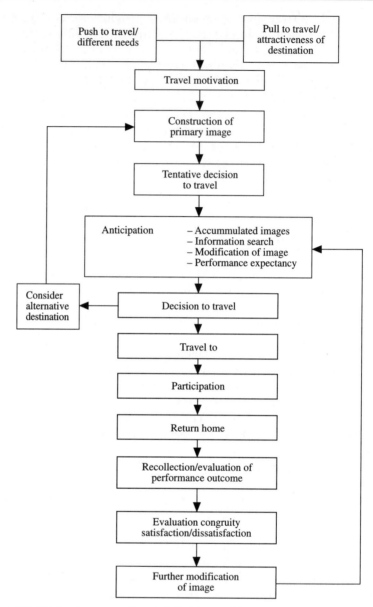

Figure 5.1 Destination perception and decision making process.
Source: redrawn after Chon 1991.

Perceptions

An important aspect within the travel destination choice process is the perception of the destinations (Chon 1989, 1990, 1991). In the literature the terms 'perception' and 'images' are sometimes used as synonyms; others use 'image' as an equivalent to a brand name, still others distinguish between both. Johnston and Tieh (1983) suggested that perceptions are beliefs held by an individual about a particular place while images or portrayed images are somewhat more generic and often 'generated' by the destination itself.

> 'Perceived images', on the other hand, are the sum of the ideas, beliefs and impressions that people possess about particular places. They are by their very nature, subjective and probably highly individualistic.
>
> (Johnston and Tieh 1983, p. 280)

Studies on perceptions of developing countries date back to the late 1970s. Crompton (1979) measured the image of Mexico using 18 different attributes. He extended his research to contrast the perceptions of Mexico as held by residents in different parts of the United States (Crompton 1979). Goodrich (1978) was among the first to research comparative perceptions of several developing countries with regard to 10 destination attributes. Unfortunately few researchers have followed along the lines of these early comparative studies of several developing countries and/or different originating regions. It appears worthwhile to extend research in this area, and direct links with the actual tourist flows may yield improved insights into the importance of perceptions on the destination decision process.

Barriers to travel

Crime, pollution, terrorism and infrastructure are just some variables which are likely to play an important part in the perception formation process and, therefore, the tourism destination choice process. Tourism can only thrive in a trouble free environment and any negative events are likely to affect the industry. This has been realized by violent opposition groups in, for example, Egypt and Turkey. Random violence purposely aimed at tourists is intended to hurt the successful tourism industry and, therefore, the government through a loss of income and negative international publicity. With the nature of today's media, any harmful event to international tourists is prone to create international headlines.

Reported high crime rates and pollution are often also deterring tourists as Brazil had to realize in the 1980s. It suffered a major setback in international tourist arrivals as a result of the negative publicity of the prevalence of violence and crimes as well as serious pollution of beaches in Brazil's primary tourism icon, Rio de Janeiro. Until 1994, it has not managed to attain its 1986 record level of tourist arrivals (Oppermann 1997). Italy is another example of how pollution can affect tourism arrivals. It suffered a major setback in tourist arrivals as a result of the reported algae which infested many of its beaches in 1989 (Becheri 1991)

Another set of barriers include the transportation infrastructure to and within developing countries. The main variables here are the cost and time involved to reach a destination. While many destinations have become more accessible over the last decades, other places experienced setbacks in the process. Kissling (1989) shows how the move towards non-stop flights across the Pacific Ocean between North America and Australia/New Zealand has hurt the tourism industry in the south Pacific islands, most notably Fiji. The latter used to be the primary stopover destination and the simple availability of a stop there induced many tourists to spend a few days there. A similar effect is likely to have occurred in Western African countries which used to be stopover destinations on flights between Europe and South America.

Closely linked to infrastructure development and competition of transportation companies is the cost of travel. A quick look into the price structure for any place of origin to other destinations readily reveals that cost is not fully dependent on distance. Some more distant destinations may be less expensive than closer ones. The competition on certain air routes and the lack of such competition on others are major determinants of the final cost. Similarly the availability or unavailability of charter flights may determine the cost structure and consequently the number of tourist arrivals.

Political reasons are another barrier to travel. These may be in the form of the destination country restricting the access to its country. Current and past examples are Tanzania, Myanmar and Vietnam. Such a restriction may come in different forms. It can be a limited time visa (e.g. one week), a screening of visitors through visa applications, the imposition of travel itineraries upon tourists, and declaring parts of the country off-limits amongst others.

Another type of political barrier to travel are restraints or embargoes by the government of the source country. The most famous case is the United States' embargo of Cuba where US citizens are not able to travel from the United States to Cuba. Sometimes this is circumvented by using other countries as a stopover destination. Another form of restraint is the imposition of high departure taxes on leaving residents. France and Israel resorted to this measure in the past in order to reduce the outflow of money.

Travel itinerary

Inextricably interlinked with the destination choice process is the decision on the form of the travel itinerary. This may range from a single destination, single country to a multi-destination, multi-country itinerary. Very little research has focused along these lines and most of the conceptual work has been based on domestic travel in the United States which tends to ignore the multi-country dimension (e.g. Mings and McHugh 1992; Lue, Crompton, and Fesenmaier 1993). Obviously different forms of tourists' interest require different itineraries. A person only interested in sun, sand and sea is likely to choose a single destination that provides all these attractions. Somebody curious about the scenery and landscape is liable to choose a multi-destination itinerary. And somebody eager to see several places and cultures is prone to opt for multi-country travel. In some instances, the availability of several places of interest in relative proximity may actually weight the destination decision towards this cluster of destinations and/or countries.

As already indicated above, the prevalent mass tourism to developing countries in the form of sun, sand and sea is doubtlessly of the single destination type, while forms of educational and religious travel commonly involve multi-destination itineraries. This distinct difference between them and a shift in the last few decades towards the three 'Ss' tourism has resulted in a concentration of tourism activity in Morocco (Berriane 1990). Pearce and

Johnston (1986) showed that many travellers to Tonga are involved in a multi-destination itinerary and that significant differences existed between single and multi-destination travellers. Hence, developing countries could obtain a better idea of what changes a shift in visitor composition will bring.

The understanding that some tourists are involved in a multi-destination and multi-country itinerary is also very advantageous for tourism promotion. Destinations or countries that share a high percentage of their visitors may be well advised to poll their precious advertising budgets and efforts rather than attempting to compete with each other. Of all the tourist to Western Samoa, for example, 43 per cent were visiting at least one other country on the same trip. This ranged from as low as 5 per cent for tourists from American Samoa to as high as 98 per cent for Germans. Fiji (50 per cent of those that visited other countries), Tahiti (27 per cent) and Tonga (22 per cent) were the most favourite other Pacific islands for German tourists, indicating that these countries may be well advised to look into joint promotion efforts in that market (Table 5.3).

Quite useful in this context is Oppermann's (1995d) model of travel itineraries which actually accounts for the multi-country nature of some itineraries (Figure 5.2). He also tested the validity of the proposed itineraries with data from visitors to Malaysia. The analysis disclosed that these itinerary types do exist and that significant differences occurred between different segments (Oppermann 1995d). For example business and vfr travellers were much more likely to be on a single destination itinerary than were pleasure tourists. Similarly, visitors from the other ASEAN countries often had just one destination while tourists from Europe, North America and Australia engaged in multi-destination itineraries. The study also revealed that the majority of the tourists had multi-country itineraries where Malaysia was just one of several countries visited.

Table 5.3 Multi-country itineraries of tourists to Western Samoa (%)

Destinations	Australia	New Zealand	USA	Japan	Germany	American Samoa	Total
Single	29	69	24	33	2	92	55
2 destinations	39	18	37	40	7	7	19
3 destinations	13	5	23	13	28	–	10
4 destinations	14	5	10	–	21	1	8
5 or more destinations	4	2	6	13	43	–	8
Average number of destinations[a]	1.7	1.7	2.0	1.7	3.5	1.6	2.3
American Samoa	20	49	43	6	2	n/a	22
Cook Islands	28	7	8	17	35	18	16
Fiji	28	23	32	50	26	27	26
Tahiti	5	2	14	6	18	9	9
Tonga	37	29	32	22	61	36	35
Other Pacific islands	10	12	13	22	5	27	16

[a] Measured in per cent of those who engaged in multi-country itineraries.
Source: extracted from TCSP 1995

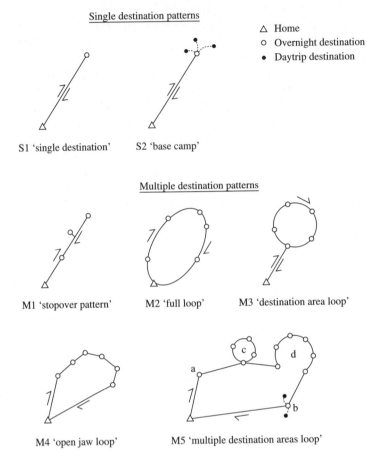

Figure 5.2 Tourist flow patterns.
Source: Oppermann 1995d.

TRAVEL VOLUME

The majority of international tourism is still occurring among the industrial-ized countries of Europe and North America. Nevertheless, their share has been consistently declining over the last few decades with many Asian coun-tries being the main beneficiaries. As Tables 1.3 and 1.5 indicated, not only has the flow of tourists from the traditional source markets of North America and Europe to Asia increased, but a large proportion of the overall increase in Asian inbound travel comes from within the region. Obviously Japan's emer-gence as a major source market in the 1980s has been one factor. However, other Asian countries have followed this path and in 1993 the four 'Asian tigers' (Hong Kong, Singapore, South Korea and Taiwan) generated almost as many outbound tourists as did Japan (Oppermann 1996b). Using other estimates, the number of outbound tourists from the Asian tigers actually exceeded Japan's considerably (WTO 1994a). China is often touted as the

new outbound tourist dragon. Given its vast population base and the growing
affluence among its upper and middle classes this appears quite realistic provided there isn't any radical political shift. In 1993, China had already deliv-
ered already 3.7 million outbound tourists, mostly to its neighbouring
countries as well as to Malaysia and Singapore, with their high ethnic
Chinese populations (Wang and Sheldon 1995). In addition, countries like
Malaysia, Thailand and Indonesia are fast becoming net outbound generators.

Major international demand sources

In terms of international outbound travel, Germany and the United States are
by far the most important source markets. In 1990, some 62 million German
residents travelled to foreign lands as did 42 million US citizens (Hudman
and Davis 1994). However, a lot of this travel is destined to neighbouring
countries and a considerably smaller proportion is actually medium- or long-
haul travel to developing countries.

Table 5.4 displays the world's top 25 tourism spenders. While the top
order countries may not come as a surprise, notable is the prevalence of
developing countries among the top 25 countries. Most of these developing
countries were able to increase their share significantly. Exceptions are the

Table 5.4 The world's top 20 tourist spenders

Country	1980 US$ million	Percentage of world share	1993 US$ million	Percentage of world share
United States	10 385	10.1	40,564	15.1
Germany	20 599	20.1	37 514	13.9
Japan	4 593	4.5	26 860	10.0
United Kingdom	6 893	6.7	17 431	6.5
Italy	1 907	1.9	13 053	4.9
France	6 027	5.9	12 805	4.8
Canada	3 122	3.0	10 629	4.0
Netherlands	4 664	4.6	8 974	3.3
Austria	2 847	2.8	8 180	3.0
Taiwan	818	0.8	7 585	2.8
Belgium	3 272	3.2	6 363	2.4
Switzerland	2 357	2.3	5 803	2.2
Mexico	4 174	4.1	5 562	2.1
Spain	1 229	1.2	4 706	1.8
Sweden	1 235	1.2	4 464	1.7
South Korea	350	0.3	4 105	1.5
Australia	1 749	1.7	4 100	1.5
Norway	1 310	1.3	3 565	1.3
Denmark	1 560	1.5	3 214	1.2
Singapore	322	0.3	3 022	1.1
Argentina	1 791	1.8	2 445	0.9
Israel	533	0.5	2 313	0.9
Thailand	244	0.2	2 092	0.8
Venezuela	1 880	1.8	2 083	0.8
Malaysia	470	0.5	1 960	0.7

Source: extracted from WTO 1995

Latin American countries which had a higher share in the overall world tourist expenditure in 1980 than in 1993.

Yet tourist arrivals is only one measure and not necessarily the best. Differing length of stay among the source countries and varying preferences for accommodation and transportation media as well as destinations within the country mean that the actual impact or importance of the source country may vary significantly. In Tunisia, for example, Algeria constitutes the second most important market of tourist arrivals at its frontier. However, few of them actually stay at hotels and Algeria's market share of hotel arrivals is just 4.1 per cent as compared to 18.5 per cent of all tourist arrivals (Table 5.5). The huge differences in the ratio of hotel to frontier arrivals among the selected origin countries indicate the completely different travel patterns of these visitors. Tourists from nearby African countries appear to make little use of hotels. Most tourists from European countries, however, stay in at least one hotel (ratio >1.0). The higher the ratio, the more active are the intranational travel patterns of the visitors as exemplified by multiple hotel stays.

Intraregional travel

Intraregional tourist demand commonly constitutes a large share of the overall arrivals. As was shown in Table 1.5, European countries derive the majority of their arrivals from within Europe. Similarly, many developing countries receive the majority of their visitors from other developing countries within the region, if not from their directly neighbouring countries alone. Table 5.6 shows tourist arrivals to selected South American countries. The majority are intraregional tourist, and in some cases this group was as high as 80 per cent.

South East Asian countries usually constitute a demanding share of tourist arrivals in their neighbouring countries (Figure 5.3). Only the Philippines tourist arrivals from the other ASEAN countries are very few. In the Malaysian case, the percentage is about 75 per cent. Figure 5.3 also illustrates that this phenomenon is not very recent. Intraregional travel in 1992 was about as important as it was more than a decade earlier. Thus, the two examples of South America and South East Asia suggest that the notion of

Table 5.5 Tunisia's varying importance of origin countries using different measures

Market	Frontier tourist arrivals	Market share (%)	Hotel arrivals	Market share (%)	Ratio hotel/ border arrivals
Germany	711 872	19.5	1 032,819	28.8	1.45
Algeria	676 873	18.5	148 287	4.1	0.22
France	447 830	12.3	661 155	18.4	1.48
UK	245 839	6.7	291 499	8.1	1.19
Italy	241 819	6.6	443 851	12.4	1.84
Morocco	151 055	4.1	43 719	1.2	0.29
Total[a]	3 655 698	100	3 584 093	100	0.96

[a] Total figure includes arrivals from other markets.
Source: extracted and calculated from WTO 1995

Table 5.6 Tourist arrivals in selected South American countries

Source country	Destination country (%)						
	Argentina	*Brazil*	*Chile*	*Peru*	*Uruguay*	*Venezuela*	*South America*[b]
Argentina	–	40.6	60.7	5.2	72.8	3.6	n/a
Brazil	11.1	–	3.4	3.1	6.8	2.9	n/a
Chile	18.7	1.9	–	10.1	1.0	1.3	n/a
Peru	n/a	1.0	8.6	–	n/a	1.5	n/a
Uruguay	31.7	10.4	n/a	0.7	–	0.3	n/a
Venezuela	n/a	0.7	0.4	2.6	n/a	–	n/a
South America	72.7	62.4	78.3	36.1	81.3	16.5	68.5
Americas	82.9	72.4	89.8	61.9	83.2	54.9	79.6
Europe	12.1	23.2	8.0	30.5	2.7	43.2	14.1
Other regions	5.0	4.5	2.2	7.6	14.1[a]	1.9	6.3

[a] Includes 13.8 per cent Uruguayan citizens (non-resident) returning from abroad.
[b] For lack of data excludes Colombia, Guayana and Suriname.
Source: Oppermann 1995c

international tourist flows from the industrialized to developing countries is somewhat hypocritical; most travel to developing countries originates in neighbouring developing countries.

Intranational demand

Another aspect of tourism demand is the intranational level. The issue of where tourists go once they have cleared customs is largely neglected by tourism organizations and researchers (Oppermann 1992d). However, it is an issue of critical interest when regional development is an objective of tourism development (see Chapter 3). Furthermore, for developing countries it is of particular interest to discern who their tourists are, not only with respect to where they come from and how much money they spend in the country, but also where and on what they spend it and who is to benefit from it. As Din (1992) showed, not all population segments benefit from tourist spending to the same extent. And some forms of tourism and tourists may incur considerably higher leakages than others (Berriane 1978; Milne 1987, 1992; Widmer-Münch 1990). While little information is generally available on where the tourists travel within the country, even less data is obtainable on the expenditure/leakage pattern by the tourists.

Turning to the intranational travel patterns by international tourists, a study by Oppermann (1992d) suggests that tourism is very concentrated in a few locations and that many tourists actually do not travel within the country. The latter should not be too surprising as much tourism in developing countries is based on the three 'Ss' which tends to be a rather stationary tourism type. However, Oppermann also showed that different types of tourists vary significantly with respect to their intranational travel patterns (Oppermann 1992a 1995d). For example, European tourists visited notably more destinations that did their Asian counterparts (Oppermann 1995d). Figures 5.4 and 5.5 illustrate differences in intranational travel patterns between package and individual tourists in Malaysia. They demonstrate the very concentrated

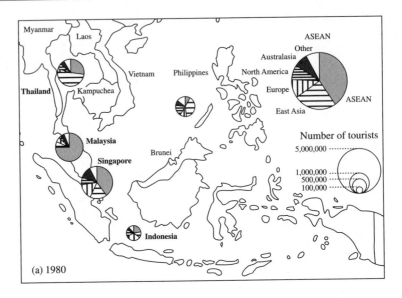

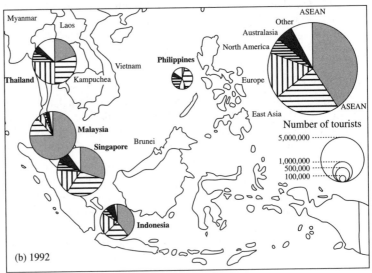

Figure 5.3 Tourist arrivals in ASEAN: (a) 1980; (b) 1992.
Source: Chon and Oppermann 1996.

flows of package tourists and the more dispersed pattern of the individual travellers.

Weightman (1987) argues that in India package tours are characterized by strong spatial and temporal biases. 'Tourists are directed towards the North, the city, and the past. Current realities provide a dim or even unnoticed context for directed experience' (1987: 232). Further, she argues that tour itineraries always include the 'must see' places and sites.

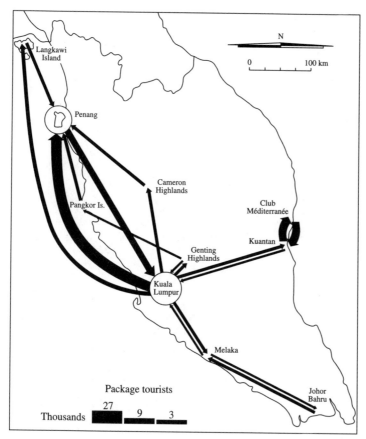

Figure 5.4 Intranational flows of package tourists in Malaysia.
Source: after Oppermann 1992b.

MEASURES OF DEMAND PATTERNS

A number of indices have been proposed over the years which measure demand patterns at international and national levels. Among them are the Concentration Index and the Travel Dispersal Index.

Concentration Index

The Concentration Index gauges the dependency of a tourist destination on one or several origin countries (Pearce 1995a). An over-reliance on only a few markets is usually considered unfavourable as any changes in the those markets, such as economic depressions, perception changes, changes in travel behaviour, will have a tremendous impact on the destination country and are often outside its control.

$$CI = (TA_p/TA_{all}) \times 100$$

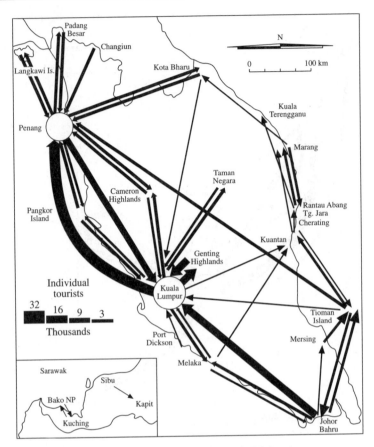

Figure 5.5 Intranational flows of individual tourists in Malaysia.
Source: after Oppermann 1992b.

where   TA$_p$ = tourist arrivals from primary markets;
    TA$_{all}$ = all tourist arrivals to the destination country.

Table 5.7 lists the Concentration Index of several developing countries. It shows that in the case of the Bahamas the primary market accounts for over 80 per cent of all tourist arrivals and the top three markets for more than 90 per cent. Yet only a few countries seem to have a CI higher than 50 for their primary markets although the CI of the top three markets commonly exceeds this mark.

Country Potential Generation Index

Hudman (1979) developed the Country Potential Generation Index (CPGI). It is a ratio of a country's trips generated and population size as measured in its world's share.

$$CPGI = (N_c/N_w)/(P_c/P_w)$$

Table 5.7 Market dependency by selected developing countries, 1993

Country	Market dependency (% of total tourists) from	
	Primary market	Top three markets
Bahamas	81.2	90.4
Chile	56.2	74.6
Aruba	56.1	78.7
Cyprus	51.6	62.3
Zimbabwe	50.1	83.1
Comores	45.4	83.9
Antigua and Barbuda	35.7	64.8
Costa Rica	35.5	55.9
Bangladesh	33.4	55.3
Argentina	32.0	60.3
Morocco	30.7	48.4
Tonga	28.3	63.0
Fiji	27.0	56.0
Maldives	25.2	52.0
Indonesia	25.2	46.9
Venezuela	25.2	42.3
Bhutan	23.8	57.7
China	19.9	48.1
Kenya	16.8	43.9
Thailand	14.4	33.6

Source: extracted from WTO 1995

where N_c = number of trips generated by the country;
N_w = number of trips generated in the world;
P_c = population of the country;
P_w = population of the world.

In a an update of the original study, Hudman and Davis (1994) compared CPGI values from 1974 and 1990 (Table 5.8). They showed that 19 of the top 50 countries were developing countries in 1990 as compared to 18 in 1974. Singapore achieved the highest score and was ranked 12th. It was followed by Hong Kong (21st) and Taiwan (30th).

Travel Dispersal Index

The Travel Dispersal Index (TDI) integrates five variables of tourists' travel behaviour as compared to just one in the Trip Index (Oppermann 1992e). The parameters number of overnight destinations (OD), length of stay (LS), number of different types of accommodation (A) and transportation (T), and travel organization (TO) are weighted and integrated to form one overall measure (Table 5.9):

TDI = LS + OD + A + T + TO.

According to Oppermann (1992e, p. 45), 'with these variables the impact and distribution of tourism can be measured not only in its spatial aspects, but also according to its sectoral effects'. He sees the usefulness of the TDI in

Table 5.8 Country Potential Generation Index

Rank 1990	Country	1990	1974
1	Switzerland	19.2	10.1
2	Austria	18.5	6.5
3	Belgium	15.4	7.2
4	Portugal	12.7	7.6
5	Netherlands	11.8	9.7
6	Luxembourg	11.7	8.0
7	Germany	10.2	11.8
8	Canada	9.2	8.0
9	Hungary	8.8	5.9
10	Denmark	8.0	7.4
12	Singapore	7.4	3.0
21	Hong Kong[a]	4.2	n/a
30	Taiwan[a]	1.7	n/a
31	Lebanon	1.4	0.7
32	Jordan	1.2	4.0
33	Mexico	1.1	0.6
35	Turkey	1.0	0.8
36	Kuwait	0.9	2.5
37	Malaysia	0.9	0.8

[a] Hong Kong and Taiwan were not among the listed top 50 countries in 1974.
Source: extracted from Hudman and Davis 1994

two areas: it can be used as a tourist typology in which tourists are classified along a scale of spatial behaviour from inactive to very active, with the latter having the greatest interest in the visited country; or it may be applied as a market segmentation tool to identify those markets whose spatial patterns conform the most with the goals of national tourism development strategies. Using data from Malaysia, Oppermann (1992e) disclosed substantial differences in TDI among tourists from different countries of origin and different group size. He also established that travellers with a high TDI were considerably less concentrated in the two major destinations Kuala Lumpur and Penang (Table 5.10).

Table 5.9 Parameters of the Travel Dispersal Index

Parameter	Weighting (in points)					
	0	1	2	3	4	5
Number of overnight destinations	0	1	2	3–5	6–10	>10
Number of nights	0	1–3	4–7	8–14	>14	
Number of different accommodation forms	0	1	>1			
Number of different transportation forms	0	1	>1			
Travel organization:						
Package		x				
Individual			x			

Source: Oppermann 1992e, p. 45

Table 5.10 Characteristics of Malaysian tourists according to their Travel Dispersal Index

Variable	Travel Dispersal Index			
	4–6 N=251	7–9 N=117	10–12 N=39	13–15 N=32
Individual travellers (%)	45.0	50.4	74.4	96.9
Sex (% female)	38.6	42.7	46.2	46.9
Repeat visitors (%)	38.6	38.5	33.3	6.2
Degree of concentration (in per cent of nights in Malaysia)				
Kuala Lumpur	37.4	38.2	26.7	14.0
Penang	41.3	35.8	21.6	16.4
Kuala Lumpur and Penang	78.7	74.0	48.3	30.4
Average nights in Malaysia	3.5	8.2	13.1	28.9
Number of overnight destinations	1.1	2.2	3.5	8.2

Source: Oppermann 1992e: 47

The Travel Dispersal Index has one major flaw, however; it has been developed in the Malaysian context and with a weighting of the five parameters that reflect the situation in Malaysia. This problem has already been addressed by the author and he suggests that to overcome this problem and to facilitate cross-national comparisons it may be necessary to change the weighting scale of one or the other variable (Oppermann 1992e).

CHANGING TOURIST TYPES

While changes in the economy and society of the origin countries and the tourism development stage and attractions of the destination countries undoubtedly contribute to changing demand patterns over time, another factor is the changing tourists themselves. This is an issue rarely examined although it is an integral issue of several theories (Cohen 1972, 1973; Oppermann 1995a; P. Pearce 1993; Plog 1991). Implicit in many destination choice models are backward linkage of actual travel towards travel experience as an input in the destination perception and selection process (Figure 5.1). Hence, with every additional trip, the person's travel experience changes and, therefore, possibly the basis of future travel decisions.

The distinctive impact of dissimilar tourist types was already the major theme of Cohen's (1972) tourist typology. He forwarded four tourist types: organized mass tourist, individual mass tourist, explorer and drifter. He summarized the first two as institutionalized tourist roles since 'they are dealt with in a routine way by the tourist establishment' (1972, p. 168). Further, he noted that mass tourism requires a high infrastructure investment (see Chapters 2 and 6).

Hence, whatever country aspires to attract mass tourism is forced to provide facilities on a level commensurate with the expectations of the tourists from those countries. A tourist infrastructure of facilities based

on Western standards has to be created even in the poorest host countries.

(Cohen 1972, p. 171)

The two other tourist types are summarized as non-institutionalized tourists
as they are only loosely attached to the tourist establishment during their
travel. Unfortunately, most research has focused on the mass tourists whereas
the explorers and drifters have attracted very limited interest despite their
potentially high contribution (for example discussion on backpackers,
Chapter 8).

Family life cycle

While travel experience is one factor in the changing tourist behaviour over
an individual's life span, the actual family life cycle stage the person is in
also determines to some extent travel behaviour and travel destinations
(Lawson 1991; Oppermann 1995e). A number of different approaches have
been used to analyse travel patterns by family life cycle stage (Table 5.11).
Due to a not fully conclusive classification scheme, many of these have an
inherent problem with unclassifiable cases. However, Oppermann's (1995e)
typology is comprehensive. Applying his methodology to travel patterns by
German residents, he showed that travel destination choice was significantly
different between different family life cycle stages. For example, those with
children were more likely to choose closer destinations and use cars as the
transportation medium. In addition, differences emerged with respect to
travel purpose, accommodation, seasonality, group size and trip duration.
Furthermore, he showed that people between 25 and 63 (retiring age) without
children had a profound higher incidence of travelling overseas to developing countries than did any other group.

Travel life cycle

Another concept applied to changing travel patterns is the travel life cycle
(Oppermann 1994c, 1995a, 1995f). Essentially it is a recognition that travel
behaviours change with respect to three time dimensions: period, life cycle
and cohort effects.

● Period effects refer to changes over the years. An example of such an
  analysis would be a plot of the growing number of tourist arrivals to
  developing countries over the last 30 to 50 years.
● Life cycle effects are the above discussed developments over the life span
  and/or family life cycle.
● Cohort or generation effects refer to distinct travel patterns by specific age
  cohorts or generations. For example, the baby boomers are likely to have
  a quite different travel pattern and choose different destinations than
  Generation X or preceding generations. As Oppermann already noted,
  'while in other social science fields the generation factor has received
  due attention … in tourism research it has almost remained a "terra incog-
  nita"' (1994c, p. 83). He illuminated how different age cohorts choose

Table 5.11 Comparison of family life cycle categories applied in tourism studies

Bojanic (1992) 8 stages	Lawson (1991) 8 stages	Oppermann (1995) 9 stages
Bachelor (18–39 years, single, no children)	**Young single** (< 25 years)	**I** (15–25, single, no children, dependent on parents and taking holidays with parents)
Newly married (18–39 years, married, no children)	**Young couples** (no no children)	**II** (15–25, single/ couple, no children, working) **III** (26–40, single/couple, no children, working)
Full nest I (18–39 years, married, children)	**Full nest I** (preschool children)	**IV** (varying age, singles/couples, only preschool children, working)
Single parents (18–49 years, divorced/sep., children)		
Full nest II (40–49 years, married, children)	**Full nest II** (school-age children) **Full nest III** (older children, possibly non-dependent)	**V** (<40, single/couple, children, working) **VI** (41–62, single/couple, children, working)
Middle-aged couples w/o children (40–49 years, married, no children)		**VII** (41–62, single/ couple, no children, working)
Empty nest (50+ years, married, no children)	**Empty nest I** (still working, no children)	**VIII** (varying age, single/couple, children take independent holidays, working)
Solitary survivor (50+ years, widowed, no children)	**Empty nest II** (retired) **Solitary survivor** (retired)	**IX** (63+, single/couple, no children, retired)

Sources: Bojanic 1992; Lawson 1991; Oppermann 1995e

significantly different destination regions with a general tendency that the 'younger' German generations were more likely to choose destinations outside Europe and particularly outside Central Europe. Furthermore, additional differences emerged with regard to transportation choice and trip generation (Oppermann 1994c, 1995a).

The travel life cycle is especially useful for destinations to realize their position in a multitemporal perspective. A destination which relies primarily on a specific cohort, for example, may soon find itself facing declining visitation as this cohort 'dies out'. Hence, a strategic analysis of the destination's position in the market should not only examine market share with respect to age groups, but integrate a three dimensional time perspective (Oppermann 1995a).

DATA PROBLEMS

A major problem with any tourism research is the gathering and obtaining of data. Tourism is a multi-faceted industry, spanning many other 'traditional' industry sectors such as construction, agriculture and transportation. Hence, few statistics exist on the actual economic contribution of tourism. The provision of secondary data is, therefore, generally limited to number of tourist arrivals and/or nights, hotel rooms and other accommodation capacity or demand. Through exit surveys some countries are able to obtain more data on tourist expenditure and sometimes other travel pattern variables such as group size and length of stay.

Compounding the general lack of comprehensive data on tourism and tourists is the dilemma that definitions tend to change over time, hampering longitudinal analysis of tourism development. International comparative studies are rarely undertaken because definitions of what constitutes tourism and who are tourists vary between countries. In South East Asia, for example, Singapore does not consider Malaysians arriving by road or train as tourists. Malaysia, on the other hand, does include Singaporean overland visitors and bases its tourists arrivals on estimates of the proportion of tourists and excursionists. However, until 1970 it too did not include overland Singaporean visitors. Furthermore, while the WTO uses the 'official' data from the Malaysian Tourism Promotion Board, Pacific Asia Travel Association excludes Singaporean arrivals to Malaysia via the causeway in its statistics. Similarly, Singaporean outbound statistics do not include its residents going overland to Malaysia. Consequently, as Oppermann (1996b) points out, the official number of Singaporean outbound tourists is already less than the number of Singaporean tourists to Malaysia. Analogous is the case of Hong Kong residents visiting Macao.

In many ways a more important shortcoming of most tourism statistics is the dearth of information available on domestic tourism. Such data tends to be very sparse as many tourism departments have as their main purpose to increase the number of international tourist arrivals and not to monitor, further or support domestic tourism.

Data sources

Summaries of international tourism statistics can be found in the official World Tourism Organization (WTO) publications such as the *Yearbook of Tourism Statistics* and the *Compendium of Tourism Statistics*. General tourism arrivals and expenditure statistics can also be found in other statistical publications such as the *International (European) Marketing Data and Statistics* by the Euromonitor and the *Statistical Yearbook* by the United Nations. Regional tourism associations also provide statistics, for example the Pacific Asia Travel Association publishes its *Annual Statistical Report*.

The *International Tourism Report* and *Travel & Tourism Analyst*, both published by the Economic Intelligence Unit in London, are essential reading if they do include the country or topic of interest. They not only provide statistical information but often very interesting background and additional insights as well. The major problem with this source is that the reports do not cover all countries (and many developing countries have never been included) and there is a long time lag between successive coverages for the same country. Similar country reports are published in the *Pacific Tourism Review* (Cognizant Communication Corporation, New York), focusing on countries in the Pacific area.

National tourism organizations (NTOs) usually make data available and this often goes beyond the statistics available in the above worldwide publications. However, the level of detail depends on each individual NTO and some are more concerned with tourism data than others. Then there are a wide range of other organizations that may collect and publish tourism data, for example airlines and statistics departments. A good source for tourism data from such sources detailing the variables used, cost of the data and contact address is the statistical report series in the above mentioned *Pacific Tourism Review*. Although not comprehensive for the whole world and particularly lacking information on many developing countries, it does provide an excellent starting point for the countries covered and may give the reader some idea of what sort of organization to contact for other countries not included.

QUESTIONS

1. Discuss the major motivators of today's pleasure travel and reflect on the implications of the travel destination decision process.
2. Why is it important to understand travel itineraries of tourists? What benefits can be gained from an improved knowledge of tourists' travel patterns?
3. Explain the concept of a travel life cycle. Discuss all three time dimensions and relate how travel behaviour changes in one might affect tourism destinations.
4. Identify one demand measure index and explain its usefulness and limitations.
5. What are the major reasons for data insufficiencies in the field of tourism?

FURTHER READING

Johnson, P. and Thomas, B. (eds) (1992) *Choice and Demand in Tourism*. Mansell, London.

> This collection of papers provides the reader with a crucial background in tourists' motivations and tourist typologies as well as destination related issues of tourism demand.

Ross, G.F. (1994) *The Psychology of Tourism*. Hospitality Press, Elseternwick.

> This book is essential reading for anybody wanting to know more about tourists' motivations, personalities and attitudes. In addition, it addresses the societal and organizational contexts of tourism and tourism demand.

German outbound travel patterns

Germany is the most important tourist generating country worldwide (Hudman and Davis 1994). It accounts for one-third of all overnight trips abroad in Europe (Aderhold 1992). With 62 million trips in 1990, it generated almost 50 per cent more trips than the second ranked United States (Hudman and Davis 1994). A high average household income, a large middle-class population, and their long holidays in particular (5–7 weeks/year) are important factors contributing to the large number of trips generated each year not only to European but also non-European destinations. In 1993, Germany was the most important source of foreign tourists arrivals to developing countries such as Tunisia, the Maldives and Sri Lanka (Table 5.12). Its economic contribution often exceeds its share in tourist arrivals owing to a usually longer length of stay of German tourists and their above average expenditure per trip. Hence, changing travel trends in the German market are of major concern to many countries.

Table 5.12 Importance of German tourist arrivals in selected developing countries in 1993 as compared to arrivals from France, Japan, UK, and USA.

Destination country	German share	German rank	UK rank	French rank	USA rank	Japanese rank
Maldives	25.18	1	4	6	*	3
Sri Lanka	24.35	1	2	3	*	5
Tunisia	19.47	1	5	4	*	*
Kenya	15.73	2	1	7	4	*
Nepal	10.90	2	3	6	4	5
Seychelles	15.90	3	2	1	9	*
Tonga	9.80	4	7	*	2	8
Venezuela	7.02	4	7	6	1	*
Morocco	5.51	4	6	2	7	*
Peru	5.38	4	8	*	1	*
India	4.72	4	2	6	3	7
Jamaica	3.69	4	2	*	1	6
Thailand	5.55	5	10	*	6	2
Costa Rica	5.32	5	*	*	1	*
Bonaire	4.89	5	*	*	1	*
Brazil	5.19	6	*	8	3	*
Indonesia	3.91	7	8	*	6	2

* = not among top 10
Source: WTO 1995

Travel destinations

In absolute numbers, Spain was the favourite foreign country for West German respondents followed by Italy, Austria and France (Table 5.13). In 1992, every eighth person's primary vacation trip led to Spain, representing 18.4 per cent of all trips to foreign destinations. This has not always been the case. Until 1980 Austria was the most visited country. Although its share of total trips was 15 per cent in 1970, only slightly more than Spain's 12.6 per cent in 1992, it represented 30 per cent of all vacation trips to foreign countries. The large increase in number of foreign vacation trips is causing this discrepancy. The 30 per cent is also an indicator of the dominant position Austria once held with regard to German outbound tourism.

The decrease in number of primary vacation trips does not necessarily imply, however, that a destination receives less tourists from Germany today than it did some years ago. The increase in travel intensity and travel frequency at least partly offsets losses from primary trips. Austria, for example, attracted a total of 3.2 million German tourists in 1990. This is only slightly less than the 3.4 million in 1970 although Austria's share of main vacation trips dropped from 15.2 per cent to 7.0 per cent in the same time period. Hence, while its share declined the number of Germans visiting Austria remained almost the same.

Table 5.13 German holiday destination choice (in % of primary holiday trips)

Year	AU	IT	SP	FR	YU	GR	CH	TU	NA
West Germany									
1970	15.0	12.0	5.0	2.0	2.0	2.0	2.0	na	na
1975	15.1	8.8	8.5	3.7	3.6	1.4	2.1	na	na
1980	13.0	9.9	9.2	4.3	4.3	2.2	2.8	na	na
1981	13.0	10.7	10.3	6.1	3.8	2.7	1.9	na	na
1982	9.9	12.0	11.1	5.3	4.2	2.3	1.5	na	na
1983	11.7	12.9	10.5	3.7	3.6	2.4	2.1	na	na
1984	9.7	13.2	10.9	5.5	4.2	2.9	2.7	na	na
1985	9.6	12.3	11.5	5.4	6.0	3.1	2.1	0.4	na
1986	9.3	12.3	12.6	5.3	5.5	3.4	1.5	0.7	na
1987	9.7	12.4	13.5	5.8	5.1	3.8	2.1	1.3	na
1988	8.2	11.3	11.7	6.6	5.0	3.4	1.9	2.5	na
1989	9.2	11.1	13.5	5.3	4.2	3.5	1.8	2.3	na
1990	7.0	10.2	13.0	5.9	5.3	4.2	1.6	2.5	2.4
1991	8.8	10.5	13.8	5.8	0.9	4.0	1.6	2.8	2.4
1992	6.8	9.7	12.6	5.8	0.7	4.6	1.7	3.1	3.2
East Germany									
1990	4.3	2.5	3.0	1.4	0.5	0.6	0.4	*	0.2
1991	9.8	4.9	7.4	2.3	*	1.2	1.1	0.5	0.8
1992	10.3	4.7	6.2	3.9	*	2.4	1.7	0.8	0.7

AU = Austria, IT = Italy, SP = Spain, FR = France, YU = Yugoslavia, GR = Greece, CH = Switzerland, TU = Turkey, NA = North America
* below 0.1 per cent
Source: StfT, various years

A rapid alteration of travel destination preferences among East German residents can be observed between 1990 and 1992. All foreign destinations are benefiting from an increase of East German tourists. Among foreign destinations, Austria is most favoured by East Germans followed by Spain and Italy. The strong showing of Austria is explained by its proximity, lack of language barriers (East Germans are less fluent in Western languages than their West German counterparts), and a favourable value perception. East German residents are first exploring destinations which are more familiar and less expensive. Spain's lead over Italy is most likely the effect of the large number of inexpensive package flights to the Balearic Islands, Canary Islands and mainland Spain which makes a holiday there more affordable.

Travel inertia and destination familiarity

Although Germans are travelling to a wider variety of countries, a high travel inertia can still be observed. The majority of all trips are to destinations which they previously had visited. A large number (26.9 per cent) of tourists reported that they had experienced visiting their destination more than three times in the past (Table 5.14). Among East German respondents this figure is naturally not quite as high owing to their drastic changes in destination availability since unification.

Table 5.14 Familiarity with travel destination (in %)

Year	First time visit	1–2 previous visits	3 or more previous visits
1976	48.2	26.6	24.3
1984	40.7	23.3	35.0
1988	41.3	25.6	32.5
1992 – West	47.1	25.4	26.9
1992 – East	69.0	19.2	11.3

Source: StfT, various years

Another aspect of destination familiarity is previous travel experience with any destination country not only the one visited on the last vacation. In 1974 and in several surveys in the late 1980s respondents were asked which countries they had previously visited (Table 5.15). The results indicate an ever growing familiarity with many destination countries among a large proportion of West German respondents. In 1988, for example, 57.8 per cent stated that they had visited Austria at least once during their life. This was up from 36.6 per cent in 1974. More than one-third of Germans had previously travelled to Spain, Italy and France. Almost 10 per cent of the surveyed population had some travel experience with destinations in Tunisia, Africa and North America as compared to 0.8 per cent, 1.9 per cent and 1.4 per cent 16 years earlier. This indicates the expansion of the German 'tourist sphere'. Unfortunately, the 1990 survey was not completely comparable to surveys in earlier years because destinations were grouped differently. It allows, however, for a comparison of West and East German respondents. It shows how novel many destinations (mostly in the Western countries) were to East

Table 5.15 Previous travel experience with travel destinations (in %)

| Year | West Germany | | | | | | | |
	Austria	Italy	Spain	France	Tunisia	Africa	Asia	North America
1974	36.6	22.1	13.3	11.3	0.8	1.9	0.6	1.4
1985	52.0	37.8	27.1	28.7	2.4	5.8	1.7	3.8
1988	57.8	42.8	35.2	34.4	5.7	8.2	2.6	6.5
1990	55.2	44.8	38.8	34.5	9.6	9.9	3.3	9.6
	East Germany							
1990	8.3	3.7	2.8	2.9	0.5	0.4	0.2	0.9

German travellers in the year after the fall of the 'Wall'. Only 8.3 per cent stated that they had visited Austria, including visits in the year 1990. A comparison of the 1990 East German destination familiarity percentages with the ones in West Germany for the year 1970 indicate that in many respects the West Germans 20 years ago were more 'well-travelled' than their East German counterparts in 1990. Obviously, a similar table showing Eastern European countries would likely reveal the high destination familiarity of East Germans with many of those and the low percentages of West Germans who had ever visited Eastern European countries. As Hudman (1979) had shown in a comparative study of many origin countries, East Germany was ranked at that time almost on par with West Germany among the countries with the highest outbound travel volume.

Table 5.15 also suggests that even a country such as Austria has not managed to penetrate more than 60 per cent of the potential German market. Although three million Germans visit Austria every year many of them are return visitors. Thus, Germany still provides for a large untapped market which may just need to be explored. And it may be easier and less expensive to attract some of these German travellers than to turn to countries overseas.

6 Tourism impacts

Tourism has many facets and apparently generates as much criticism as praise: tourism as an economic development agent, a job generator, and a white industry, but also tourism as an evil industry, a destructive force, etc. Three areas of impacts are usually identified: economic, socio-cultural and physical effects. The issues within these three domains will be discussed in this chapter in order to illustrate the potential positive and/or negative impacts of tourism development. First, however, a brief overview of tourism resources and methods of resource evaluation are given.

RESOURCE EVALUATION

Resources constitute the 'pull' factors of tourism. These resources take a wide range of different forms and what may be a tourism attraction to some does not have the same effect on others. 'Resources are not, they become; they are not static but expand and contract in response to human wants and human actions' (Zimmermann 1951, p. 15). This important notion by Zimmermann is very obvious in tourism. An island with its beaches and tropical climate is not a tourism resource until it is made accessible to tourists and it is something desired by tourists. 'Availability for human use, not mere physical presence, is the chief criterion of resources. Availability, in turn, depends on human wants and abilities' (Zimmermann 1933, p. 4). In the nineteenth century, for example, such an island, even if accessible, would not have been considered a tourism resource. The individual and societal perceptions of tourism attractivity did not include sun-bathing. Another example are the many hill-stations in the Orient. Only because the colonialist perceived the need of having a retreat from the humidity and heat of the tropics, did they make the higher altitudes accessible and establish summer resorts. Hence, any evaluation of tourism resources will always be a dynamic one which will require an update every few years or decades.

Historically, the physical resource base has been considered as the major factor in the development of tourism (Mathieson and Wall 1982). Today, the preponderance of non-natural tourist attractions adds an even more dynamic element to the resource base. Casinos, theme parks, ski-resorts, and shopping centres all are tourist attractions that are built quickly and can change the tourism resource base within months or a few years. Except for its casinos, Las Vegas would attract only a few visitors and not almost 30 million as it did in 1994. Genting Highlands in Malaysia pulls visitors for the same reason.

And the promotional efforts of not only Singapore but of Hong Kong, Jakarta, Bangkok and Kuala Lumpur emphasize the ready availability of large shopping complexes; attractions completely detached from the physical environment.

Resource inventories

In tourism planning and site selection it is of great importance to know the availability and location of resources in order to make effective decisions (Gearing, Swart and Var 1974). This seems particularly important in many developing countries which have a shortage of financial resources and, therefore, need to make a sound decision the first time. A common method is resource inventory. It involves gathering of information and data on all sorts of tourism attractions.

Pearce (1989) suggests seven broad categories in the analysis of tourism resources: climate, physical conditions, attractions, access, existing facilities, land tenure and use, and other considerations such as government incentives. A literature review indicates that a large number of different variables have been used which generally do not include all categories suggested by Pearce. For example, Cha and Uysal (1994) utilized 24 parameters to analyse regional tourism resources in South Korea. However, their list covered mostly urban supply variables such as retail establishments, travel agencies, tourist accommodations, medical facilities, water supply per person and restaurant and hotel employees. The list of included parameters leaves the reader with the distinct impression that the availability of data was paramount in deciding which ones to include rather than a sound approach towards covering all different aspects.

Another approach to resource inventory in the face of lack of time and financial resources is to scan tourism guidebooks for features and activities and to measure the amount of space allocated for different types of tourist attractions (e.g. Ferrario 1979).

Lew (1987) provided a detailed discussion of different attraction typologies ranging from idiographic to organizational and from cognitive to cross-perspective approaches. Table 6.1 is an example of the 'idiographic perspective. Lew argues that 'idiographic approaches are the most frequent forms of attraction typologies encountered in tourism research' (1987, p. 558). It illustrates the wide range of tourist attractions that may be considered in a resource inventory while not even addressing issues such as authenticity, visitors' perceptions, accessibility and capacity.

Landscape evaluation and touristic attractiveness

Commonly considered as one of the most important tourism resources is the scenery or landscape. However, not all respondents prefer the same landscapes. Some appreciate mountainous terrain whereas others favour open space. Approaches to landscape evaluation often involve the use of representative photos (Mitchell 1979). Respondents are given a series of pictures depicting different scenes, for example different beaches, which they have to

Table 6.1 Composite ideograph of tourist attraction typology

Nature	Nature–human interface	Human

General environment:
1 Panoramas
    Mountain
    Sea coast
    Plain
    Arid
    Island
	4 Observational
	    Rural/agriculture
	    Scientific gardens
	      Animals (zoo)
	      Plants
	    Rocks and archaeology
		7 Settlement infrastructure
		    Utility types
		    Settlement morphology
		    Settlement function
		      Commerce
		        Retail
		        Finance
		      Institutions
		        Government
		        Education and science
		        Religion
		      People
		        Way of life
		        Ethnicity

Specific Features:
2 Landmarks
    Geological
    Biological
    Flora
    Fauna
    Hydrological
	5 Leisure nature
	    Trails
	    Parks
	      Beach
	      Urban
	      Other
	    Resorts
		8 Tourist infrastructure
		    Forms of access
		      To and from a destination
		      Destination tour routes
		    Information and receptivity
		    Basic needs
		      Accommodation
		      Meals

Inclusive Environmental:
3 Ecological
    Climate
    Sanctuaries
      National parks
      Nature reserves
	6 Participatory
	    Mountain activities
	      Summer
	      Winter
	    Water activities
	    Other outdoor activities
		9 Leisure superstructure
		    Recreation entertainment
		      Performances
		      Sporting events
		      Amusements
		    Culture, history and arts
		      Museums and monuments
		      Performances
		      Festivals
		      Cuisine

Source: Lew 1987, p.558

evaluate. Peterson and Neumann (1969) discovered two very distinct user groups among their respondents: those with a preference for urban beaches and those with an inclination towards more natural beaches.

Landscape evaluation could also mean a resource inventory which is then subjected to a grading. Grosjean's (1986) landscape evaluation study is an excellent example of such an approach. In a first step, the study area was subdivided into small areas and for each a rigorous inventory of current tourism resources was undertaken including geomorphology, glaciers and water bodies, vegetation, fauna, buildings (historic, new, industry), infrastructure, and psychological experience value. It also covered not only the actual presence of attractions within each area but also the distance from such attractions in the vicinity. In addition, he used historic data for 1850 and 1906 in the form of maps and pictures to derive the resource base for earlier times. Taking three tourist types (nature oriented, tradition oriented and activity oriented) with their different assessment scales of the resource base, Grosjean weighted the existing resources within the region for the three time periods and, in addition, he developed two future scenarios. The 15 resulting maps are a fine example of how resource evaluation and preference analysis can be applied. The maps can easily be used for tourism planning, for example in the identification of areas that may be under imminent threat of losing their appeal to one or several groups of tourists.

Gearing *et al.*'s (1974) study on the attractiveness of Turkish cities and regions is another example of how importance-performance or expectancy value analysis (Fishbein 1963; Martilla and James 1977) may be applied to tourism attraction research.

ECONOMIC EFFECTS

The economic benefits to be derived from tourism are generally heralded as the prime reason by developing countries to become involved in tourism. Tourism appears as an attractive proposition in earning much needed foreign exchange, stimulating employment and investment, and contributing to the balance of payments (Cater 1987). Yet these positive effects are often accompanied by other less favourable effects such as inflation, leakages and dependency. These need to be weighted carefully, based on accurate assessments of the actual economic effects. Too often, multiplier effects are overestimated, leakages misjudged and costs for infrastructural developments and induced leakages through demonstration effects are not considered.

Foreign exchange earning and government revenues

Tourism's potential to positively contribute towards the national balance of payments is perhaps the most important reason why governments support and encourage tourism development (Long 1991; Vorlaufer 1984; Wood 1979). Few countries and especially few developing countries, feature a positive trade account and many are in dire need to improve it. Although tourism does not fit the pattern of traditional export industries, it does generate foreign exchange earnings through tourists' expenditure in the destination country. Thus, tourism is an export industry where the product is produced and consumed within the country and the travel experience is exported.

Three types of balance of payment effects can be identified, namely direct, indirect and induced. Most studies and statistics usually examine only the primary effects. Table 6.2 shows the tourism receipts and expenditures of selected countries. The difference between these two is called the travel balance or travel account. It is positive when the residents of country A spend less money on their trips overseas than do all the visitors to country A.

In 1993, Germany had the highest negative travel account in the world. Its residents spent some US$27 003 million more on their trips than all the visitors to Germany spent during their visit in Germany. Japan is another country with an extremely high negative travel account whereas the United States featured a high positive balance.

Table 6.2 Travel account of selected countries, 1993 (in US$ million)

Country	Tourism receipts	Tourism expenditures	Travel account
Germany	10 509	37 512	−27 003
Japan	3 557	26 860	−23 303
Canada	5 897	10 629	−4 732
Taiwan	2 943	7 585	−4 642
United Kingdom	13 451	17 431	−3 980
South Korea	3 510	4 105	−595
Brazil	1 449	1 842	−393
Malaysia	1 876	1 960	−84
Chile	744	560	184
Egypt	1 332	1 048	284
Mexico	6 167	5 562	605
Puerto Rico	1 628	776	852
Tunisia	1 114	203	911
Morocco	1 243	245	998
India	1 487	400	1 087
Argentina	3 614	2 445	1 169
Singapore	5 793	3 022	2 771
Thailand	5 014	2 092	2 922
Turkey	3 959	934	3 025
China	4 683	555	4 128
Italy	20 521	13 053	7 468
Spain	19 425	4 706	14 719
United States	57 621	40 564	17 057

Source: calculated from WTO 1995

Taiwan and South Korea were leading the list of developing countries with a negative travel account balance. On the other end, China, Turkey and Thailand recorded the largest surplus in their travel account. In many instances, tourism is a major contributor to the total foreign exchange earnings. Tourism's contribution may range as high as 52 per cent (Seychelles) or relatively low as in Sri Lanka with just 5 per cent (Agel 1993).

Governments also benefit directly from tourism. Income taxes from tourism employees and operators, accommodation and airport taxes, sales tax, and customs duties are among the primary income generators for governments. Then there are indirect tax benefits as the tourist expenditure ripples through the economy and generates further income and spending with their associated taxes.

But there are also costs involved which are often not considered. General infrastructure needs to be supplied or upgraded and is often a general prerequisite to most forms of tourism development. Airports, harbours, railways, roads, fresh water supply, electricity and sewage plants are but a few infrastructural costs incurred by tourism. These costs or at least the share attributed to tourism, since other users also benefit from them, never enters into the input–output analysis of tourism's profitability from a government perspective (Ruf 1978). It has been estimated that in some countries infrastructural investments amount to about 80 per cent of hotel capital costs (Wood 1979). Government incentives in the form of tax holidays, investment subsidies, duty-free imports, etc. (see Chapter 2) also reduce the potential economic effects. Some authors even doubt if an input–output analysis of tourism's economic benefits to the government would provide a positive balance (Voss 1984). Other commentators have critically remarked that infrastructure development may not be beneficial to the surrounding areas and may lead to negative sentiments at best and open hostility at worst (e.g. Aziz 1995).

Another cost factor that detracts from the benefits of tourism's earnings are the promotional costs. Since tourism is a very competitive industry with more and more entrants to the marketplace, promotional presence in the major source countries is often a necessity and promotional spending may be as high as US$ 10 per arriving tourist (Wood 1979).

Employment and skills

The second most important economic benefit of tourism is its employment generation potential. Tourism is usually considered a labour intensive industry (Culpan 1987; Kasse 1973; Mings 1969; Vorlaufer 1979). In developing countries with high unemployment this benefit may even outweigh other financial considerations. Particularly in view of generally high population growth, some commentators have considered job generation as the primary benefit (Vorlaufer 1979). In countries with labour shortages, however, any tourism development is prone to tighten the labour market even further and, because of its perceived attractiveness and ease of work, to negatively effect the labour situation in agriculture and other industries.

Other authors have argued, however, that tourism is capital intensive and provides less employment than investments into other industry sectors (e.g. Ruf 1978). In addition, it has been criticized that positions in the tourism industry are primarily low-wage jobs that do not require any skills and seldom contribute to skill improvements and that managerial positions are often given to expatriates (e.g. Ruf 1978). Robinson (1994) reports, however, that a large share of travel and trekking agencies in Nepal are controlled by Sherpas and explains how Sherpas are able to move through the hierarchical structures in Nepal's trekking industry.

The most obvious areas of tourism employment are hotels, souvenir shops, restaurants, travel agencies and transportation and entertainment facilities. These jobs are directly generated through tourism. Indirect employment is where jobs are generated in the tourism supply area but do not result directly from tourist expenditures, such as in the construction of hotels. Induced employment results from the re-spending of income earned through tourism by local residents.

A number of studies have provided data on direct and indirect employment effects, often measured as number of full-time equivalent (FTE) jobs per hotel room or bed (Table 6.3). The available data suggests a wide range of potential employment impacts and some figures certainly appear to be on the high side.

Table 6.3 Direct and indirect employment effects

Country/region	Full-time equivalent jobs	Reference parameter
Bali	1 500	1000 tourists
Sri Lanka	220	1000 tourists
South Pacific islands	77	1000 tourists
Guatemala	68–75	1000 tourists
Kenya	57	1000 tourists
Puerto Rico	4.1	hotel room
Tunisia	4.0	hotel room
Peru	3.5	hotel room
British Virgin Islands	2.3	hotel room
Mexico	2.0	hotel room
Jamaica	1.5	hotel room
Guatemala	1.25	hotel room

Sources: Bastin 1984; Craig-Smith and Fagence 1994; Cukier and Wall 1994; Vorlaufer 1979; Voss 1984

Seasonality

One of the major disadvantages of the tourism industry is its usually high seasonality. Closed hotels, restaurants and other tourism supply facilities in the off-season are a sure sign for a high seasonality. Other evidence includes drastically reduced hotel rates and airfares through which the tourism operators attempt to attract at least a few travellers to their destination.

A high seasonality means that many employees have only seasonal jobs and that the high investments required for international standard hotels lay idle for several weeks or months. In turn, this implies that any profit to be made from tourism has to come from a shorter time period and not the whole year since the good 'hotel room' cannot be resold next season.

Reasons for seasonality are manifold. On one hand, there are causes related to the tourists' countries of origin. Families with children are commonly dependent on the school holidays which tend to fall into the respective summer months. In some countries, companies and government enforce vacation leaves during similar time periods by closing down for several weeks. Thus, a destination that depends mostly on one or several countries of origin with similar holiday patterns tends to experience a very seasonal demand pattern. This is, for example, the case in Tunisia. The majority of its international tourists come from Germany, France and other European countries. Consequently, the summer months July to September account for the majority of all tourist arrivals whereas the winter months attract only a small share of the overall demand. Hence, many hotels close down for the season. In Turkey, 70 per cent of arrivals are counted in the period April to October with the ensuing problem of excess capacity during the rest of the year (Sezer and Harrison 1994). Thompson, O'Hare and Evans (1995) report that in The Gambia about one-third of the hotels close down completely from April through October.

Seasonality may be determined by the climate and/or attractions of the destination itself. In countries with a monsoon season tourists tend to avoid the rainy season and would rather travel during the rest of the year. The Club Méditerranée and several other hotels on the east coast of peninsular Malaysia shut down operations for several months between November and March. And the tourist season in Antarctica lasts only a few summer months.

Some countries are fortunate in deriving their visitors from different parts of the world, for example from the southern and northern hemisphere, with different vacation times. Several South East Asian and Pacific island countries are in that situation with their visitors coming from both Australia/New Zealand and North East Asia, North America and Europe.

Inflation

Another detriment often associated with tourism development is inflation. Tourism induced inflation comes mostly in two areas: land values and tourism related goods. Any tourism development requires land. Since most tourism development occurs on coastlines and/or in the vicinity of urban centres, it is likely to be in competition with other forms of land use such as residential, industry, and agriculture. The increased demand for land forces the land prices to rise which is a benefit to landowners, real estate agents and perhaps builders. But local residents are also forced to pay higher prices for their homes and possibly higher taxes as well (e.g. Long 1991; Mathieson and Wall 1982; Ruf 1978).

Tourists are often willing and able to pay more for the same product than local residents. When tourism demand is strong, retailers start charging more for their products. Sometimes a dual price system is introduced where (foreign) tourists are charged a higher price and locals a lower one. More often they simply increase their prices for everybody and, therefore, tourism contributes to inflation of those products. An example of such a product is firewood in Nepal. Tourists compete with locals for this product ensuing in a price increase for firewood (e.g. Curry and Morvaridi 1994).

Inflation caused by tourism is particularly hard on residents who are not engaged in tourism and do not derive any benefit or income from it. These residents are faced with the increased costs of living with no increased income balancing the equation. Even in the Nepal example where many of the Sherpa families benefit from trekking tourism, 'inflation of food and supplies in Khumbuhas financially burdened those poorer families not involved in tourism' (Robinson 1994, p. 694).

Market dependency

The high dependency by developing countries on one or a few tourist originating countries is often criticized. Sometimes it is compared with high dependency on one or few export commodities. And true enough, most developing countries draw the majority of their visitors from just one or a handful of originating countries which causes a high dependence on these markets (Table 5.7). As a consequence, tourist arrivals in the destination country depend on the primary holiday seasons, destination fashions and economic well-being in these markets. A sudden negative downturn in any of these may critically affect the destination country. Hence, the wider the arrivals are distributed among a number of originating countries, the easier it is for the destination to grapple with a downturn in one market.

Leakages

Tourism leakage refers to income from the purchase of goods lost to the local or national economy through required and/or existing money transfers overseas. High leakages are the primary reason for the disenchanting performance of tourism in developing countries. A large share of the tourists' spending is often directly lost to the economy through imports for tourist goods, profit transfer, expatriate labour earnings (Voss 1984). Accordingly, the direct earnings derived from tourism are a lot less with resulting lower multiplier effects. Reasons for high leakages are:

- the lack of availability of goods and services at the required quantity and quality;
- foreign ownership of tourism plants;
- vertical integration of tourism suppliers and multinational corporations;
- the lack of a skilled labour force.

In some instances, almost everything consumed by tourists during their stay is imported.

The import propensity or leakage rate differs among different forms of tourism and among countries. Widmer-Münch (1990) and Milne (1992) showed in completely different contexts how small-scale tourist accommodations are better integrated in the local economy and have a lower import propensity than do large-scale hotels. Differences in leakage rates among countries arise from their size, resource availability and economic development stage. In general, smaller and less well endowed countries are prone to feature a higher leakage rate (Vorlaufer 1990). And the more a country is industrialized and developed, the more it is capable of producing the goods and services required in international tourism. In Singapore, for example, the leakage is estimated to be between 38 per cent (Khan, Seng and Cheong 1990) and 27 per cent (Heng and Low 1990). Leakage rates may also vary depending on the country's ownership of a national airline (Sinclair 1991).

Multiplier effect

A number of different multipliers are being used to derive the value of tourism to the economy beyond a look at the immediate tourist spending. Transaction multipliers, income multipliers, government revenue multipliers and employment multipliers are perhaps the most commonly used ones (Frechtling 1994). Most multipliers are a ratio of the effect of tourism spending vis-à-vis the original amount spent. The concept of a multiplier is based on the notion that the money spent by the tourists is respent by the tourism operators on suppliers and labour who in turn spend their income on other items. Hence, the tourist dollar is being turned over several times as it ripples through the economy. In the context of the overall economy, the transaction and income multipliers are the most important ones:

- **Transaction multiplier:** Ratio of the total change in business sales in an area to the initial tourism expenditure. A simple equation for this multiplier is TM = (1/L) where L represents the leakage rate. Thus, if a region has a leakage rate of 50 per cent, the transaction multiplier (TM) is 2.
- **Income multiplier:** Ratio of income (e.g. business profits, labour income, dividends) to the tourist spending that generated them.

The many links between tourism and a wide range of other industries, such as agriculture, construction and handicrafts, are thought to be very beneficial to the whole economy in the case of tourism development. Accordingly, the multiplier effect of tourism is often considered as a positive development as it is thought to be relatively high. This viewpoint was encouraged in early studies when multiplier effects of more than 2.0 were disclosed (Zinder 1969). However, these studies were soon countered by others which showed considerably lower multiplier effects and severely criticized the earlier approach (Bryden and Faber 1971; Levitt and Gulati 1970). In general, the income multiplier effect is unlikely to be much higher than 1.00 in many developing countries. Table 6.4 shows the multipliers for several developing countries. In the case of Singapore, it has been estimated to be 0.94 (Khan, Seng and Cheong 1990) or 0.98 (Heng and Low 1990). It gives an indication that the multiplier effect is closely interlinked with the leakage rate. The

Table 6.4 Income multiplier effects for selected developing countries

Country	Income multiplier
Turkey	1.96
Egypt	1.23
Island nations	
Jamaica	1.23
Dominican Republic	1.20
Cyprus	1.14
Bermuda	1.09
Hong Kong	1.02
Singapore	0.94–0.98
Mauritius	0.96
Antigua	0.88
Seychelles	0.88
Papua New Guinea	0.87
Bahamas	0.79
Vanuatu	0.56
Cook Islands	0.43
Tonga	0.42
Kiribati	0.37
Niue	0.35

Sources: Archer 1982; Archer and Fletcher 1995; Fletcher 1989; Heng and Low 1990; Khan *et al.* 1990; Milne 1991

higher the leakage, the less money is available to ripple through the economy and multiply the effects of the original tourist expenditure.

Another aspect to be considered is that multiplier effects are often a lot lower on regional levels as leakages out of regional economies are higher (Mathieson and Wall 1982; Oppermann 1993). Others have argued that multiplier effects also differ significantly between different types of tourists (e.g. Milne 1992; Widmer-Münch 1990). Heng and Low (1990) suggest that multipliers among different nationalities vary little. However, their methodology hardly warranted such conclusions as they did not give due consideration to differing expenditure patterns within each sector. For example, they failed to differentiate between accommodation expenses on five or four star hotels and those of lower quality. Similarly, any expenses incurred for food and beverages were treated the same irrespectively if they were incurred in a hawker stand or in a deluxe restaurant where the guests consumed imported wine and steak. This example demonstrates the difficulties involved in multiplier assessments.

Archer and Fletcher (1995) provide a very detailed analysis of tourism's impact in the Seychelles, based on a much more detailed input–output analysis. They illustrated how tourists from different origin countries have a varying employment multiplier effect although their income multipliers differed only slightly.

Regional development

Many developing countries face severe regional economic imbalances within their countries. As a result, migration occurs from the less towards the better endowed regions. Often this means migration from the rural to the urban areas and from the smaller to the larger cities. Consequently, the large metropolises face not only strong population growth due to high birth rates but also additional pressure through migration. As a result, any urban planning and provision of infrastructure is prone to be outdated and inadequate by the time it is completed. To reduce the migration pressure, many governments of developing countries attempt to bring economic development to the less developed regions so that the people feel less inclined to migrate elsewhere (Long 1991). Tourism has been traditionally given much credit for the development of peripheral and economically lagging regions. And in the case of several industrialized countries it has achieved this objective (Christaller 1955). To what extent tourism is a useful tool in regional development in developing countries remains to be thoroughly investigated. Current evidence suggests that it may be less successful in developing countries (Oppermann 1992a; 1993).

Distribution of tourist spending

An interesting aspect of tourism spending is the area in which it is spent. The distribution of tourist expenditure in the areas of accommodation, food, transportation, amusement and shopping may be quite different from country to country and between developing and industrialized countries. Table 6.5

Table 6.5 Distribution of tourist expenditure (in %)

Item	Thailand	South Korea	Hong Kong
Accommodation	23.0	33.3	27.4[1]
Food and beverages	15.1	19.3	11.7[2]
Sightseeing	5.2		
Local transportation	5.5	7.0[3]	2.8[3]
Shopping	42.8	23.7	50.5
Entertainment	5.1	11.3	n/a
Miscellaneous	3.5	5.3	7.6

[1] Hotel bills;
[2] Meals outside hotel;
[3] Sightseeing and local transportation.
Sources: Bailey 1995; McGahey 1995; Muqbil 1995

presents the distribution pattern for several developing countries. It reveals that accommodation often accounts for a large share of the total tourist expenditure and together with shopping for food and beverages is likely to comprise almost 70 per cent. This high proportion and the preponderance of fully inclusive tourism resorts in developing countries has been used by some authors as an argument that tourism is very much an enclave industry with few benefactors outside the hotel operators (Oppermann 1993).

SOCIO-CULTURAL EFFECTS

If there is a domain of tourism research associated with developing countries then it is the socio-cultural effects that tourism has on these countries. While it has been recognized that tourist–host interactions not only have an effect on the hosts and the host society, but also on the tourists and the tourists' society, the dominant majority of all studies are concerned with the former. In contrast to the study of economic effects, socio-cultural impacts are generally depicted with a disapproving connotation. Few studies highlight the positive aspects of host–guest interactions and these are mostly concerned with the rejuvenation of interest in handicrafts, native art and cultural shows.

UNESCO (1976) suggests that host–guest interactions in mass tourism are characterized by four properties: transitory nature; temporal and spatial constraints; lack of spontaneity; and unequal and unbalanced experiences. These properties appear especially valid in the context of mass tourism to developing countries. The primary problems associated with tourism are the demonstration effect, increases in crime and prostitution, general host irritation and the commercialization of culture.

Demonstration effect

Tourists to developing countries, especially if they come from very different societies, introduce and display a very foreign way of life to the host population. This may be positive when it stimulates certain behaviours or inspires people to work for things they lack.

More commonly, it is detrimental and most authors indicate concern for the effects of foreign domination of the industry and the impacts of tourists who parade symbols of their affluence to interested hosts.

(Mathieson and Wall 1982, p. 143)

The demonstration effect also has economic implications. Local people often tend to imitate the seemingly rich tourists (Jafari 1974). A shift in the local consumption patterns occur (Wood 1979) towards 'Western' products. Instead of locally produced lemonade it has to be imported coke, instead of the traditional clothing jeans, t-shirts, etc., are fashionable. Robinson (1994) reports that Sherpas purchase more readily available manufactured items (i.e. cooking items, clothes) than before. This economic implication of the demonstration effect is routinely overlooked in studies on the economic impact of tourism.

Tourism and crime

To what extent tourism contributes to an increase in crime remains yet to be thoroughly investigated (Mathieson and Wall 1982). It appears, however, that especially on a seasonal basis tourism raises the crime level as the tourist influx provides for more targets and possibly easier and wealthier targets.

Ryan (1993, p. 173 f.) lists five different relationships between crime and tourism:

(a) tourists as accidental victims of criminal activity;
(b) a venue which is used by criminals because of the nature of the tourist location;
(c) tourists as easy victims of crime but crime is opportunistic;
(d) organized criminal activity to meet certain types of tourist demand; and
(e) organized criminal and terrorist groups commit specific violent actions against tourists and tourist facilities.

Thus, tourists may be accidental or specific victims of crime or violence or because they are easier victims, crime occurs because of the nature of tourism, and tourists themselves are engaged in criminal or illegal activities such as drugs and prostitution. Ryan also answered the question of tourism giving rise to crime:

It would seem that some of the very forces that motivate tourism contain the seed for criminality. However, for the potential to be actualized, specific forces within the host destination must also be present.

(Ryan 1993, p. 181)

Sex tourism and prostitution

Prostitution undeniably existed before the onset of mass tourism or even tourism to developing countries (Cohen 1982; Phongpaichit 1981). However, in many countries tourism has undoubtedly contributed to an increase in prostitution although it is difficult to determine exactly how much. This already brings up the data issue in this specific area of tourism research. More often than not, prostitution is illegal and, therefore, prostitutes are not registered and official data is non-existent. The illegality also hampers attempts of primary data gathering as prostitutes are very wary of undercover police or other informants. Apparently it is also a profession in which few insiders are willing to talk and to specify numbers of customers, turnover, etc. It appears to be even more difficult to survey the customers. Thus, a great deal of the literature on this topic relies on second hand or estimated data and systematic and methodologically sound investigations are desperately required (Cohen 1982).

Sex tourism to developing countries is only one side of the coin, the other is the marriage trade towards industrialized countries or the more obvious temporary transfer of sex workers from developing countries to developed countries (Agisra 1990; Latza 1987). Probably the most famous and best documented sex tourism destinations are Thailand and the Philippines, and to a lesser extent South Korea, Kenya, the Dominican Republic and Brazil. Sex tourism often involves both sexes, male and female tourists looking for female and/or male prostitutes (e.g. Latza 1987; Leheny 1995; Meisch 1995; Pruitt and LaFont 1995) and the often unidirectional viewpoint of some authors is bothersome (e.g. Agisra 1990; Hall 1992; Thiemann 1989). Mings and Chiulikpongse (1994) highlight the fact that most sex tourists in southern Thailand are not Westerners or Japanese as is so often reiterated but residents from Malaysia and Singapore.

Sex tourism comes in many forms and the most obvious and notorious is the one where the tourist reimburses the prostitute for services rendered (Latza 1987). However, many tourists go into holidays with the inner hope of finding a partner for a sexual relationship, even if temporary (Clark 1994). This partner may or may not be a resident of the host society; it often is a fellow tourist. Cohen (1982, 1986) shows how women involved in 'open-ended' prostitution may be able to establish longer-term relationships with several foreigners through faking romantic involvement.

The scare of AIDS had a dramatic effect on prostitution (Cohen 1988). Tourists wanted younger and younger prostitutes in the hope that there was a lower likelihood of contracting this disease (Thiemann 1989). In recent years, however, several industrialized countries (for example Sweden and Germany) have finally passed legislation which allows for the prosecution of their residents for sex with minors overseas. It is hoped that this will serve as a disincentive.

Changing culture

The culture of a destination can constitute a major draw for tourists. On the other hand, tourism can have a tremendous effect on culture, both positive and negative (Cater 1987). Some governments have recognized this potential threat and tried to limit tourism development to selected areas through zoning or limited access. In Bali (Indonesia), the official policy was until recently to favour tourism concentration in the very south. However, as Wall and Dibnah (1992) note, the marked concentration of tourism and growing regional imbalances contributed to a reversal in this policy with the identification of 16 additional centres of tourism development.

A change in culture may also simply mean a changing composition with respect to income earners in the family (Long 1991; Cukier and Wall 1994). Tourism often brings paid jobs for females which, in several developing countries, is almost a novelty. Although commonly at the bottom end of the pay scale, such a modification is bound to have a tremendous impact on family structures and the society as a whole. Where women gain financial independence, their whole perspective of life and marriage is prone to change (Richter 1995).

Cultural rejuvenation

On the search for souvenirs, tourists often look for arts and crafts. This demand may preserve, stimulate or even rejuvenate the local arts and crafts industry as many additional customers demand local products (Long 1991; Swain 1989). In South East Asia, hand-batik of clothes is very popular and a small cottage industry has developed to cater to the needs of the tourists. In some places, tourists are encouraged to gain hands-on experience. Since demand often determines production, tourists may have a guiding influence on what specific types of arts and crafts are produced. This may result in a bias towards some products, designs and technologies whereas others suffer or may be forgotten because of a lack of demand.

Another area where tourism demand may instigate a revival of tradition are cultural shows. On the other hand, the repeated performance of ceremonial rituals may cause the loss of their traditional significance (Long 1991). Sometimes, traditions are modified to facilitate a show to be performed within the tourists' limited available time span and to accommodate tourists' expectations (Stymeist 1996).

Gayle (1993) reported that Jamaican citizens living in the primary tourist resort areas viewed the benefits of tourism as mostly economic, accompanied by social costs such as drug trafficking, acute shortage of housing, prostitution, water pollution and other environmental problems. Workers at smaller hotels and street vendors considered the all-inclusive nature of tourism as of little benefit because it limits their potential share in tourism's benefits.

PHYSICAL EFFECTS

The environmental effects of tourism in developing countries are among the least documented. However, they have attracted considerable attention in the developed countries where high intensity usage and demand by tourism has transformed many landscapes. Sometimes, tourism has an indirect impact on the physical environment (Hunter and Green 1995). The increased fuelwood demand in Nepal, for example, places more pressure on the resource wood (Pawson, Stanford, Adams and Nurbu 1984; Robinson 1994). In the high altitudes of the Himalaya, however, forests grow very slowly and any usage beyond the reproductive capacity means a loss of protective tree cover for the soil. In a worst case scenario, valuable soil is being washed off and the reproductive potential of nature even further diminished. In other instances, tourism may facilitate conservation (Mathieson and Wall 1982). Hunter and Green (1995) provide an overview of the major potential impacts of tourism on the natural environment (Table 6.6). It illustrates the wide range of potential consequences of tourism development.

Water usage and degradation

One of the most often mentioned conflicts between tourism and the environment and also other users is the availability of water. While many developing countries are located in the inner tropics with an abundant water supply, others are situated in the arid parts of the world where water is a scarce resource. The provision of water supply for hotels is a necessity in international tourism. However, the consumption per tourist day is many times higher than that of residents. If water supply to residential areas is reduced as a result of tourism development this leads invariably to negative feelings if not conflict.

Table 6.6 Major impacts of tourism on the natural environment

Impact aspect	Potential consequences
Floral and faunal species composition	• disruption of breeding • killing of animals through hunting • killing of animals in order to supply goods for the souvenir trade • inward or outward migration of animals • trampling and damage of vegetation by feet and vehicles • destruction of vegetation through the gathering of wood or plants • change in extent and/or nature of vegetation cover through clearance or planting to accomodate tourist facilities • creation of a wildlife reserve/sanctuary or habitat restoration
Pollution	• water pollution through discharges of sewage, spillages of oil/petrol • air pollution from vehicle emissions, combustion of fuels for heating and lighting • noise pollution from tourist transportation and activities
Erosion	• compaction of soils causing increased surface run-off and erosion • change in risk of occurence of land slips/slides • change in risk of avalanche occurence • damage to river banks
Natural resources	• depletion of ground and surface water supplies • depletion of fossil fuels to generate energy for tourist activity • change in risk of occurence of fire • depletion of mineral resources for building materials • over-exploitation of biological resources (e.g. overfishing) • change in hydrological patterns
Visual impact	• facilities (e.g. building, chairlift, car park) • litter • sewage, algal blooms

Source: Hunter and Green 1995

Another user conflict occurs with agriculture which usually relies on irrigation in these climates. Hence, tourism development may actually have a negative effect on agricultural production and not the frequently mentioned positive linkages.

As mentioned earlier, a large proportion of tourism to developing countries is attracted by the three 'Ss' – sun, sand, and sea. The sea water is, therefore, a major asset to developing countries, provided it is of good quality and not polluted. However, many hotel developments occur where the waste water is not adequately treated before it is released into the sea. Particularly isolated hotel resorts, which are not connected to a sewage plant, often dispose of their waste water through a pipe that extends into the sea. Obviously dependent on the currents, the waste water may be washed back ashore, threatening the very resource the hotel resort is based upon. Harris and Nelson (1993) indicate that in the case of Pangandaran (Indonesia), water supply, water disposal and litter are a major problem.

A fine example of the immediate effect of a destroyed resource base on tourism is the algae pollution of many Italian beaches in 1988 and 1989. Tourist bookings dropped by about 25 per cent and in the area of organized tourism even 50–60 per cent (Becheri 1991). It vividly illustrates the danger to any form of tourism development if the resources it is built upon are seriously destroyed and not preserved.

Wildlife and vegetation

In Africa, wildlife is a primary tourism resource. Viewing, photographing and hunting are major tourist activities and tourism has contributed towards the establishment of national parks and the conservation and protection of wildlife. Yet, the increasing demand for such activities also brings congestion to these areas with not only a detrimental effect on the visitors' experience but also a serious disruption of the wildlife, their feeding and reproductive patterns. Some species may adjust better to living under the eyes of the tourists and, therefore, may increase at the expense of others. In a balanced environment, small changes in the habitat can result in enormous modification of the whole ecosystem. Furthermore, the establishment of national parks means disruption of the local economy as they are forced to seek alternative areas for cultivation and grazing (Cater 1987).

Other ecosystems, such as coral reefs, may also need protection from tourists. Sea pollution and removal of shells and corals are among the major threats to coral reefs (Cater 1987).

Landscape and architecture

Mass tourism often transforms the whole landscape (Kulinat 1991). Multistorey hotels are built along beaches where there were only dunes, palm trees or orchards. Roads and airports need to be constructed and other tourist support infrastructure is also required. The spatial concentration of mass tourism in developing countries (Chapter 3), especially in coastal areas, brings an immense land use demand. Other more traditional land uses cannot compete.

However, eventually land pressure in existing tourism resorts increases so much that original single or double storey buildings are replaced by multi-storey skyscrapers (Uthoff 1991). Fortunately, most developing countries have learned from the negative example of Spain where, in the tourism boom years, many tourism beach resorts were transformed into Hong Kong or Rio de Janeiro look alikes: 20 or more storey hotel and apartment complexes rising immediately behind the beach with no regard for landscape aesthetics or the traditional architectural style of the region.

Singapore, in an effort to show its transformation into a modern society through construction of skyscrapers, almost lost its architectural heritage. Today, huge sums are devoted to restoration and preservation. After all, these old buildings constitute tourism attractions as well. Ungefehr (1988) reports of similar development problems in the Bahamas.

Carrying capacity

An important concept in the context of tourism resource management is carrying capacity. Four different carrying capacity types are generally identified: physical; psychological or perceptual; social; and economic. With respect to the physical carrying capacity of tourism, it denotes the maximum number of tourists that can use a specific area over a specified length of time without serious interruption of the natural habitat. If this capacity level is exceeded, the environment is seriously damaged and may never recover. It has also another meaning in the experiential sphere:

> Carrying capacity is the maximum number of people who can use a site without an unacceptable alteration in the physical environment and without an unacceptable decline in the quality of the experience gained by visitors.
>
> (Mathieson and Wall 1982, p. 21)

Tourists have very different perceptions of how many other tourists should be allowed in the area at the same time before their own experience suffers. Carrying capacities vary from setting to setting and from habitat to habitat. Especially the social carrying capacities of the host population and the experiential carrying capacity of the tourists themselves vary considerably from person to person.

> Care has to be taken to recognize that perceptual capacity of any group is part of a continuum in the general community. The continuum extends across time as well as among people.
>
> (Mitchell 1979, p. 197)

Mathieson and Wall (1982) suggest that host resentment is likely to be higher where there is limited local involvement in the tourism industry. Thus, the hosts' social carrying capacity may be directly related to their financial and social involvement in tourism. Carrying capacity levels may also be lower when tourists and hosts come from very different social, ethnic and economic backgrounds as is often the case in developing countries. Finally, economic carrying capacity denotes the ability to absorb tourism in the local economy without displacing or impeding other desirable local activities and industries.

Unfortunately few tourism studies in developing countries have ever been placed in the context of either of the aforementioned four carrying capacity dimensions. But research in recreational settings in North America suggests that the most impact upon the biophysical environment occurs within the first few years of development and that there are critical stages in the progressive change of the environment (Mitchell 1979). Thus, any research into physical effects of tourism development should start before the first development occurs in order to establish a meaningful baseline inventory. Longitudinal investigations into environmental changes are needed to allow for better planning and management of future tourism developments.

SUMMARY

What is apparently needed are studies that comprehensively investigate tourism impacts and not only one side of the coin. Almost all impact assessments examine only economic or socio-cultural or environmental effects but seldom the whole range. Another shortcoming of many past studies is that they rarely examine long-range effects. Furthermore, little research has been concerned with alternative scenarios. What would have happened if, instead of hotel development, a textile industry was established or an aluminium smelter? What are the likely effects of different development scenarios vis-à-vis tourism development? And also, is tourism or television a greater force in cultural and societal change in developing countries? Many residents in developing countries may never or rarely see, or even come in contact with, tourists from a different culture. Yet, they tend either to own a television or have access to one. The current similarities in clothing fashion around the world including developing countries among the younger generations is a sign of the increasing similarity of idols or status symbols around the globe. Often called the MTV-generation, many teenagers in developing countries share more similarities with their counterparts in the industrialized countries than with their parent generation. And television is only one influence on changes in culture and society outside tourism. Cinema, radio and fast food chains often prove to be powerful attractions to youngsters, influencing their habits and society.

A reasonable lesson learned from the examination of tourism impacts is that these effects vary from location to location depending on the overall development status, resource base, type of tourism development and tourists, and the similarity and/or differences between the hosts' and tourists' society.

QUESTIONS

1. Why is a tourism resource inventory an important step in the tourism planning process?

2. Name the major economic effects of tourism and discuss their advantages and disadvantages.
3. Why are multiplier effects independent of the original tourist spending volume and why are multiplier effects always lower on local as compared to regional or national level?
4. Discuss tourism's primary socio-cultural effects. Which aspect appears to you as the most critical one to consider when planning for tourism?
5. Define carrying capacity. What are its three dimensions?

FURTHER READING

Mathieson, A. and Wall, G. (1982) *Tourism: Economic, Physical and Environmental Impacts*. Longman, Harlow.

> Still the most comprehensive book on the topic of tourism impacts. Unfortunately it is getting rather outdated and a new edition is urgently needed. It is a detailed coverage of all three types of impacts albeit not focused on developing countries.

Mitchell, B. (1989) *Geography and Resource Analysis* (3rd. ed.). Longman, London.

> Again a fairly outdated textbook that deserves a new edition. While not directly placed in a tourism context, it provides many fine examples of such development impacts in the area of physical effects. It is a must read for anybody involved in physical resource assessment, landscape evaluation, carrying capacity, environmental impact assessments and perceptions. Again, most studies cited are North America based but the underlying concepts and approaches towards studying physical impacts are easily transferable.

7 Tourism marketing

Tourism has grown enormously and its influence has spread widely since World War II. The growth of international tourism has been strong and sustained since its initial surge in the 1960s. Although an international recession for the period of 1982 to 1983 caused a slight decline, recovery was swift and strong. In more recent years, the rate of growth in international tourism receipts exceeded the growth rate of tourist arrivals, which is indicative of increase in per capita expenditures by international tourists. International tourist arrivals increased at a phenomenal rate of 6.5 per cent from 1960 to 1990 and the World Tourism Organization (WTO) projects that international arrivals will reach over 700 million by the year 2000. The fastest growing destinations have been outside the traditionally strongest continents of North America and Europe. Most parts of Asia, Oceania, Africa and South America, which include the majority of the world's developing economies, have recently experienced rates of growth significantly above the world average. Possible explanations for the rapid growth of tourism in these regions would include the fast economic growth, relatively stable political environment, ability to finance infrastructure development, aggressive marketing efforts by NTOs and increase of tourism demand worldwide. In the following section we will first identify the general environmental factors which influence the growth of international tourism in developing countries, and will focus our discussion on the effects of these factors on the marketing of tourism products.

ENVIRONMENTAL FACTORS INFLUENCING THE GROWTH OF TOURISM

Economic environment

Economic considerations are important in international tourism because consumption patterns in tourism are largely dependent upon the economic conditions in the market. The economic condition in the countries or regions in which prospective visitors live is one of the most important factors which influence total visitor volume. Developed and growing economies sustain large numbers of trips away from home for business purposes of all kinds. Business meetings, attendance at conferences and trade shows and travel on government business are all important parts of the travel and tourism industry. The influence of economic conditions is more obvious in leisure travel where, in many countries with advanced and developed economies, average disposable income per capita has grown to a size large enough to enable a majority of the population to take vacation trips in foreign lands.

As a case in point, tourism from and within Asia showed an unprecedented growth in the 1980s stemming from very fast economic growth in many countries in the region. During the 1980–1990 period, the average annual rate of growth of the Gross Domestic Product (GDP) for the Asian region was 5.5 per cent compared with 2.4 per cent recorded by Europe for the same period, 2.8 per cent by North America and 0.9 for the Middle East. Economic growth in newly industrialized countries also made it possible for these countries to fund infrastructure development, thus increasing the capacity to accommodate international tourists. At the same time, the relatively stable political and social climate in most Asian countries combined with the rapid growth of the industrial and service sectors of the economies have contributed to a rapid development of personal disposable income and private consumption, thus considerably improving the propensity to travel for many residents in Asian countries. The Japanese market in particular showed a remarkable growth in the 1980s and early 1990s. The number of Japanese overseas travellers has shown a large increase since 1985, when the value of the yen rose sharply against other currencies. Further, riding on a favourable economy in Japan, the Japanese government in 1987 launched the 'Ten Million Program', which aimed at doubling the number of Japanese overseas travellers from the 1986 level of 5.5 million to 10 million by the end of 1991. The Ten Million Program was achieved in 1990, one year before the target year.

Technological environment

An obvious factor which influences the demand for international tourism is technology and innovation as applied to new processes. Technology and travel are natural partners. The rapid growth of travel and tourism in the post-war period has been founded upon technological developments, principally in air transport through the development and refinement of the jet engine, more sophisticated aircraft design and improved systems. For example, the world's three largest aircraft manufacturers (MacDonald Douglas, Boeing and Lockheed) all introduced the wide-bodied passenger aeroplanes such as the DC-10, Boeing 747 and Tri-star L-1011 in the early 1970s. The three airplane manufacturers have continuously modified the aircraft to fly longer distances with better fuel economy. As an example, the original Boeing 747 had to make a refuelling stop in an intermediary location in order to make a direct flight from New York to Tokyo. However, with the introduction of the Boeing 747–400, the newer version of the original jumbo jet, a non-stop flight became popular between New York and Tokyo. Without these developments in air transport, foreign travel would have remained the privilege of the wealthy and business persons.

Wide use of computer technology in recent years brought another advance to the travel industry. Computer software has been designed to cover a wide range of activities undertaken by the travel trade (e.g. information retrieval, reservation, ticketing, invoicing, etc.). There is strong evidence to suggest that these developments will result in a revolution in the distribution and marketing of the various travel and tourism services throughout all segments of the travel and tourism industry.

Political/legal environment

Government interest in tourism has sprung primarily from economic significance, particularly its tax earning and employment potentials. However, tourism demand can be largely influenced by legislative actions at various levels of government and inter-government agencies (e.g. the World Tourism Organization and International Air Transport Association). Also, international politics play a significant role in the volume of travel and tourism business. As one example, following a series of terrorist activities in Europe and elsewhere in 1985–1986, 35 per cent of US travellers with reservations to Europe cancelled their flights. Likewise, as illustrated in the case study at the end of this chapter, the Gulf War had a profound effect on Thailand's tourism industry in terms of cancelled reservations.

In the 1980s the air transport industry was liberalized in most tourist generating countries. For example, the deregulation of the airline industry in North America generated a significant increase in intercontinental flights, which in turn positively contributed to the growth of world tourism. At the same time, the adaptation of the open sky policy in Asian countries resulted in a substantial increase of air traffic within Asia and the introduction of carriers like Eva Airways (Taiwan) and Asiana Airlines (South Korea).

Relaxed travel restrictions and increased leisure time by residents in newly industrialized countries contributed significantly to a growth of tourism within and from Asia. For example, both the Taiwanese and South Korean governments in the past restricted or limited overseas travel by their citizens. However, due to a rapid economic growth and increase in consumer disposable income, the concept of leisure became widespread among their citizens and the governments gradually lifted the overseas travel ban. For instance, the Korean government in the past restricted its citizens from obtaining a passport for 'sightseeing' purposes. However, effective from January 1, 1989, the government eliminated all age restrictions on the issuing of passports to its citizens. Previously, to obtain a passport for pleasure travel, an applicant had to be at least 50 years old in 1983, 40 in 1987 and 30 in 1988. The Taiwanese government also lifted the age restrictions on issuing passports in a similar way. As a result, the number of outbound tourists from Taiwan increased from 813 000 in 1986 to 2.8 million in 1995. During the same period, the number of South Korean outbound travellers increased from 400 000 to almost three million.

Socio-cultural environment

Social and cultural considerations involve the beliefs, value, attitudes, opinions and lifestyles of those in the market environment, as developed from their cultural, ecological, demographic, religious, educational and ethnic conditioning. As an example, while the Japanese and Koreans share similar cultural heritages, these two ethnic groups are known to be very different in travel behaviour. Japanese travellers like to travel in groups, usually with their work colleagues. On the other hand, Koreans like to travel with friends and only a few with co-workers. Also Koreans prefer free independent travel (FIT) packages rather than group packages.

Demographics is a key element in the tourism marketing process, especially in light of the significant demographic shifts affecting the population. These shifts will affect the travel and tourism market, particularly in determining target markets. For example, in 1970, 24 per cent of the US population was between 25 and 45 years of age. By 1990, this age cohort accounted for 33 per cent of the population – a 38 per cent increase. This kind of demographic shift is evident in many other countries as well. A careful analysis of the shifting age categories is a critical source of information for an NTO in determining the marketing process. Moreover, as social attitudes change, so too do the leisure patterns of consumers. The popularity of ecotourism in recent years is one good example.

THE ROLE OF NTOs

At the national level, governments promote their countries in the international tourist market through national tourism organizations (NTOs). For example, Korea National Tourism Corporation (KNTC) is the NTO for South Korea. In some countries, such as Mexico, government leaders have recognized the importance of tourism to the nation's economy and have elevated the status of the NTO to cabinet level, instituting a Ministry of Tourism. Regardless of the position in their government, NTOs have similar objectives. They promote their countries through publicity campaigns, conduct research and develop plans for destinations. Due to increased competition in world tourism, NTOs today spend much more on their tourism marketing budget. A significant part of NTO budgets is spent publicizing the destinations. They work to make the public in their target markets aware of the destinations and to promote positive images of the destinations.

Importance of image promotion

A tourist destination's image has a profound effect on tourism marketing. This is because many tourists, especially the first time visitors, have limited knowledge of the destination and thus rely upon the image of the destination when they make their travel decisions. Studies indicate that a destination's image is driven by two primary sources – organic and induced. Generally, non-tourist directed communication sources, including any political, geographical, or social events and activities in the destination, comprise the organic image source. On the other hand, deliberately created, tourist-directed communications (e.g. advertisements and marketing communications) comprise the induced sources.

Images of tourist destinations play a pivotal role in marketing at least from the point of attracting enough tourists to the destination and also in terms of influencing the visitors' overall satisfaction or dissatisfaction with the destination (Chon 1989, 1990, 1992b). Every time someone is exposed to anything related to a destination, it helps in forming an image of that place. Books, movies, television, postcards, songs, photographs, news stories and advertising all contribute to images of various destinations. Favourable images of the destinations would greatly improve the chance of increasing tourist traffic. For example, Austria became a popular vacation destination for many Americans as a result of the favourable images portrayed in the movie *The Sound of Music*, while Kenya enjoyed a substantial increase in tourism after the movie *Out of Africa*. On the other hand, negative images can have a profound impact on the country's tourism. The 'war image' of Korea associated with the television drama *M.A.S.H.*, even 25 years after the Korean War, was a detrimental factor for Korea to promote the country as an ideal tourist destination to Americans in the 1970s. Likewise, one of the difficulties in promoting India as a tourist destination is the image of poverty people associate with the country. The scenic beauty and many cultural attractions in the country are overshadowed by negative scenes of starving people and squalor. This negative image makes it a challenge for India's tourism marketers to promote the country's tourism overseas.

Images of a destination are so important that states and countries spend millions of dollars to build positive images of their destinations. Some researchers postulate that a tourist's experience is nothing but a constant modification of the destination image (Table 7.1). As illustrated in Figure 5.1, a tourist makes a destination choice based on his previously held images of the destination. The tourists' actual experience in the destination allows them to compare their previous images with the 'reality', which in turn influences their satisfaction or dissatisfaction with the overall experience. The following example illustrates this process.

Suppose a married couple in Japan decide to take a vacation in Bali, Indonesia. They have never been to Bali or Indonesia and are excited about the idea of going to Bali. At this point, their image of Bali is mainly based on two things – the written information from the tour package brochure and their previous knowledge about Bali and Indonesia acquired through books, mass media and friends. The couple's image of the destination is most important here because their expectations of Bali (and also the country of Indonesia in general) are based on their previously held images of the destination. The couple finally arrive in Bali and participate in various touristic experiences.

When they return home, they go through a 'recollection' stage. In the recollection stage, they evaluate their overall experience of the destination. The evaluation process includes a comparison of their expectations and their actual experiences. When the actual experiences live up to the expectations (based on images of the destination), there is satisfaction. If the actual experiences do not live up to expectations, there is dissatisfaction. Depending on their level of satisfaction or dissatisfaction, the couple will decide whether to return to Bali as well as other places in Indonesia in the future. More importantly, they will talk about their experiences with their friends. The couple's descriptions of their experiences to friends will in turn

Table 7.1 Perceptual differences of South Korea between pre- and post-visit American tourists

Perceptions	Pre-visitors (n = 204)	Post-visitors (n = 240)	t-value
Shopping opportunities	4.71	5.43	9.65*
Friendly people	5.19	5.40	3.68*
Safety/security	4.70	5.28	6.23*
Scenic beauty	3.96	4.87	9.86*
Historical/cultural attractions	5.27	6.16	9.43*
Travel related resources	4.37	4.63	2.77*
General attitude toward Korea	4.13	4.99	10.65

* significant at 0.01 level.
Based on a scale of 1 to 7; the larger the number, the more favourable the responses.

help their friends form images of Bali and Indonesia. As illustrated above, the primary images of a destination as perceived by a tourist have a lot to do with the tourist's ultimate satisfaction or dissatisfaction.

Research indicates that an initial impression (or the image) of a destination is hard to change. That is, everything that happens, good or bad, is ultimately based on the original image! In a study which attempted to determine the image of South Korea as a tourist destination by American visitors, pre- and post-visit surveys were administered to American tourists visiting the country. The country's image by both pre- and post-visit American tourists was measured on the seven areas of shopping opportunities, friendliness of the Korean people, historical and cultural attractions, safety and security concerns, scenic attractions, travel conditions and the tourists' general attitudes toward the country. As Table 7.1 shows, post-visitors rated each of the seven areas more favourably; however, interestingly enough, patterns of perception for each of the seven areas remained similar to the perception held by pre-visitors. This tends to confirm that a destination's image, once established in the mind of the public, is hard to change.

Marketing functions of NTOs

Historically the principal marketing role of NTOs has been seen in the fairly narrow promotional terms of creating and communicating overall appealing destination images and messages to the target market. However, traditional NTO functions are changing as today's international tourism industry becomes more competitive and tourists are becoming increasingly sophisticated in their destination choice behaviour. In many countries leaders of the tourism industry recognize the importance of collaboration between the public and private sectors and they launch and implement various collaborative marketing programmes. A good example would be Thailand's 'The World

Our Guest' programme in 1992 which is illustrated in the case study at the end of this chapter. Thailand's tourism industry in the early 1990s was adversely affected by the Persian Gulf War, the spread of AIDS in the country, and the political unrest that occurred in early 1992. In an attempt to offset the adverse situation, the Tourism Authority of Thailand (TAT) in collaboration with airlines, hotels and tour operators launched 'The World Our Guest' programme, which was a massive familiarization trip campaign aimed at travel intermediaries. More than 11 000 individual tourists and travel agents were invited to Thailand and were given free hotel rooms, airline tickets, meals and tours as part of the promotion, which was declared by the TAT to be an unqualified success.

As we discussed above, the marketing activities of an NTO are mainly centred around the promotion of the country as a whole. A natural extension of such efforts is the 'facilitation role' which typically includes collecting, analysing and disseminating market research data, establishing a representation in the markets of origin, participating in trade shows, organizing and coordinating familiarization trips and supporting the private sector with literature production and distribution.

The growth and traffic pattern of international tourism is largely influenced by environmental trends related to economic, technological, political and socio-cultural factors of the world. Therefore, in order to make sound marketing decisions, an NTO needs to constantly monitor any changes occurring in the environment and take a proactive posture in their marketing programmes (Chon and Olsen 1990, Chon and Singh 1995). In this chapter we have reviewed the role of NTOs in marketing countries as tourist destinations. Because of the importance of building positive destination images, NTOs in the future will continue to play the image building and image communication role in the market place. At the same time, NTOs in the future will play a greater role as facilitators for market research and collaborators for marketing efforts by the private sector of the tourism industry.

MARKETING IN THE PRIVATE SECTOR: THE HOTEL/RESORT INDUSTRY

While marketing at the national level primarily focuses on promoting the country's overall image as a tourist destination and creating a favourable climate for marketing of the tourism products, the private sector – comprising hotels and resorts – typically focuses on actual sales and the promotional aspects of marketing. As the 'global village' concept of marketing became a reality in the 1990s, the importance of local markets took on a different role. The phrase 'think global – act local' became a part of business language. This overly simplistic phrase attempted to define a broad range of activities that international hoteliers used in their marketing efforts. The phrase implied that anyone involved in international hotel marketing needed to remain current on global activities as they related or affected local market conditions. Keeping track of world-wide trends required the organization of information by developing a system of categories so that the information could be used in a manner that was expedient to the hotel.

Establishing an organized information gathering system, or an environmental scanning system, is very important in today's fast paced business world. It allows the organization the opportunity to plan, to navigate the system, and to catch and collate the information. To be successful in international marketing, a manager must have the necessary information quickly and efficiently to out-manoeuvre the competition by creating his own race. Remember that the competitors have access to the same information that the operators have. Thus, the system becomes the competitive edge.

INFRASTRUCTURE OF THE TRAVEL INDUSTRY

In his book, *Relationship Marketing*, Regis McKenna (1991) talks about the relationship infrastructure of the computer business and its invisible, but very important marketing role, as demonstrated by the early success of Apple Computers. The relationship infrastructure of any business plays a role which is often overlooked and can cause problems. The tourism industry relationship infrastructure consists of the following six major components:

- airlines;
- tour wholesalers for both foreign independent tours (FITs) and groups;
- tour operators;
- retail travel agents for all segments of leisure, business travel and groups;
- travel journalists and trade publications representatives;
- other special interest groups.

Airlines

Airlines play a dual role: first, they play a part in the distribution system vis-à-vis their role in the reservation systems; and, second, they transport guests to a destination. Therefore, airlines play a critical role in marketing by linking hotels in the international market to relationships with major carriers in the local market. The relationship with any airline is triangular. The tourism business operator's day-to-day relationship is established with the local office, the reservation system is handled through a central reservation office, and in major feeder markets a relationship needs to be developed with a regional or national sales office. This triangular relationship results from the following. The local office of the airline is responsible for outbound business, and as such the offices in the feeder markets actually have measurable business potential with the airline reservation system. The airline reservation system, in this case, is the distribution channel for reservations since they have all the necessary information and records. A relationship is often needed within the domestic-offices of the airlines, especially for countries with 'flag carriers' – those carriers which contract their own stopover programmes.

With a triangular relationship the operator can give more emphasis to a particular point of the triangle and still keep viable relationships with the other two points without creating too much of an imbalance. Airline reservation systems are becoming more important as more hotel reservations are being made through these systems. It is therefore important for the operator to understand the basic capabilities of the airline systems, and how the hotel is displayed in the systems. If the system is neglected, it may yield inaccurate information about the hotel or resort.

Wholesalers

Wholesalers are the mass-movers of the travel industry and in many ways are arguably the best business operators in the industry. They operate on slim margins to gain market share, and therefore, they need to move as many seats as possible to remain profitable. Their distribution channel is through retail travel agents who receive commissions from the wholesalers. Some wholesalers specialize in the higher margin travel market, but they are in the minority, and as such are the easiest to identify.

Generally, a wholesaler puts together air, hotel and land packages (sometimes tours), and then contacts retail travel agents to sell their products. Airlines, hotels, and ground operators extend non-commissionable rates to the wholesalers, who then mark up the prices to cover their costs and in turn pay commissions to the retail agents who distribute their products.

Tour operators

The basic distinction between wholesalers and tour operators is that tour operators market their packages directly to the public. The very large wholesalers such as JTB in Japan and DER in Germany are examples of tour operators who often provide multiple services. Whether the tour operator is a wholesaler or not, the pricing and relationships with tour operators are the same as with wholesalers. Remember, tour operators play an important role in building the positive perceptions of the hotel or resort with the public. This is compounded by the travel/tourism infrastructure, and, therefore, cultivating long-term relationships with tour operators should become part of the operator's strategy for long-term success. A subsegment of tour operators relates to companies that put together group trips for organizations such as alumni groups or groups solicited through advertising media. For the hotel, these types of groups are lucrative due to the high yield factor or due to the fact that these groups choose prospective hotels during slow periods to get better rates.

Retail travel agents

This segment of the travel industry has a tremendous influence on international travellers, because many travellers rely on their travel agents, as experts or consultants. Often, a traveller is influenced to stay or not stay at the hotel based upon their agent's perception of the establishment.

Journalists and travel writers

This part of the travel industry network is quite interesting since hotels, all too often, underestimate or overestimate the value of journalists and travel publications. This is easily done, as there are many journalists who present themselves as being more than they really are, or travel publications and magazines which are started for the purpose of selling advertisements rather than journalistic purposes, solely using advertisements to finance the magazine. Therefore, many hotels underestimate and overestimate the power of the media. One strategy for dealing with the press is to hire a professional public relations or advertising agency which can handle all media inquiries for the operator. Regardless of the situation, developing a positive relationship with journalists and travel publications will play a key role in the development of long-term positive perceptions of the hotel.

Special interest groups

One important segment in this category is the incentive travel market. This segment is viewed by many as the glamour part of the travel industry. It is high yield, very visible, and generates lots of attention. Its participants are those who earned the chance to take a trip that the 'general public' was unable to take. The Society for Incentive Travel Executives (SITE) defines incentive travel as travel offered by an employer in recognition for an employee's high performance. It is often used as a motivational tool for employees, primarily in the sales intensive industries (Society of Incentive Travel Executives 1990). However, most hotels define incentive travel in much broader terms which often include groups – for example, an annual company-wide group tour. If this is the case, the number of incentives, as defined by SITE, is somewhat limited.

Another important segment in the special interest group category is the corporate business travel market. This segment makes up the greater part of most hotels' markets 'except for resorts or other leisure destinations', and therefore gets most of the attention. The emphasis on this segment, which includes group travel, includes the many meetings held by business companies. The distribution system and rate structure for this segment is quite varied, depending upon which part of the world the operator resides in. However, in all parts of the world one common factor remains in that the majority of all corporate business is booked locally. From 60 to 80 per cent of all corporate reservations are made through local company offices. The phrase 'think globally – act locally' seems rather appropriate within this segment. Again, developing relationships is the key to building success in this segment. How well the operator is perceived 'at home', allows the operator the opportunity to maximize the business from this segment.

The embassy and government segment presents another category of markets in the international hotel business. Hotels that are located in cities which serve as capitals of their countries or in cities supported by international business will benefit from this segment. In many instances, business from this segment is low-rated, but it has high visibility which helps enhance local perceptions of the hotel. To attract embassy business, relationships need to be developed with the administration section of the embassy first, and then with the industrial sections such as commerce, agriculture, protocol, etc. For government business (this is true for embassies as well, but less so), the hotel's reputation, services, amenities and rates will help determine what types of government business the operator can get. No matter what type of business the operator gets from this segment, it will ultimately benefit the operator's overall business if it is handled properly. Too often, hoteliers take this segment for granted, and as a result, they find that the business that they once had is now gone. Conversely, during difficult times they are unable to attract this segment's business, because they ignored it during prosperous times.

Lastly, convention related businesses should be treated as a separate special interest group in the larger business traveller segment. In many cities around the world, this segment might be a very profitable portion of their business mix. In other cities it may have little or no impact. Factors such as the size of the city's convention centre/exhibition hall, the size of the hotel, the location of the hotel in relationship to the convention centre/exhibition hall and the capacity of the local airport will determine to what extent this segment will impact on the hotel's business.

First, determine if the business the operator receives from an event is indirect or direct. Basically, if the hotel is located away from the venue of the event and the size of the event is large enough to fill the hotels near the venue, then there will be enough pressure in the city to cause the hotel to get indirect business. If the operator receives indirect business, they should manage the inventory properly to avoid giving blocks of rooms to travel companies operating group packages for the event, since a room block in the hotel could be one of the last ones to fill. The operator is in a better position by saving rooms available for FIT business related to or unrelated to the event. However, if the event is not so large as to cause the previously mentioned pressure, then it is important not to hold rooms for a demand which might not materialize.

ORGANIZATION AND DEPLOYMENT OF THE SALES AND MARKETING DEPARTMENT

The structure of the sales and marketing department in a hotel which has international business is dependent upon the size of the hotel, the market mix of the hotel, and the quality of personnel available. The basic organization to fit these factors would be general manager, director of sales or marketing, sales managers or executives and administration staff. Also, reservations and banquet sales should be included either directly or through a 'dotted line' responsibility to the director of sales or marketing as these three departments interact daily. The opportunity for the three departments to develop a synergy of operations is far greater when they are co-ordinated under one division. In the sales department organization, it is important to have as few layers of management as possible. It is recommended to avoid having sales executives who report to sales managers, who report to a director of sales. All sales personnel should report directly to the director of sales, and thus each person is responsible for a market. This allows all sales personnel to concentrate on selling. To function properly, this system requires hiring individuals with good hotel operations experience. Also, the sales team must have good communication skills, an understanding of the hotel's profit and loss statement and basic selling skills.

MARKET MIX AND YIELD MANAGEMENT

It is critical to know where the business is generated so that the operator can manage it profitably. To do this, a market mix needs to be tracked daily so that a yield management system can be implemented. A market mix can be tracked by a rate type or by a reservation source. However, in the opinion of the authors, tracking by rate type is preferable, as this assists with the development of a yield management system. A market mix based on rate type would have categories for each of the rates. An example could include volume corporate, preferred corporate, overseas corporate, wholesale corporate, wholesale FIT, packages, airlines, government/embassy, special rates, group tour, group trade show, group corporate, group incentive and complimentary rooms.

These categories are only examples, as there are certainly many more variations as to how market mix occurs. The most important aspect of developing a market mix for a yield management system is to identify and to track the most important market segments that make up the room revenue. The more specific the tracking, the better the yield management system will be. In addition, tracking business based upon 'rate paid' is another way that tracking should be done.

Developing a system to track the nationality of guests and their country of residence is an effective marketing tool because this information assists with determining the effectiveness of the reservation distribution systems, advertising and rate structures for geographical markets. By developing systems to track rate segments, geographical markets and distribution channels, a yield management system can be effectively implemented. The purpose of the system is to maximize rate and occupancy on a daily basis, which requires accurate and detailed information.

Sales plan

Many hotels write lengthy sales plans which are mistakenly called 'marketing plans'. The basic distinction is that a sales plan deals primarily with action plans and personnel deployment. The identification of markets and tactics is mentioned in sales plans but only in the context of justifying actions. This being said, a sales plan may sound unimportant as a stand-alone document when compared to a detailed marketing plan. However, there are instances where sales plans are far more effective than marketing plans. A typical sales plan has one to three basic strategies:

1. it identifies markets to solicit;
2. it establishes goals for the various segments; and
3. it details action plans for each segment.

The plan should be short and concise. The plan becomes a working document that is used daily. Also, the plan should be a 'living' document in that it is constantly updated and perfected by the sales team. The plan should have very little statistical information and should be integrated into the financial projections or goals of each segment. The plan should be composed of action plans serving as the guides for the sales team. As the business situation changes and/or the sales team matures, the operator can then develop more sophisticated marketing plans.

Marketing plan

The common thread that runs through every marketing plan meshes in determining 'who' is the target customer. How does the operator get that customer? How does the operator keep that customer? Put simply, the marketing plan tells the operator how to identify, create and keep customers. The plan starts with a brief review of the global market condition as it relates to the local market based upon a detailed description of local market conditions. From this, the operator can begin to match the product(s) with the market(s) that show the greatest potential. Once the markets are determined, sales plans are developed for each market taking into consideration distribution channels, pricing strategies, public relations activities, advertising and goals. Also, the plan takes into consideration past performance, past strategies and past successes.

As with the sales plan, it is important to keep the marketing plan simple and concise so that the hotel managers can understand the plan and thus build clarity of purpose. This then is the major distinction between the marketing plan and the sales plan. The marketing plan is for the entire hotel to follow. It is the guide by which all major decisions from capital expenditures to service developments are made.

QUESTIONS

1. What is the special role of NTOs in destination marketing?
2. What is a destination image and why is it difficult to change once established?
3. Why is the role of airlines so important in the tourism distribution system?
4. Name two special interest group segments and discuss their advantages and disadvantages.

FURTHER READING

Morrison, A.M. (1996) *Hospitality and Travel Marketing*. (2nd ed.). Delmar Publishers/International Thomson Publishing, Albany, NY.

This book, now in its second edition, provides a comprehensive approach and overview to marketing tourism and hospitality operations on all levels, ranging from individual operators to countries. Its advantage is the direct approach taken by the author in addressing the critical issues.

Gartrell, R.B. (1994) *Destination Marketing for Convention and Visitor Bureaux*. (2nd ed.). Kendall/Hunt Publishing, Dubuque.

This book, also in its second edition, is of special value for those interested in the more general destination level marketing perspective.

Marketing international tourism in Thailand

A country's tourism development and growth can be both positively and negatively affected by a number of factors. This has been certainly the case in Thailand, a country often referred to as a success story in tourism development and marketing. This case study examines the environmental constraints and factors which have affected the growth and development of tourism in Thailand.

The beginning of international tourism in Thailand can be traced back to as early as the seventeenth century. By this time European travellers began visiting the country and marvelled at its exquisite temples. As a result of the beautiful gold-tipped stupas of the temples and the vast amount of wealth amassed, Thailand became a hub for international travellers. These merchants came from England, Portugal, Holland and France. However, it was not until the Vietnam War era in the 1960s that tourism was developed on a large scale. In the late 1960s, the United States' armed forces participating in the Vietnam War began utilizing locations in Thailand as sites for rest and relaxation visits. Thailand in the 1970s and 1980s enjoyed a healthy development of tourism. Nonetheless, the country's tourism industry in the late 1980s and early 1990s faced new environmental challenges. Political instability, the spread of AIDS among the Thai population, and the over building of hotels adversely affected the country's tourism industry. In response, the Thai Prime Minister's Office, the national tourism organization, and the private sector made vigorous efforts to re-establish Thailand's image and promote the country as a tourism destination. The lesson that Thailand's tourism industry provides should assist other developing countries in establishing their tourism policy and tourism management strategies.

A favourable economic climate in the 1980s propelled the Thai economy into achieving one of the highest growth rates in the world with an average annual gross domestic product (GDP) of 10 per cent between 1986 and 1990 (Asia Year Book 1992). The contribution of tourism to the Thai economy cannot be underestimated. Tourism plays an ever increasing and crucial role in the growth and development of the country's economy as the country shifts from an agricultural base to a more industrialized and service based economy. Tourism is Thailand's largest source of foreign exchange earnings with receipts accounting for about 5 per cent of the country's GDP (Friedland 1992). A rapid growth of tourism in conjunction with a strong international demand has yielded high economic returns, stimulated the nation's economy, created jobs, encouraged investments and raised the standard of living.

Through strong marketing efforts by both the public and private sectors, the number of international visitors increased from 1.85 million in 1980 to over 6 million in the early 1990s, an average annual growth rate of 15 per cent. Likewise, tourism receipts jumped by over 70 per cent annually from $1.2 billion in 1985 to $4.3 billion in 1990 (Economic Intelligence Unit 1991a).

Thailand's tourism industry faced new challenges in the early 1990s. While the government pushed both tourism growth and export industry growth to improve the economy, it did so at the expense of the long-term benefits of the tourism industry. As the economy grew pollution and traffic worsened and these problems were not addressed. The AIDS problem and political unrest also added to the problem. At the same time as the government was promoting tourism, it was not addressing the issues that would eventually lead to the challenges which the tourism industry faces today.

Tourism development in Thailand

Tourism development and promotion in Thailand attracted the attention of the Thai government beginning in 1979 when tourism was included in the fourth National Economic and Social Development Plan (1972–81) (Tourism Authority of Thailand 1991). The plan was aimed at strengthening the Thai economy in the areas of international trade, investment and tourism to boost foreign exchange earnings and to create and expand employment opportunities. The success of the policy was evident when tourism became the fastest growing and most important sector of the Thai economy. Throughout the 1980s, international tourist arrivals to Thailand increased at an average of 10.5 per cent annually. Tourist arrivals expanded from under 2 million in 1980 to 3.4 million in 1987 before rising to 4.8 million in 1989, an average annual increase of 15 per cent (Tourism Authority of Thailand 1991). The number of arrivals peaked in 1990 to 5.3 million before declining by 3.75 per cent to 5.1 million in 1991.

Along with the increase in arrivals, tourism income increased more than three and a half times from US$1.2 billion in 1985 to US$4.3 billion in 1990 (Tourism Authority of Thailand 1991). The success of tourism promotion in Thailand from 1987 to 1988 rests largely on the high level of cooperation between the Thai public and the private sector. To celebrate the auspicious sixtieth birthday of King Rama IX, his status as the longest reigning monarch of the Chakri dynasty was commemorated by declaring the year 1987 as 'Visit Thailand Year'. As part of the celebrations, festivals, fairs, processions and cultural displays were organized throughout the country. A diversity of tourist experiences in national parks and historical sites was provided, while the scope of activities was expanded to promote the cultural heritage, history, folk arts and crafts and natural environment of Thailand. Special tour packages were also introduced, combining several Thai destinations such as Bangkok plus Chiang Mai, Pattaya or Phuket. International marketing efforts through a strong presence at trade shows in the main tourist markets of Europe, North America, Asia and Australia were equally instrumental in promoting Thai tourism. The marketing campaign continued with the promotion of the 'Thailand Arts and Crafts Year' in 1988–89. The marketing efforts were fruitful as evidenced by the increase of visitor arrivals during those years.

Asia and Pacific markets represented about 60 per cent of all arrivals in 1990 with 3.3 million tourists, an increase of 12 per cent over the previous year. The region's overall travel growth remained at the impressive levels of 10 to 15 per cent annually. Taiwan and South Korea recorded the largest growth rates largely due to the lifting of overseas travel restrictions in these two countries. Visitor arrivals from Australia, Hong Kong and Singapore continued to grow during the period. European visitors increased 11 per cent over 1989, and this increase coincides with a relative decline of European arrivals in Mediterranean destinations (Economic Intelligence Unit 1992).

Tourist expenditure patterns also exhibited a change as tourists spent more time and money on shopping. In 1986, international tourists spent almost 44 per cent of their budget on lodging/food and 27 per cent on shopping. By the 1990s, shopping expenditure accounted for 43 per cent while spending on accommodation and food decreased to 38 per cent as shown in Table 6.5. Inexpensive arts and crafts are some of the most popular shopping items for international visitors. Increased marketing efforts to Asian visitors, who typically stayed only half as long as European and North American visitors, resulted in an increase in the length of stay from 6 nights in 1987 to 7.6 nights in 1989 (Tourism Authority of Thailand 1991). In terms of purpose of visit, business travel surged ahead of leisure travel due to an increase of international trade and convention business in the country. In 1990, business travellers increased 27.8 per cent while leisure travellers showed an increase of only 8.5 per cent. Convention attendees account for approximately 70 per cent of business travellers from Asian/Pacific countries (Economic Intelligence Unit 1992).

The rapid growth and success of the Thai tourism industry can be attributed to a number of factors. The prosperity and high economic growth rate of Asian countries was a major factor in encouraging regional travel. Asian economic growth recorded the world's largest average annual expansion at 5.5 per cent. As a result, Asian tourists from newly industrialized countries (South Korea, Taiwan, Hong Kong and Singapore) travelled in greater numbers. At the same time, tourists from West Germany and Japan, Thailand's major markets for many years, recorded increases in arrivals as their countries continued to lead in world economic performance. A rising trend in long-haul travel in Europe and North America, spurred by larger and more fuel efficient jet aircraft which facilitate non-stop travel, increased Thailand's role as a popular commercial aviation hub. Thailand also occupies an advantageous geographical location because it is a convenient stop-over or transit point between Europe, Australia and the Far East. Accordingly, new air links were established with other airlines that created new markets in Canada, Finland, Spain and Switzerland.

In line with the expansion of the tourism sector, there was a corresponding boom in the accommodation industry. Average occupancy rates in Thailand increased from about 60 per cent in 1986 to 87 per cent in 1990. At the same time, average room rates more than tripled from about $30 in 1986 to $114 in 1990 but posed no threat to demand due to a shortage of rooms. Thus, the Thai government introduced policies that promoted hotel construction through special incentives in order to encourage investment in the accommodation industry.

New challenges

After four years of extensive tourism growth from 1987 to 1990, the Thai tourism industry started experiencing difficulties that led to lower arrivals and depressed market conditions in 1991 and 1992. The rapid expansion of tourism that brought forth mass tourism resulted in the deterioration and disorderliness of the tourism industry. The Persian Gulf War and world economic recession in the USA and Europe as well as political unrest, pollution, high prices, competition and an excess supply of hotel rooms disrupted tourism. Fairly expensive airfares and hotel room rates especially in Bangkok made European packages to Thailand more expensive than those to alternative destinations such as Singapore. In addition, the country's tourism industry failed to market itself aggressively after the successful campaigns which occurred from 1987 to 1990. Thailand's woes continued with the crash and pillaging of a Lauda Air 767 jet in late May 1991, which attracted widespread media and public attention in key markets. Together with an ongoing image problem over AIDS, the sex industry and environmental neglect at some destinations, Thailand's positive tourist image began to decline in the minds of visitors, primarily from the negative publicity. Consequently, tourists were avoiding Thailand in favour of Singapore, Malaysia and Indonesia (especially Bali). From 1989 to 1990, visitor arrivals in Indonesia increased from 1.6 million to 2.2 million, while the visitor arrivals in Malaysia increased from 3.9 million to 7.5 million (ASEANTA 1991).

Another major contributing factor for the slow to moderate growth of Thailand's tourism industry is the winding down of Thailand's economic and investment boom. The effects of the various constraints listed below led to a decline in tourist arrivals in 1991 by about 4 per cent to 5.1 million.

1. The Persian Gulf War dealt a severe blow to European and Middle East airlines by forcing the suspension of services to Thailand and re-routeing others. Potential visitors from major tourist generating countries cancelled their flight reservations in fear of terrorist activities associated with the war.

2. The spread of AIDS in Thailand, primarily among Thai citizens, coincided with the boom in international tourism toward the late 1980s. Thailand found itself facing a 'sexual paradise' image problem connected with AIDS and prostitution. The risk of contracting AIDS discouraged many tourists from visiting Thailand. Facing the downfall in tourist arrivals, the Thai tourism authorities minimized the existence and threat of the disease so that Thailand would not lose its attractiveness as a tourist destination. The tourism industry sensed no threat from AIDS and consequently did not take any restrictive or preventive measures to protect those at risk.

3. The effects of overbuilding was obvious in major Thai cities including Bangkok. Lower occupancies and average room rates are the result of the tourism slump and the industry's over-built state. The arrivals slump could hardly have come at a worse time.

4. The ravaging of Thailand's environment by rapid industrialization has contributed to problems of pollution in cities, resorts and beaches. The air

in Bangkok is highly polluted and European tour cancellations are attributed to the high level of pollution in Bangkok and at some resorts such as Pattaya.

5. International investors are seeking alternative countries in South East Asia for their investment, citing inability of successive Thai administrations to correct severe infrastructure defects, especially Bangkok's rapidly deteriorating traffic network. Additionally, tourists are spending more time in the northern city of Chiang Mai or in the resort islands of Phuket or Ko Samui in the south to avoid the traffic congestion in Bangkok.

6. Since the fall of the absolute monarchy in 1932, Thailand has experienced 10 successful coups, a number of failed ones, and 14 new constitutions. Another bloodless military coup in late February 1991 resulted in the overthrow of the government. Tourists from Japan, Taiwan and Hong Kong who were highly conscious of political instability chose other destinations over Thailand. Coupled with the Persian Gulf War, tourist arrivals from Asia fell by 20 per cent (Economic Intelligence Unit, 1991).

The pro-democracy uprising in late May 1992 resulted in a major blow to the Thai economy and tourism industry. As a result of the uprising, the National Economic and Social Development Board (NESDB) revised its pre-May projection of GDP growth from 7.9 per cent to 7.6 per cent for 1992 (Pura and Owens 1992). The most immediate effect, however, was on the tourism industry which was likely to incur a potential loss of millions of dollars in tourism revenues. Tourism revenue, which in 1991 brought in US$4.48 billion, was expected to fall to US$4.28 billion from a previously estimated US$5 billion. Tourist arrivals were forecast to be at 5.1 million visitors for 1992 (or no growth over 1991) and down about 4 per cent from 1990 (Carey 1992).

The severest blow has come from cancelled bookings by Japanese tour groups who constitute the lion's share of Thailand's tour market. Cancellations by the Japanese tourists, who comprised the second largest group of arrivals after Malaysia at 559 000 in 1991, ran as high as 40 per cent. Airlines were also affected; Singapore Airlines cancelled a number of flights while Thai Airways had to cancel more than 200 scheduled flights during the crisis. Thai Airways furthermore cut its profit forecast by 20 per cent for 1992 as a result of the crisis. A combination of the above listed factors gave a severe blow to Thailand's tourism industry. In 1992 and 1993, Bangkok's premier hotels reported occupancies of 20 to 30 per cent, down from normal occupancy rates of about 60 per cent.

Marketing strategies

The most important aspect of the tourism revival campaign is the cooperation between the private and public sector, a cooperative effort that has been absent since the highly successful 'Visit Thailand Year' in 1987. The Tourist Authority of Thailand (TAT), the main tourism agency responsible for marketing and promoting Thailand, has embarked on a tourism recovery programme to restore the tourism industry. TAT's first objective, aimed at the high spending Japanese tourists, is to assure them that Thailand is safe to visit. Advertising and promotion in major tourist markets is also aimed at restoring confidence among tourists that Thailand is now a safe and stable country. The second objective addresses the problems of pollution, cheating, touting and tourist hijacks that were becoming rampant and gaining notoriety.

Familiarization trips to Thailand for the foreign press and travel agents were conducted by Thai tourism representatives to encourage travel to Thailand. The TAT has also increased its presence in Japan, South Korea and Taiwan by opening three new sales offices in 1992. Airlines, travel agents and hoteliers have restructured low cost holiday packages to entice visitors. To avoid sparking rate wars, hotels are emphasizing value by offering free upgrades and complimentary extra room nights.

A major public relations and promotional campaign called 'The World Our Guest' was developed in August 1992 to coincide with the sixtieth birthday of Queen Sirikit. An estimated 11 000 visitors to Thailand were given free hotel rooms, airline tickets, meals and tours as part of the promotion, which was declared an unqualified success by the TAT. The campaign was intended to kick-start Thailand's declining tourism industry.

Due to the AIDS crisis, the government has attempted to change the tourist image by stressing the cultural and natural attractions and bargain shopping in Thailand rather than sexual attractions. At the same time, the TAT increased its cooperation with the national tourism authorities of the Association of South East Asian Nations (ASEAN) to promote multi-destination travel. The inauguration of 'Visit ASEAN Year 1992' is an example of cooperative marketing by the tourism agencies of the six member ASEAN countries which comprise Thailand, Malaysia, Indonesia, Brunei, the Philippines and Singapore. Furthermore, the year 1992 was designated as 'Women's Visit Thailand Year' in order to encourage more women to visit Thailand, a country where the ratio of male tourists is higher. These marketing campaigns were reportedly most successful in enhancing the country's image and maintaining the growth of new markets.

With relatively inexpensive accommodation, first class Thai hospitality, an increase in international flights, a growing economy and infrastructure improvements, the country will be able to maintain tourism growth through the 1990s. One asset that Thailand can be proud of is that Thailand and hospitality service appear to be a perfect match, one in which every employee wants a guest to be happy. Thailand's past experience shows that tourism demands self-discipline, planning and marketing to be successful. Whether or not it will fulfill its promises as Asia's biggest holiday destination will also depend upon the depth of commitment from the tourism industry and the lessons learned about the results of inadequate planning.

8 The future of tourism in developing countries

As the third millennium is approaching, the future of tourism in developing countries looks promising (Richter 1992). The developing countries' share in international tourism is slowly increasing. More and more people in the developed world, but also in the more affluent developing countries, are packing their luggage and travelling farther and farther. The younger generations gain a completely different travel experience in their childhood and early adulthood, setting them on a unique stage in their travel career or travel life cycle. Research has shown that they are likely to travel to more distant destinations in later stages of their life cycle as well (Oppermann 1995a, 1995f). Furthermore, tourism has rapidly emerged as a social status symbol with a high resistance to monetary self-discipline in recession years. In particular long-haul travel appears little affected by recession. Thus, tourism demand in the 1990s and presumably well into the next millennium is much more stable than many commentators over the last few decades have thought it to be. This does not mean that destinations can relax and watch the tourists flock to their beaches, temples, mountains, cities and forests. The rapid expansion of tourism destinations around the world with more and more countries opting for tourism developments denotes an increasing competition for the tourists. And many countries have yet to enter the competition in a serious way. India, most African countries and the newly formed republics in the territory of the former USSR are but a few examples of countries with great tourism potential, but which have not been able or willing to tap into the tourism market yet. Hence, while tourism demand for developing countries will most certainly be expanding, the competitors and new entrants to the tourism industry are waiting to take a share of the pie. Some countries are likely to benefit from their engagement in tourism over the last few decades and their consistent work on their tourism image. Others have to overcome their non-image or even a negative image in the markets before they will be able to gain a larger share of the market. Whatever the situation, developing countries have to be aware of some of the basic underlying currents of changing travel behaviour and its influencing factors. Another important concept to realize is that tourist does not equal tourist. The issue of quantity versus quality has taken on a new meaning in the tourism demand discussion in the 1990s as a result of the recognition of tourists' impacts and the social and physical carrying capacity levels of host countries (e.g. AIEST 1991). This chapter addresses all these issues by examining some factors influencial in changing travel behaviour, the effect of health and safety issues on tourism in developing countries, and, after a general deliberation on the quality versus quantity debate, by examining two different forms of tourism that, depending on the context, may be considered quality tourism – convention tourism and backpackers.

CHANGING TRAVEL BEHAVIOUR

Probably the most important impact on tourism demand in the Pacific basin region and its developing countries is the rapid emergence of the Asian Tigers as large outbound generating markets. Between 1990 and 1993, the number of outbound travellers from these four countries (Hong Kong, Singapore, South Korea and Taiwan) grew by 50 per cent. In the same time period, international arrivals in the whole world increased by just 9 per cent. And in 1993, the Asian Tigers already generated as many tourists as the outbound-wonder Japan (Oppermann 1996b). Thus, countries in that region have seen and will experience a further shift in their visitor composition with certain spatial, sectoral and service implications (see Chapter 5). The growing affluence and still rapid expansion of the economies in Malaysia, Thailand and Indonesia signifies yet another wave of outbound tourism growth in the region. And China is already dubbed as the country with the greatest outbound generation potential (e.g. Wang and Sheldon 1995). In some countries, Chinese outbound tourism has certainly already had a major impact. In Malaysia, for example, arrivals from mainland China approached the 100 000 mark in 1994, exceeding other secondary markets such as the United States, South Korea and Germany (MTPB 1995). Within a few years, China climbed from virtually nothing (less than 7000 arrivals in 1990) to became the tenth most important source country.

However, because the great outbound growth among the Asian markets is currently only felt in the Pacific basin area, other developing countries should still be aware of these source markets and, depending on their location, may be wise to actively promote their country in these markets and/or establish direct flight links. As the Japanese outbound tourist wave conquered and left behind many countries in the area on the search for newer and more remote places (Oppermann 1996b), a similar occurrence can be expected for the other Asian markets as well.

Socio-economic factors

Among the socio-economic factors that are prone to sway demand for specific vacation products and destinations, one needs to distinguish those in the traditional markets (i.e. North America and Europe) and the newly emerging markets (i.e. North Asia, South East Asia and other economically advanced developing countries). While net incomes and disposable incomes are unlikely to expand significantly in the former, profound increases are expected among the latter. Economic growth in North and South East Asia is generally expected to remain high, far above world averages. The growing prosperity in this region, and especially an expanding middle class with sufficient disposable income for pleasure travel, will induce a growing demand not only for domestic but also international tourism. Furthermore, there appears to be a prevailing tendency towards increasing paid holiday leave which will amplify the disposable income effect. Hence, western Pacific Rim countries can expect an even higher share of intraregional travel over the next few years. Similarly, if economic growth stabilizes in South American countries, the neighbouring countries will benefit from it.

Trends in North America and Europe will be more influenced by other factors as paid holiday and disposable income are not expected to increase significantly. Existing trends towards dual income families will reinforce the popularity of short breaks, which has been growing strongly for several years (King 1994), because of difficulties in synchronizing holiday leaves for two. Obviously, not many developing countries will be able to benefit from short breaks from these two important source regions as they are too far away to make the trip worthwhile. However, countries in the Caribbean and North Africa may be well suited for such short breaks and may be well advised to position themselves accordingly.

Another trend in these markets is towards having fewer and fewer children and having children at later stages in the life cycle. As a result, potential pleasure travellers are more flexible in their vacation times and can afford to take their trips in the off-season rather than during the main holiday breaks. Thus, demand may become somewhat more balanced and less concentrated in a few weeks or months which will contribute towards a lower seasonality, better occupancy throughout the year and therefore improved profitability. In addition, young couples or singles with no children tend to have some of the highest disposable incomes and are more apt to take vacations overseas owing to their more adventurous nature (Oppermann 1995e). Developing countries should be able to capitalize on this trend.

Some developing countries should also be aware of another trend, namely the impact of outbound travel by their own citizens on the travel account and thus balance of payments. Especially in countries with rising disposable incomes, locals may be inclined to travel to foreign countries. Table 8.1 compares outbound with inbound tourist figures for several developing countries. It shows that several developing countries have a negative tourist balance, most notably Taiwan. Even Egypt, which is one of the major tourist destinations in the Mediterranean region, features a negative saldo – more Egyptians are travelling overseas than foreign tourists coming to Egypt.

This list of factors influencing travel behaviours and demand patterns is not meant to be exhaustive. It is rather intended to provide some glimpses of a range of variables to be pondered when considering the future of tourism and tourism demand. It is also meant to indicate areas that require more research as many of these facets are not fully understood or have just emerged as issues in tourism.

HEALTH AND SAFETY

Perceived safety and political stability are among the major variables that influence international travel patterns.

Table 8.1 Outbound versus inbound travel (in thousands), 1993

Country	Inbound tourists	Outbound tourists	Net balance
Bolivia	269	264	5
Brazil (1991)	1 192	1 309	−117
Botswana	607	327	280
Chile	1 412	842	570
China (1992)	4 006	2 930	1 076
Colombia	1 047	877	170
Ecuador (1992)	403	216	187
Egypt	2 291	2 676	−385
Mexico	16 440	10 185	6 255
Morocco	4 027	1 375	2 652
Papua New Guinea	40	52	−12
Peru	273	443	−170
Philippines (1992)	1 043	1 231	−188
Syria	703	1 521	−818
Taiwan	1 850	4 654	−2 804
Vanuatu	45	9	36
Venezuela	396	457	−61

Source: WTO 1995b

Sun, sand, sea and sex ... are often seen as the core of a developing nation's appeal ... A fifth 's' is even more critical: security. Tourism as a discretionary activity is incredibly vulnerable to political instability.

(Richter 1992, p. 36)

Richter also argues that another factor affecting perceptions is how the violence in question is labelled. Politically inspired violence, urban guerrillas, terrorism or civil strife strike irrational fears among potential tourists, deflecting travel decisions away from controversial destinations. Safety checklists for overseas travellers (Japan) or lists of countries considered unsafe (United States) are but two examples of how governments in the source countries attempt to provide their citizens with information on safety aspects in destination countries. Richter (1992) identifies several areas where political instability and safety issues can seriously affect tourism development: regional conflicts, areas of turmoil, tourists as political pawns and tourism as a rationale for political unrest.

Regional conflicts often have an impact on the tourism industry beyond the immediate conflict area, particularly in cases where countries depend on other countries for passage of tourists. The Iraq–Iran war terminated the popular land route from Europe to Pakistan and India. And any civil unrest in India has immediate effects on the number of tourist arrivals in Nepal. The Gulf War affected many countries around the world and not only in the immediate region. In Africa and many Central and South American countries, tourism development is seriously hampered by the recurrence of political instability in the form of military coups, civil war and national liberation wars (Oppermann 1997; Richter 1992). For distant markets such events may be associated with the whole region and not only the country in question, especially when there is a repetition of such incidents in a number of countries in the region. Richter (1992) also suggests, however, that nations sometimes benefit from instability in neighbouring countries as tourists may change their travel plans in their favour. An excellent example is the recent case of the former Yugoslavia. Tourist flows were diverted to other countries with a similar attraction base (Oppermann and Chon 1995a).

In Fiji, the two coups in 1987 not only reduced tourist arrivals to Fiji itself but also to several neighbouring countries since many flights were routed through Fiji. While tourists were never really in danger, the long-term future of the tourism industry was. Several international airlines not only temporarily re-routed their flights but dropped Fiji as a stopover between North America and Australia/New Zealand altogether.

More threatening to the tourists themselves are instances where the tourists become political pawns in fights between the government and opposition groups. Tourists have been kidnapped by opposition groups in countries such as China, India, Pakistan, the Philippines and Turkey in order to compromise the government and to destroy a major income generator. In more radical cases, tourists are purposely attacked and killed as examples from Algeria, Egypt, Kenya, Peru and the Virgin Islands illustrate (Butler and Mao 1995; Ryan 1993). The Shining Path in Peru, for example, has not only crippled tourism to the famous ruins of Macchu Picchu (Richter 1992), but affected the nation as a whole (Oppermann 1997).

Health concerns are and have always been among the deterrents to travel in general and to some destinations in particular. Many developing countries are not free from infectious diseases like cholera, hepatitis, yellow fever, typhus and malaria (Figure 8.1). The simple fact that one or the other disease may be prevalent in a specific destination country can prove to be an effective obstacle. In some major tourism source countries, specific medical centres have been established which advise on the existence of diseases around the world and provide immunization and health risk guidelines for all countries around the world (e.g. CfR 1993).

The advent of AIDS has placed a major scare on the tourism industry in countries where a considerable share of demand is for sex tourism. Tourists infect locals and vice versa, leaving AIDS as a lasting souvenir for both. To what extent AIDS has reduced the demand for sex tourism is unclear. Countries often closely associated with sex tourism such as Thailand, the Philippines, the Dominican Republic and Kenya have not experienced a dramatic downturn in visitors. In contrast, if not for other reasons such as natural disasters or political unrest, they have been able to show consistent increases in tourist arrivals. Only a tendency for demanding younger and younger prostitutes who, presumably, have not had many sexual encounters, has been observed (Thiemann 1989). Other observers suggest that 'tourists have modified their conduct in the sphere of sex ... They seem to engage less intensely in promiscuous activities and protect themselves more carefully' (Cohen 1988, p. 480). Cohen also mentions that the sex industry has experienced a decline, affecting the composition of tourist flows to, in that instance, Thailand: family tourism is on the rise with a simultaneous decline in single-male tourism.

Health and physical recuperation are also becoming more important travel

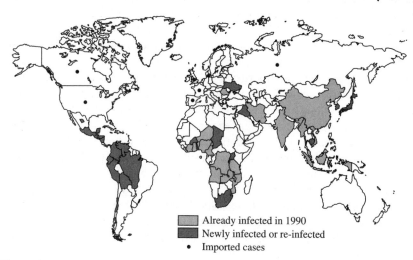

Figure 8.1 Distribution of cholera in 1991.
Source: after CFR 1993.

motivators (King 1994) and some developing countries with the appropriate resources are well poised to take advantage of this. Cuba, for example, is emphasizing its health tourism industry and others are sure to follow.

QUALITY VERSUS QUANTITY

Many developing countries have realized that not all tourists are the same. Depending on their origin, travel purpose, length of stay, activities, etc. they spend dissimilar amounts during their stay. Japanese and other North Asian tourists are often thought to be particularly great spenders, especially with respect to souvenirs. Some countries have purposely developed their tourist attraction base to include shopping. At least in many South East Asian countries, shopping is a major tourist activity that helps to form the architectural landscape and control tourism activity in cities (Oppermann, Din, and Amri 1996).

In some countries the discovery that not all tourists are the same went hand in hand with a recognition of their limited resource base. In some island countries such as the Seychelles, there is a ceiling to the number of tourists simply because of physical space limitations. As a result, many developing countries, and also developed countries, state that they want quality tourists: those who are sensitive towards the host country and its culture, society and environment and, most importantly, who spend the most money. After all, if one tourist spends as much as two others combined, the absolute impact and resource use of the former is likely to be smaller and, therefore, the cost–benefit ratio more favourable. Or is it? It really depends on several factors, such as the time reference unit of expenditure (i.e. per day, per trip), what the money is spent on and the cost and leakages involved in producing it, the regional and sectoral distribution of expenditures, and what the government's objectives are.

Before a country decides what type of tourism constitutes quality tourism it should clearly define the objectives of tourism and tourism development. Without such a framework, there can be no quality tourism as any measure to distinguish quality tourists from other tourists becomes arbitrary. Yet what most countries seem to associate quality tourism with is the expenditure of the tourists, usually on a per day expenditure basis. To some extent this is congruent with the most often mentioned objectives of tourism development, namely increase in foreign exchange earnings, improving the balance of payments and increasing income earned through tourism. However, per day expenditures of tourists may be the wrong measure as high daily expenditures routinely go hand in hand with short lengths of stay. In many instances this results in the fact that those with the highest per day expenditure are not those with the highest per capita or per trip expenditure. Hence, focusing on the former tourist type may actually reduce the income earned from tourism.

A preoccupation with tourists' expenditures as a measure of quality tourism also obscures other issues, such as where do tourists spend, how much do they spend on what and who is benefiting from it? As several commentators have noted, tourism does not benefit everybody in the host community equally and some forms of tourism may be more regionally, sectorially and ethnically biased than others (e.g. Din 1990; Oppermann 1994a, 1994d). Expenditures by tourists with a short length of stay are more likely to be concentrated in the primary tourist destinations and international gateways (e.g. Oppermann 1994a). Travel purpose, travel organization and country of residence have been proven to be major influencing variables in the spatial distribution as well (e.g. Oppermann 1992a, 1992e; Pearce and Johnston 1986). If regional development is a primary objective, then quality tourists may need to be defined as those who actually travel to those peripheral regions in question. These may turn out to be visitors with a very low daily expenditure but a very long length of stay, or those with a specific travel motivation (i.e. want to stay on a farm) or purpose (i.e. visiting friends/ relatives).

Some forms of tourism may be better adapted to the country using services and goods that are mostly produced locally and do not need to be imported. Accordingly, the leakage rate is much lower, the multiplier effect higher and the net effect may be the same as that of other tourism types where higher initial expenditures are incurred which are consequently subject to high leakages.

Hence a guideline to the governments' objectives for tourism is imperative in the establishment of criteria for quality tourism. The issue of quality versus quantity in tourism should not and cannot just be reduced to who spends the most money per day. Two widely different examples of what may constitute quality tourism are provided on the next few pages. These are just examples of what could be quality tourism in a specific country or destination context and not universally applicable. Again, it depends on the country itself, its tourism resources, infrastructure, international access, image, and possibly most importantly, what the government wants to derive from international tourism.

Convention tourism

Several hundred million people travel each year to attend a conference, convention and/or congress. Undoubtedly the largest market for this type of travel is in North America where some some 85 million trips are undertaken for meetings and conventions (Oppermann 1994e). But conference tourism in and to developing countries is also on the increase. Seemingly the most successful country in this respect is Singapore. It has ranked among the top 10 conference destinations for the last few years (Table 8.2). Other developing countries that have a relatively successful convention industry are the Philippines, Thailand and South Korea. The Philippines were also among the first developing countries to built a conference centre in order to capitalize on this newly emerging tourism sector (Oppermann 1994/95).

The major advantages commonly associated with convention tourism are the high per day expenditure of conference attendees and the seasonality of demand. Conferences are often held in the off or shoulder season and, therefore, contribute to a better occupancy in otherwise slack times. Besides having a high per day expenditure, many conference participants also combine their conference business with pleasure travel. They may not only take in the sights during the conference, but add a few nights before or after the conference for leisure purposes.

An obvious sign that convention tourism is not strictly business tourism and has wider impacts beyond the number of participants and length of the conference is the number of spouses accompanying the conference attendees. Approximately one-third of association attendees in North America are accompanied by spouses (Association Management 1993). And the Association of

Table 8.2 International conference destinations

1954	1968	1982	1988	1990	1992
Paris	Paris	Paris	Paris	Paris	Paris
Geneva	Geneva	London	London	London	London
London	London	Geneva	Madrid	Brussels	Brussels
Rome	Brussels	Brussels	Brussels	Vienna	Vienna
Brussels	Strasbourg	Vienna	Geneva	Geneva	Madrid
New York	Vienna	New York	W. Berlin	Berlin	Geneva
Vienna	Rome	Copenhagen	Rome	Madrid	Amsterdam
Amsterdam	New York	Rome	Sydney	Singapore	Singapore
Copenhagen	Mexico City	Tokyo	Singapore	Amsterdam	Washington
The Hague	W. Berlin	Strasbourg	Washington	Washington	Barcelona
Munich	Tokyo	W. Berlin	Vienna	Strasbourg	Copenhagen
Zürich	Prague	Hong Kong	New York	Rome	Strasbourg
Stockholm	Washington	Washington	Strasbourg	New York	Hong Kong
Liège	Madrid	Dublin	Amsterdam	Copenhagen	Budapest
Washington	Copenhagen	Singapore	Seoul	The Hague	Prague

Source: Oppermann 1996d

International Scientific Tourism Experts, with meetings held around the globe, registers a similar spouse turnout. Another sign is that many conference programmes provide for spouse activities and agenda. Hence, an attractive destination can draw additional benefits from conferences beyond the attendees.

Oppermann and Chon's (1997) models of convention location choice and the participation decision making process illustrate the actors and factors involved in the association meetings market. Clark and McCleary (1995) elaborated on the buying decision process in the corporate market although they failed to address the consequential issues of destination perceptions and perception building processes. In a rare case of analyzing meeting destination images in developing countries, Bonn, Brand and Ohlin (1994) analysed the perceptions of corporate and association planners with regard to ten Caribbean islands. Distinct differences emerged between the destinations in respect to the utilized attributes included, which arguably have vital impacts on the destination selection process.

Convention tourism is a valuable tourism sector and some developing countries are placing great hopes on it. Important pre-requisites for a successful development to a convention destination include several factors, such as easy and relatively inexpensive access from the relevant source markets, adequate conference, accommodation and restaurant facilities and an image of a safe and exciting destination to name a few (Association Management 1993; Oppermann 1996c, 1996d; Oppermann and Chon 1995b).

Backpackers

A rarely examined tourist type are backpackers (e.g. Ross 1997). Sometimes called drifters (Cohen 1973; V. Smith 1990) or budget travellers (Ross 1993), backpackers are often disliked because of their low per day expenditure, and sometimes even met with open hostility (e.g. Cohen 1973; Hoivik and Heiberg 1980; Wood 1979, 1980). However, they really deserve a closer look by most developing countries.

First of all, their low per day expenditures are often compensated by a much longer stay (Wood 1979) bringing their per trip expenditure often close to or even higher than that of other tourists. In the cases of backpackers in Australia and New Zealand, for example, backpackers spend a significantly higher amount within these countries than any other market segment.

Second, their expenditures tend to go to smaller restaurants, small hotels or other accommodation forms, and local transportation companies (Hoivik and Heiberg 1980). All these enterprises are characterized by their higher integration into the local economy with significantly lower leakages (Wood 1979) and, therefore, a higher multiplier effect. Thus, each dollar spent by backpackers is more beneficial to the developing countries than those by ordinary mass tourists.

Third, the regional impact of backpackers is much wider due to their more active intranational travel patterns and longer length of stay. Hence, peripheral and non-traditional tourist areas primarily benefit from this tourist type whereas most expenditures by mass tourists are incurred in the major gateways and resorts.

Fourth, backpackers are commonly considered the explorers or pioneers of tourism development (Butler 1980; Cohen 1973; Oppermann 1993; Plog 1991). Except for instant resorts, it is these unusual tourists who discover locations for tourism and set the path for the later arrival of mass tourism through relating their experiences at home to virtually hundreds of friends and relatives. Hence, to ignore these trendsetters of tourism development is imprudent.

Fifth, because of their generally lower comfort standards, investments into this sector are profoundly lower than in four or five star hotels. They prefer smaller and less expensive accommodations not unlike many domestic tourists (e.g. Wood 1980). From a resource point of view, developing countries can engage in backpacker tourism without having to resort to the foreign financial investments and management capabilities. One may consider it as a bottom-up strategy of tourism development versus the top-down approach of modern mass and five star tourism. The people involved in small-scale tourism can gain valuable working experience and enhance their entrepreneurial skills (Wood 1979). The latter, especially, seems a priceless advantage.

FINAL REFLECTIONS

This book provides an overview of the main issues of tourism in developing countries. The limited space necessitated a cursory approach with few opportunities to discuss specific issues in detail. The systematic approach adopted, however, facilitates a discussion of issues of general concern to developing countries and does not restrict the lessons learned to individual case studies.

Tourism in developing countries and particularly international tourist flows from the developed to the developing world remains a highly controversial topic in the popular and academic press. As with perceptions of destinations, the perception of the advantages and disadvantages appears to be highly individualistic in nature. Discussions of tourism effects are too often hampered by the lack of holistic approaches that encompass more than just economic or cultural impacts. Even within each of these, serious research is routinely hampered by a lack of data, both in-depth as well as longitudinal. Analyses of tourism's economic contribution remain only rough estimates until a serious effort is made at tracking tourist expenditures and the direct, indirect and induced effects of tourism as it ripples through the economy, with a close examination of leakages and important contents for every product. Similarly, any study of the cultural impacts of tourism will need to consider not only tourism as an agent of change but also other influencing variables such as television, music, movies and the changing workplace.

One recurrent issue in writing this book was that most authors seem to work in their own world and, apart from referencing the major works in the same field, neither attempt to systematically replicate previous studies in the same or other environments nor exalt tourism science by model and theory building. These shortcomings urgently need to be addressed if researchers want to make a greater impact and if one country or destination is to learn from others without needing to replicate all the trials and errors. In this context, developing countries are encouraged to systematically collect data on all aspects of tourism and not only on the number of tourist arrivals and their expenditure. Data deficiencies in international inbound and outbound tourism as well as on domestic travel are among the primary obstacles to systematic tourism research and our deeper understanding of tourism.

Finally, the World Tourism Organization forecasts that by the year 2010 international tourist arrivals will have increased to 937 million, 65 per cent or 370 million more than in 1995. While much of this growth volume will again be in Europe and North America, developing countries are prognosticated to gain a larger share of the pie. Especially countries in the Asia-Pacific region and in Central and South America appear poised to benefit from this growth. And Europe's share in world tourist arrivals is expected to drop to just above 50 per cent from 60 per cent in 1995. While this continuing boom in world tourism may convince yet more developing countries to embark on tourism development, other countries and regions are well advised to plan for the continued tourism onslaught as pressure on land resources, physical and socio-cultural effects are prone to increase at at least the same rate. The issue of quality tourism will gain more and more importance and only a well planned and managed tourism development can prevent or minimize negative side-effects of the continuing tourism boom.

QUESTIONS

1. Discuss the major trends in the world's major tourism source markets and their likely impact on tourism arrivals trends in the near future.
2. Reflect on the importance of safety in the tourism industry.
3. Consider the major advantages and disadvantages of convention tourism to a tourism destination.
4. What is quality tourism and what are quality tourists?
5. Deliberate on the advantages of backpacker tourism vis-à-vis mass tourism.

FURTHER READINGS

Theobald, W. (ed.) (1994) *Global Tourism: the Next Decade*. Butterworth-Heinemann, Oxford.

   This is an excellent collection of papers that discuss a wide range of future tourism developments ranging from management to education, and from behavioural to planning issues.

Bibliography

Aderhold, P. (1992) Trends in German Outbound Tourism. *World Travel and Tourism Review*, **2**, 113–21.

Adu-Febiri, F. (1994) Developing a Viable Tourist Industry in Ghana: Problems, Prospects and Propositions. *Tourism Recreation Research*, **19**(1), 5–11.

Agarwal, S. (1994) The Resort Cycle Revisited: Implications for Resorts. *Progress in Tourism, Recreation and Hospitality Management*, **5**, 194–208.

Agel, P. (1993) Dritte-Welt-Tourismus. In G. Haedrich, C. Kaspar, K. Klemm, and K. Kreilkamp (eds), *Tourismus-Management, Tourismus-Marketing und Fremdenverkehrsplanung*. Walter de Gruyter, Berlin/New York, pp. 715–28.

Agisra (1990) *Frauenhandel und Prostitutionstourismus*. Trickster, München.

Ahmed, Z.U. (1991) Indian Tourism: A Victim of Mismanagement. *Cornell HRA Quarterly*, 32(3), 75–81.

Alleyne, F. (1974) The Expansion of Tourism and its Concomitant Unrealised Potential for Agricultural Development in the Barbadian Economy. *Proceedings 9th West Indies Agricultural Economic Conference*, pp. 143–52.

Anschütz, H. (1965) Wachsender Tourismus im Iran. *Zeitschrift für Wirtschaftsgeographie*, **9**, 211–13.

Archer, B.H. (1982) The Value of Multipliers and their Policy Implications. *Tourism Management*, **3**, 236–41.

Archer, B.H. (1985) Tourism in Mauritius: An Economic Impact Study with Marketing Implications. *Tourism Management*, **6**(1), 50–4.

Archer, B. and Fletcher, J. (1995) The Economic Impact of Tourism in the Seychelles. *Annals of Tourism Research*, **23**, 32–47.

Arndt, H. (1978/79) Definitionen des Begriffes Fremdenverkehr im Wandel der Zeit. *Jahrbuch für Fremdenverkehr*, **26/27**, 160–74.

Arnold, A. (1972) Der Fremdenverkehr in Tunesien. Entwicklung, Struktur, Funktion und Fremdenverkehrsräume. *Würzburger Geographische Arbeiten*, **37**, 453–89.

ASEAN Tourism Association (1991) *ASEANTA Annual Report '91*. ASEANTA, Singapore.

Ashworth, G. (1989) Urban Tourism: An Imbalance in Attention. *Progress in Tourism, Recreation and Hospitality Management*, **1**, 33–54.

Asia Year Book (1992). Review Publishing Co., Hong Kong.

Association Internationale d'Experts Scientifiques du Tourisme [AIEST]

(1991). *Quality Tourism – Concepts of a Sustainable Tourism Development, Harmonizing Economical, Social and Ecological Interests*. AIEST, St Gallen.

Association Management (1993) The Impact of Association Meetings. *Association Management*, **45**(7), 85–8.

Aziz, H. (1995) Understanding Attacks on Tourists in Egypt. *Tourism Management*, **16**, 91–6.

Bailey, M. (1995) Hong Kong. International Tourism Reports, No. 4, 4–21.

Barrett, J.A. (1958) The Seaside Resort Towns of England and Wales. Unpublished PhD thesis, University of London.

Bastin, R. (1984) Small Island Tourism: Development or Dependency? *Development Policy Review*, **2**, 79–90.

Becheri, E. (1991) Rimini and Co. – The End of a Legend? Dealing with the Algarve Effect. *Tourism Management*, **12**, 229–35.

Benzing, B. (1973) Tourismus für oder gegen Kamerun? *Afrika Heute*, **11**(3), 29–32.

Berger, M.T. (1994) The End of the 'Third World'? *Third World Quarterly*, **15**, 257–75.

Bernklau, T. (1991) *Tourismus auf den Philippinen. Eine kulturgeographische Untersuchung unter besonderer Berücksichtigung des Binnentourismus*. Peter Lang, Frankfurt/M.

Berriane, M. (1978) Un type l'espace touristique marocain: le littoral méditerranéen. *Revue de Géographie du Maroc*, **29**(2), 5–28.

Berriane, M. (1990) Fremdenverkehr im Mahgreb: Tunesien und Marokko im Vergleich. *Geographische Rundschau*, **42**, 94–9.

Bianchi, R. (1994) Tourism Development and Resort Dynamics: An Alternative Approach. *Progress in Tourism, Recreation and Hospitality Management*, **5**, 181–93.

Bleasdale, S. and Tapsell, S. (1994) Contemporary Efforts to Expand the Tourist Industry in Cuba: The Perspective from Britain. In: A.V. Seaton (ed.), *Tourism: The State of the Art*. John Wiley & Sons, Chichester, pp. 100–9.

Blume, H. (1963) Westindien als Fremdenverkehrsgebiet. *Die Erde*, **94**, 48–72.

Boeckh, A. (1993) Entwicklungstheorien: Eine Rückschau. In: D. Nohlen and F. Nuscheler (eds), *Handbuch der Dritten Welt*. Verlag J.H.W. Dietz, Bonn, pp. 110–30.

Bojanic, D.C. (1992) A Look at a Modernized Family Life Cycle and Overseas Travel. *Journal of Travel and Tourism Marketing*, **1**(1), 61–79.

Bonn, M.A., Brand, R.R. and Ohlin, J.B. (1994) Site Selection for Professional Meetings: A Comparison of Heavy-Half vs. Light-Half Associations and Corporation Meeting Planners. *Journal of Travel & Tourism Marketing*, **3**(2), 59–84.

Boyd, A. (1993) Vietnam – Tied Up in a Tangle of Land Titles. *Asian Hotelier*, August, p. 6.

Branagan, J. (1992) Growing up painfully. *Time*, June 1, p. 70.

Britton, S. (1980) The Evolution of the Colonial Space Economy: The Case of Fiji. *Journal of Historical Geography*, **6**, 151–74.

Britton, S. (1982) The Political Economy of Tourism in the Third World. *Annals of Tourism Research*, **9**, 331–58.

Britton, S. (1991) Tourism, Capital, and Place: Towards a Critical Geography of Tourism. *Environment and Planning*, **D9**, 451–78.

Bryden, J.M. (1973) *Tourism and Development: A Case Study of the Commonwealth Caribbean*. Cambridge University Press, Cambridge.

Bryden, J.M. and Faber, M.L. (1971) Multiplying the Tourist Multiplier. *Social and Economic Studies*, **20**, 61–82.

Burkart, A.J. and Medlik, S. (1974) *Tourism: Past, Present and Future*. Heinemann, London.

Butler, R.W. (1980) The Concept of a Tourism Area Cycle of Evolution. Implications for the Management of Resources. *Canadian Geographer*, **24**, 5–12.

Butler, R.W. (1990) Alternative Tourism: Pious Hope or Trojan Horse. *Journal of Travel Research*, **28**(3), 40–5.

Butler, R.W. (1993a) Tourism Development in Small Islands: Past Influences and Future Directions. In: D.G. Lockhardt, D. Drakakis-Smith and J. Schembri (eds), *The Development Process in Small Island States*. Routledge, London, pp. 71–91.

Butler, R.W. (1993b) Tourism – An Evolutionary Perspective. In: J.G. Nelson, R.W. Butler and G. Wall (eds), *Tourism and Sustainable Development: Monitoring, Planning, Managing*. Dep. of Geography, University of Waterloo, pp. 27–43.

Butler, R.W. and Mao, B. (1995) Tourism Between Quasi-States: International, Domestic or What? In: R.W. Butler and D.G. Pearce (eds), *Change in Tourism: People, Places, Processes*. Routledge, London, pp. 92–113.

Carey, S. (1992) Recent Slump Could Bring Needed Dose of Reality to Thailand's Tourist Industry. *Asian Wall Street Journal*, July 13, p. 2.

Cater, E.A. (1987) Tourism in the Least Developed Countries. *Annals of Tourism Research*, **14**, 202–26.

Centrum für Reisemedizin [CfR] (1993) *Reisemedizinischer Informationsservice – Reisesaison 1993*. CFR, Düsseldorf.

Cha, S. and Uysal, M. (1994) Regional Analysis of Tourism Resources: A Case Study of Korea. *Journal of Hospitality & Leisure Marketing*, **2**(3), 61–74.

Chon, K.S. (1989) Understanding Recreational Traveller's Motivation Attitude and Satisfaction. *Tourist Review*, **44**(1), pp. 3–7.

Chon, K.S. (1990) The Role of Destination Image in Tourism: A Review and Discussion. *Tourist Review*, **45**(2), 2–9.

Chon, K.S. and Olsen, M.D. (1990) Applying Strategic Management Process in Tourism Organizations. *Tourism Management*, **11**(3), pp. 206–13.

Chon, K.S. and Olsen, M.D. (1991) Functional Congruity and Self Congruity Approaches to Consumer Satisfaction/Dissatisfaction in Tourism. *Journal of the International Academy of Hospitality Research*, **3**, pp. 2–18.

Chon, K.S. (1991) Tourism Destination Image Modification Process. *Tourism Management*, **12**, 68–72.

Chon, K.S. (1992a) Self-Image/Destination Image Congruity. *Annals of Tourism Research*, **19**, 360–3.

Chon, K.S. (1992b) The Role of Destination Image in Tourism: An Extension. *Tourist Review*, **43**(1), pp. 2–8.

Chon, K.S. and Sparrowe, R. (1995) *Welcome to Hospitality: An Introduction*, Southwestern Publishing Company. Cincinnati, Ohio.

Chon, K.S. and Singh, A. (1995) Marketing Resorts to 2000: Review of Trends in the USA. *Tourism Management*, **16**(6), pp. 463–9.

Chon, K.S. and Oppermann, M. (1996) Tourism Development and Planning in the Philippines. *Tourism Recreation Research*, **21**(1), 35–43.

Christaller, W. (1955) Beiträge zu einer Geographie des Fremdenverkehrs. *Erdkunde*, **9**, 1–19.

Christaller, W. (1964) Some Considerations of Tourism Location in Europe: The Peripheral Regions – Underdeveloped Countries – Recreation Areas. *Regional Science Association Papers*, **12**, 95–103.

Clark, J.D. and McCleary, K.W. (1995) Influencing Association's Site-Selection Process. *Cornell HRA Quarterly*, **36**(2), 61–8.

Clark, N. (1994) Youth Travel and the 3Ss. In: J. Cheyne and C. Ryan (eds), *Proceedings Tourism Down-Under: A Tourism Research Conference*, Massey University, Palmerston North, New Zealand, pp. 373–83.

Cockerell, N. (1993) Germany Outbound. *EIU Travel & Tourism Analyst*, No. 2, 19–34.

Cohen, E. (1972) Towards a Sociology of International Tourism. *Social Research*, **39**, 164–82.

Cohen, E. (1973) Nomads from Affluence: Notes on the Phenomenon of Drifter Tourism. *International Journal of Comparative Sociology*, **14**, 89–102.

Cohen, E. (1982) Thai Girls and Farang Men: The Edge of Ambiguity. *Annals of Tourism Research*, **9**, 403–28.

Cohen, E. (1986) Lovelorn Farangs: The Correspondence between Foreign Men and Thai Girls. *Anthropological Quarterly*, **59**(3), 115–27.

Cohen, E. (1988) Tourism and AIDS in Thailand. *Annals of Tourism Research*, **15**, 467–86.

Collin-Delavaud, A. (1990) L'espace touristique uruguayen et la consolidation de la station de Punta de l'Este. *L'information géographique* **54**(4), 153–67.

Cooper, C. and Jackson, S. (1989) Destination Life Cycle: The Isle of Man Case Study. *Annals of Tourism Research*, **16**, 377–98.

Craig-Smith, S.J. and Fagence, M. (1994) A Critique of Tourism Planning in the Pacific. *Progress in Tourism, Recreation and Hospitality Management*, **6**, 92–110.

Crompton, J.L. (1979) An Assessment of the Image of Mexico as a Vacation Destination and the Influence of Geographical Location upon that Image. *Journal of Travel Research*, **17**(4), 18–23.

Crompton, J.L. (1992) Structure of Vacation Destination Choice Sets. *Annals of Tourism Research*, **19**, 420–34.

Cukier, J. and Wall, G. (1994) Informal Tourism Employment: Vendors in Bali, Indonesia. *Tourism Management*, **15**, 464–7.

Culpan, R. (1987) International Tourism. Model for Developing Countries. *Annals of Tourism Research*, **14**, 541–52.

Curry, S. and Morvaridi, B. (1992) Sustainable Tourism: Illustrations from Kenya, Nepal and Jamaica. *Progress in Tourism, Recreation and Hospitality Management*, **4**, 131–9.

Defert, P. (1954) Essai de localisation touristique. *Tourist Review*, **9**(1), 110–19.

De Kadt, E. (1979) *Tourism: Passport to Development?* Oxford University Press, New York.

Dernoi, L.A. (1991) About Rural & Farm Tourism. *Tourism Recreation Research*, **16**(1), 3–6.

Deutsche Stiftung für internationale Entwicklung [DSE] (1993) *Literatur zum Themenbereich Entwicklungspolitik/Entwicklungsländer: Auswahl-bibliographie Nr.60 – Tourismus 1980–1992*. Deutsche Stiftung für internationale Entwicklung, Bonn.

Din, K.H. (1990) *Bumiputera Entrepreneurship in the Penang-Langkawi Tourist Industry*. Unpublished PhD dissertation, University of Hawaii.

Din, K.H. (1992) The 'Involvement Stage' in the Evolution of a Tourist Destination. *Tourism Recreation Research*, **17**(1), 10–20.

Dove, R. (1992) Asia's next tiger. *Asian Review*, May, pp. 12–14.

Economic and Social Commission for Asia and the Pacific (1991) *Economic Impact of Tourism in Thailand*. ESCA. Bangkok.

Economic Intelligence Unit (1991a) Thailand. *International Tourism Reports*, No. 1, 69–87.

Economic Intelligence Unit (1991b) Mauritius. *International Tourism Reports*, No. 4, 47–71.

EIU Travel & Tourism Analyst (1995) Real Exchange Rates and International Tourism Demand. *EIU Travel & Tourism Analyst*, No. 4, 66–92.

Eriksen, W. (1967) Landschaft, Nationalparks und Fremdenverkehr am Ostpatagonischen Andenrand. *Erdkunde*, **21**, 230–40.

Eriksen, W. (1973) Bodenspekulation und exzessive Grundstücksparzellierung in argentinischen Fremdenverkehrsgebieten. *Mitteilungen der Österreichischen Geographischen Gesellschaft*, **115**(1–3), 21–37.

Ferrario, F.F. (1979) The Evaluation of Tourist Resources: An Applied Methodology. *Journal of Travel Research*, **17**(4), 24–30.

Fishbein, M. (1963) An Investigation of the Relationship Between the Beliefs About an Object and the Attitude Toward that Object. *Human Relationships*, **16**, 232–40.

Fletcher, J.E. (1989) Input–Output Analysis and Tourism Impact Studies. *Annals of Tourism Research*, **16**, 514–29.

Forschungsgemeinschaft Urlaub und Reisen [FUR] (1995) *Urlaub und Reisen 94. Kurzfassung*. Gruner+Jahr, Hamburg.

France, L. (1991) An Application of the Tourism Destination Area Life Cycle to Barbados. *Tourist Review*, **46**(3), 25–31.

Franz, J.C. (1985a) The Seaside Resorts of Southeast Asia. *Tourism Recreation Research*, **10**(1), 15–24.

Franz, J.C. (1985b) Pattaya, Penang, Bali: Asia's Leading Beach Resorts. *Tourism Recreation Research*, **10**(1), 25–30.

Frechtling, D.S. (1994) Assessing the Impacts of Travel and Tourism – Measuring Economic Benefits. In: J.R.B. Ritchie and C.R. Goeldner (eds), *Travel, Tourism and Hospitality Research. A Handbook for Managers and Researchers* (2nd edn). John Wiley & Sons, New York, pp. 367–91.

Frentrup, K. (1969) *Die ökonomische Bedeutung des internationalen*

Tourismus für die Entwicklungsländer. Unpublished PhD dissertation, University of Hamburg.

Friedland, J. (1992) Tourists Stay Away in Droves. *Far Eastern Economic Review*, June 4, 56–7.

Gartrell, R.B. (1994) Destination Marketing for Convention and Visitor Bureaux. (2nd ed.). Kendall/Hunt Publishing. Dubuque.

Gayle, D.J. (1993) The Jamaican Tourist Industry: Domestic Economic Growth and Development. In: D.J. Gayle and J.N. Goodrich (eds) *Tourism Marketing and Management in the Caribbean.* Routledge, London, pp. 41–57.

Gearing, C.E., Swart, W.W. and Var, T. (1974) Establishing a Measure of Tourist Attractiveness. *Journal of Travel Research*, **12**, 1–18.

Gerlach, A. (1991) What Investors are up Against. *Executive*, **12**(12), 82–4.

Gerstenhauer, A. (1956) Acapulco, die Riviera Mexikos. *Die Erde*, **8**, 271–81.

Goldstein, C. (1991) Balmy Weather Ahead. *Far Eastern Economic Review*, April 11, pp. 42–3.

Goodrich, J.N. (1978) The Relationship between Preferences for and Perceptions of Vacation Destinations: Application of a Choice Model. *Journal of Travel Research*, **17**, 8–13.

Gormsen, E. (1981) *The Spatio-Temporal Development of International Tourism.* Centre des Hautes Etudes Touristiques, Aix-en-Provence.

Gormsen, E. (1983) Tourismus in der Dritten Welt. *Geographische Rundschau*, **35**, 608–17.

Grosjean, G. (1986) Ästhetische Bewertung Ländlicher Räume am Beispiel von Grindelwald. *Geographica Bernensia*, **13**.

Gunawan, M.P. (1996) Domestic Tourism in Indonesia. *Tourism Recreation Research*, **21**(1), 65–9.

Günter, W. (1982) Geschichte der Bildungsreise. In: Günter, W. (ed.) *Handbuch für Studienreiseleiter.* Starnberg: Studienkreis für Tourismus, pp. 7–27.

Haggett, P. (1985) *Geography: A Modern Synthesis.* Harper Row, London.

Hall, C.M. (1992) Sex Tourism in Southeast Asia. In: D. Harrison (ed.), *Tourism and the Less Developed Countries*, Belhaven Press, London, pp. 65–74.

Hall, C.M. (1994) Tourism in Pacific Island Microstates: A Case Study of Vanuatu. *Tourism Recreation Research*, **19**(1), 59–63.

Handley, P. (1992) Limited Damage. *Far Eastern Economic Review*, July 2, p. 48.

Harris, J.E. and Nelson, J.G. (1993) Monitoring Tourism from a Whole Economy Perspective: A Case from Indonesia. In: J.G. Nelson, R.W. Butler and G. Wall (eds), *Tourism and Sustainable Development: Monitoring, Planning, Managing*, Dep. of Geography, University of Waterloo, pp. 179–200.

Harrison, D. (ed.) (1992) *Tourism and the Less Developed Countries.* Halsted Press, New York.

Harvey, D. (1969) *Explanation in Geography*, Edward Arnold, London.

Haywood, K.M. (1985) Can the Tourist Area Life Cycle be made Operational? *Tourism Management*, **7**, 154–67.

Helbig, K. (1949) *Am Rande des Pazifik. Studien zur Landes- und Kulturkunde Südostasiens*. Kohlhammer, Stuttgart.

Heng, T.M. and Low, L. (1990) Economic Impact of Tourism in Singapore. *Annals of Tourism Research*, **17**, 246–69.

Hiebert. M. (1992) Vietnam Opening: Hong Kong vies to become Gateway. *Far Eastern Economic Review*, **155** (21 May), 26–8.

Hobson, J.S.P. and Dietrich, U.C. (1994) Tourism, Health and Quality of Life: Challenging the Responsibility of Using the Traditional Tenets of Sun, Sea, Sand, and Sex in Tourism Marketing. *Journal of Travel & Tourism Marketing*, **3**(4), 21–38.

Hoffmann, H. (1971) Die Bedeutung des internationalen Tourismus für die Entwicklungsländer. *Berichte zur Regionalforschung*, **6**, 5–13.

Höhfeld, V. (1989) Türkischer Tourismus. Ausverkauf der Küsten. *Geographische Rundschau*, **41**, 230–34.

Hoivik, T. and Heiberg, T. (1980) Centre-Periphery Tourism and Self-Reliance. *International Social Science Journal*, **32**, 69–98.

Huckendubler, M.M. (1970) Le tourisme, facteur important du développement économique de la Tanzanie. *Industries et Travaux d'Outre-Mer*, **18**(195), 103–7.

Hudman, L.E. (1979) Origin Regions of International Tourism. *Wiener Geographische Schriften*, **53/54**, 43–9.

Hudman, L.E. and Davis, J.A. (1994) World Tourism Markets: Changes and Patterns. *Proceedings TTRA 25th Annual Conference*. Wheatridge: TTRA, pp. 127–45.

Hunter, C. and Green, H. (1995) *Tourism and the Environment*. Routledge, London.

Husbands, W. (1981) Centres, Peripheries, Tourism and Socio-spatial Development. *Ontario Geography*, **17**, 37–59.

Ioannides, D. (1992) Tourism Development Agents. The Cypriot Resort Cycle. *Annals of Tourism Research*, **19**, 711–31.

Jafari, J. (1974) The Socio-economic Costs of Tourism to Developing Countries. *Annals of Tourism Research*, **1**, 227–59.

Japan International Corporation Agency [JICA] (1989) Malaysia. The study on a comprehensive National Tourism Development (unpublished). Tourist Development Corporation, Kuala Lumpur.

Jenkins, C.L. (1982) The Effects of Scale in Tourism Projects in Developing Countries. *Annals of Tourism Research*, **9**, 229–49.

Jenkins, C.L. (1991) Development Strategies. In: J. Bodlender, A. Jefferson, C.L. Jenkins and L. Lickorish (eds), *Developing Tourism Destinations: Policies and Perspectives*, Longman, Harlow, pp. 59–118.

Jenkins, C.L. (1994) Tourism in Developing Countries: The Privatisation Issue. In A.V. Seaton (ed.), *Tourism: The State of the Art*. John Wiley & Sons, Chichester.

Jenkins, C.L. and Henry, B.M. (1982) Government Involvement in Tourism in Developing Countries. *Annals of Tourism Research*, **9**, 499–521.

Johnston, D.C. and Tieh, P. (1983) Projected and Perceived Images of Tourist Destinations in Asia and the Pacific. *Proceedings 12th New Zealand Geographer Conference*, pp. 280–3.

Johnston, R.J. (1991). *Geography and Geographers*. Edward Arnold, London.

Jones, J.F. (1970) *Tourism as a Tool for Economic Development with Specific Reference to the Countries of Jamaica, Trinidad and Guyana*. Unpublished PhD dissertation, University of Florida.

Jurczek, P. (1985) Gross- und kleinräumige Auswirkungen des Ferntourismus auf Peru. *Die Erde*, **115**, 27–48.

Kasse, M. (1973) La théorie du développement de l'industrie touristique dans les pays sous-développés. *Annales africaines*, 1971–1972, 53–72.

Kermath, B.M. and Thomas, R.N. (1992) Spatial Dynamics of Resorts: Sosua, Dominican Republic. *Annals of Tourism Research*, **19**, 173–90.

Khan, H., Seng, C.F. and Cheong, W.K. (1990) Tourism Multiplier Effects on Singapore. *Annals of Tourism Research*, **17**, 408–18.

King, B. (1994) Research on Resorts: A Review. *Progress in Tourism, Recreation and Hospitality Management*, **5**, 165–80.

Kissling, C. (1989) International Tourism and Civil Aviation in the South Pacific: Issues and Innovations. *GeoJournal*, **19**, 309–15.

Kissling, C. and Pearce, D.G. (1990) Destination South Pacific. In: C. Kissling (ed.), *Destination South Pacific – Perspectives on Island Tourism*. Centre des Hautes Etudes Touristiques, Aix-en-Provence, pp. 1–11.

Körner, H. (1994) The 'Third World' in the 1990s: Problems and Challenges. *Intereconomics*, **29**, 92–7.

Kulinat, K. (1991) Fremdenverkehr in den Mittelmeerländern. Konkurrenten mit gemeinsamen Umweltproblemen. *Geographische Rundschau*, **43**, 430–6.

Labeau, G. (1970) Quelques problèmes économiques et humains de l'implantation touristique et hôtelière dans les pays en voie de développement. *Tourist Review*, **25**(1), 27–31.

Latza, B. (1987) *Sextourismus in Südostasien*. Fischer Taschenbuch Verlag, Frankfurt/M.

Lavery, P. (1971) Resorts and Recreation. In: P. Lavery (ed.), *Recreational Geography*, John Wiley, New York, pp. 167–95.

Lawson, R.W. (1991) Patterns of Tourist Expenditure and Types of Vacation across the Family Life Cycle. *Journal of Travel Research*, **29**(4), 12–18.

Lee, G.P. (1987) Future of National and Regional Tourism in Developing Countries. *Tourism Management*, **8**(2), 86–8.

Leemann, A. (1975) Fremdenverkehr auf Bali. *Zeitschrift für Wirtschaftsgeographie*, **18**, 165–72.

Lefort, E.J.E. (1959) Bright Future for Tourism in New Caledonia. *South Pacific Commission Quarterly Bulletin*, **9**(1), 25 and 70.

Leheny, D. (1995) A Political Economy of Asian Sex Tourism. *Annals of Tourism Research*, **22**, 367–84.

Levitt, K. and Gulati, I. (1970) Income Effects of Tourist Spending: A Critical Comment on the Zinder Report. *Social and Economic Studies*, **19**, 326–43.

Lew, A.A. (1987) A Framework of Tourist Attraction Research. *Annals of Tourism Research*, **14**, 553–75.

Loker-Murphy, L. and Pearce, P.L. (1995) Young Budget Travelers: Backpackers in Australia. *Annals of Tourism Research*, **22**, 819–43.

Loki, M. (1974) How Fijians can Benefit from Tourism and How To Milk the Tourists. *Pacific Perspective*, **3**(2), 48–51.

Long, V.H. (1991) Government – Industry – Community Interaction in Tourism Development in Mexico. In: M.T. Sinclair and M.J. Stabler (eds), *The Tourism Industry: An International Analysis*. C.A.B. International, Oxon, pp. 205–22.

Lubeigt, G. (1979) Economie, tourisme et environnement en Thailande. *Cahiers d'Outre Mer*, **32**, 371–99.

Lue, C.C., Crompton, J.L. and Fesenmaier, D.R. (1993) Conceptualization of Multidestination Pleasure Trips. *Annals of Tourism Research*, **20**, 289–301.

Lundberg, D.E. (1974) Caribbean Tourism: Social and Racial Tensions. *Cornell HRA Quarterly*, **15**(1), 82–7.

Lundgren, J. (1972) The Development of the Tourist Travel Systems – A Metropolitan Economic Hegemony par Excellence? *Jahrbuch für Fremdenverkehr*, **20**, 85–120.

Madras, D. (1946) Les hotels de Grand Tourisme au Maroc. *Bulletin Economique et Social du Maroc*, **8**(30), 387–91.

Malaysian Tourism Promotion Board [MTPB] (1992) *Malaysia Accommodation Directory 1992/93*, MTPB. Kuala Lumpur.

Malaysian Tourism Promotion Board [MTPB] (1995) *Visitor Arrival Statistics 1994*. MTPB, Kuala Lumpur.

Mansfeld, Y. (1992) From Motivation to Actual Travel. *Annals of Tourism Research*, **19**, 399–419.

Marquardt, W. (1976) *Seychellen, Komoren und Maskaren. Handbuch der ostafrikanischen Inselwelt*. Weltforum Verlag, München.

Martilla, J.A. and James, J.C. (1977) Importance–Performance Analysis. *Journal of Marketing*, **41**(1), 77–9.

Mathieson, A. and Wall, G. (1982) *Tourism: Economic, Physical and Environmental Impacts*. Edward Arnold, London.

Matthews, H.G. (1977) Radicals and Third World Tourism: A Caribbean Focus. *Annals of Tourism Research*, **5**, 20–9.

Mauritius Government Tourist Office (1996) *Mauritius. Information Guide*. Mauritius Government Tourist Office, Port Louis.

Mazières, M.de and Gattfossé, J. (1937) Le tourisme au Maroc. *Revue de Géographie Marocaine*, **21**, 241–51.

McGahey, S. (1995) South Korea. *International Tourism Reports*, No. 3, 22–47.

McKean, P.F. (1973) *Cultural Involution: Tourists, Balinese, and the Process of Modernization in an Anthropological Perspective*. Unpublished PhD dissertation, Brown University.

McKenna, R. (1991) *Relationship Marketing*. Addison Wesley Publishing Company, New York.

McKinnon, A. (1993) Vietnam: Construction Invasion. *Asia Travel Trade*, August, pp. 16–17.

Meisch, L.A. (1995) Gringas and Otavalenos: Changing Tourist Relations. *Annals of Tourism Research*, **22**, 441–62.

Menzel, U. (1991) Das Ende der 'Dritten Welt' und das Scheitern der grossen

Theorie. Zur Soziologie einer Disziplin in auch selbstkritischer Absicht. *Politische Vierteljahresschrift*, **21**(1), 4–33.

Mergard, C. (1986) *Tourismus der Tropen – Eine quantitative Studie zur Entwicklung von 1970 bis 1980*. Unpublished PhD dissertation, University of Bonn.

Meyer-Arendt, K.J. (1990) Recreational Business Districts in Gulf of Mexico Seaside Resorts. *Journal of Cultural Geography*, **11**, 39–55.

Michaud, J. (1991) A Social Anthropology of Tourism in Ladakh, India. *Annals of Tourism Research*, **18**, 605–21.

Milne, S. (1987) Differential Multipliers. *Annals of Tourism Research*, **14**, 499–515.

Milne, S. (1991) Tourism Development in Papua New Guinea. *Annals of Tourism Research*, **18**, 508–11.

Milne, S. (1992) Tourism and Development in South Pacific Microstates. *Annals of Tourism Research*, **19**, 191–212.

Mings, R.C. (1969) Tourism's Potential for Contributing to the Economic Development in the Caribbean. *Journal of Geography*, **68**, 173–7.

Mings, R.C. and McHugh, K.E. (1992) The Spatial Configuration of Travel to Yellowstone National Park. *Journal of Travel Research*, **30**(4), 38–46.

Mings, R.C. and Chiulikpongse, S. (1994) Tourism in Far Southern Thailand: A Geographical Perspective. *Tourism Recreation Research*, **19**(1), 25–31.

Miossec, J.M. (1976) *Eléments pour une théorie de l'espace touristique*. Centre des Hautes Etudes Touristiques, Aix-en-Provence.

Miossec, J.M. (1977) Un modèle de l'espace touristique. *L'espace géographique*, **6**(1), 41–8.

Mitchell, B. (1979) *Geography and Resource Analysis* (2nd edn). Longman, London.

Mitchell, L.S. and Smith, R.V. (1985) Recreational Geography: Inventory and Prospects. *Professional Geographer*, **37**, 6–14.

Morrison, A.M. and O'Leary, J.T. (1995) The VFR Market: Desperately Seeking Respect. *Journal of Tourism Studies*, **6**(1), 2–5.

Müller, B. (1984) Fremdenverkehr, Dezentralisierung und regionale Partizipation in Mexico. *Geographische Rundschau*, **36**(1), 20–4.

Muqbil, I. (1995) Thailand. *International Tourism Reports*, No. 3, 66–81.

Myers, N. (1974) The Tourist as an Agent for Development and Wildlife Conservation: The Case of Kenya. *International Journal of Social Economics* **2**(1), 26–42.

Naylon, J. (1967) Tourism – Spain's Most Important Industry. *Geography*, **52**, 23–40.

Nettekoven, L. (1969) Massentourismus aus der Industriegesellschaft in die Dritte Welt: Ein Faktor des sozialen Wandels. *Kölner Zeitschrift für Soziologie und Sozialpsychologie*, **21**, 257–75.

Nohlen, D. and Nuscheler, F. (1993) *Handbuch der Dritten Welt: Grundprobleme, Theorien, Strategien 1*. Verlag J.H.W. Dietz, Bonn.

Nuscheler, F. (1991) *Lern- und Arbeitsbuch Entwicklungspolitik*. Verlag J.H.W. Dietz, Bonn.

Oestreich, H. (1977) Gambia – Zur sozioökonomischen Problematik des Ferntourismus in einem westafrikanischen Entwicklungsland. *Geographische Zeitschrift*, **65**, 302–8.

Oppermann, M. (1992a) International Tourism and Regional Development in Malaysia. *Tijdschrift voor Economische en Sociale Geografie*, **83**, 226–33.

Oppermann, M. (1992b) *Tourismus in Malaysia. Eine Analyse der räumlichen Strukturen und intranationalen Touristenströme unter besonderer Berücksichtigung der entwicklungstheoretischen Problematik.* Breitenbach, Saarbrücken/Fort Lauderdale.

Oppermann, M. (1992c) Regional Aspects of the Indonesian Tourist Industry. *Indonesian Journal of Geography*, **22**, 31–44.

Oppermann, M. (1992d) Intranational Tourist Flows in Malaysia. *Annals of Tourism Research*, **19**, 482–500.

Oppermann, M. (1992e) Travel Dispersal Index. *Journal of Tourism Studies*, **3**(1), 44–9.

Oppermann, M. (1993) Tourism Space in Developing Countries. *Annals of Tourism Research*, **20**, 535–6.

Oppermann, M. (1994a) Length of Stay and Spatial Distribution. *Annals of Tourism Research*, **21**, 834–6.

Oppermann, M. (1994b) The Malaysian Tourist System. *Malaysian Journal of Tropical Geography*, **25**(1), 11–20.

Oppermann, M. (1994c) Travel Life Cycles – A Multitemporal Perspective of Changing Travel Patterns. In R.V. Gasser and K. Weiermair (eds), *Spoilt for Choice. Decision Making Processes and Preference Changes of Tourists – Intertemporal and Intercountry Perspectives.* Kulturverlag, Thaur, pp. 81–97.

Oppermann, M. (1994d) Relevance of Nationality in Tourism Research. *Annals of Tourism Research*, **21**, 165–8.

Oppermann, M. (1994e) *Modeling Convention Location Choice and Participation Decision Making Process: A Review with Emphasis on Professional Associations*, Centre des Hautes Etudes Touristiques, Aix-en-Provence.

Oppermann, M. (1994/95) Tourism in the Philippines: Development and Regional Impacts. *Ilmu Masyarakat*, **25**, 21–36.

Oppermann, M. (1995a) Travel Life Cycle. *Annals of Tourism Research*, **22**, 535–52.

Oppermann, M. (1995b) Comparative Analysis of Escorted Package Tours in New Zealand and North America Offered in Germany. *Progress in Tourism and Hospitality Research*, **1**(2), 85–98.

Oppermann, M. (1995c) Tourism Development in South America. *Proceedings 1995 STTE Conference*, Vol. 7, 38–45.

Oppermann, M. (1995d) A Model of Travel Itineraries. *Journal of Travel Research*, **33**(4), 57–61.

Oppermann, M. (1995e) Family Life Cycle and Cohort Effects: A Study of Travel Patterns of German Residents. *Journal of Travel & Tourism Marketing*, **4**(1), 23–44.

Oppermann, M. (1995f) Travel Life Cycles – A Multitemporal Perspective of Changing Travel Patterns. *Journal of Travel & Tourism Marketing*, **4**(3), 101–9.

Oppermann, M. (1996a) Rural Tourism in Southern Germany. *Annals of Tourism Research*, **23**, 86–102.

Oppermann, M. (1996b) The Changing Market Place in Asian Outbound Tourism and its Marketing Implications. *Tourism Recreation Research*, **21**(2), 53–62.

Oppermann, M. (1996c) Convention Destination Images: Analysis of Meeting Planners' Perceptions. *Tourism Management*, **17**, 175–82.

Oppermann, M. (1996d) Convention Cities – Images and Changing Fortunes. *Journal of Tourism Studies*, **7**(1), 10–19.

Oppermann, M. (1997) Tourism Development Patterns in Latin America: A Regional Perspective (forthcoming). In: W.J. Pitts (ed.), *The Political Economy of Tourism in Latin America*. Cognizant Communication Corporation, New York.

Oppermann, M. and Brewer, K.P. (1996) Location Decision Making in Hospitality using GIS – A Paradigm Shift? In *Proceedings 1996 Conf. of Australian Tourism & Hospitality Educators*. Bureau of Tourism Research, Canberra, pp. 279–88.

Oppermann, M. and Chon, K.S. (1995a) Time-series Analysis of German Outbound Travel Patterns. *Journal of Vacation Marketing*, **2**(1), 39–52.

Oppermann, M. and Chon, K.S. (1995b) Factors Influencing Professional Conference Participation by Association Members: A Pilot Study of Convention Tourism. *Proceedings TTRA 26th Annual Conference*. TTRA, Wheatridge, pp. 254–9.

Oppermann, M. and Chon, K.S. (1997) Convention Participation Decision Making Process. *Annals of Tourism Research*, **24**(1), 178–91.

Oppermann, M., Din, K.H. and Amri, S.Z. (1996) Urban Hotel Location and Evolution in a Developing Country: The Case of Kuala Lumpur. *Tourism Recreation Research*, **21**(1), 55–63.

Oppermann, M. and Sahr, W.D. (1992) Another View on 'Alternative Tourism in Dominica'. *Annals of Tourism Research*, **19**, 784–91.

Owens, C. (1992) Thai Officials Encouraged by Economy say Future Hinges on Political Stability. *Asian Wall Street Journal*, September 14, p. 4.

Page, S.J. (1994) *Transport for Tourism*. Routledge, London.

Page, S.J. (1995) *Urban Tourism*. Routledge, London.

Pavaskar, M. (1982). Employment Effects of Tourism and the Indian Experience. *Journal of Travel Research*, **21**(2), 32–8.

Pawson, I.G., Stanford, D.D., Adams, V.A. and Nurbu, M. (1984) Growth of Tourism in Nepal's Everest Region: Impact on the Physical Environment and Structure of Human Settlements. *Mountain Research and Development*, **4**(3), 237–46.

Pearce, D.G. (1989) *Tourist Development*. Longman, Harlow.

Pearce, D.G. (1993) Introduction. In: D.G. Pearce and R.W. Butler (eds), *Tourism Research: Critiques and Challenges*. Routledge, London, pp. 1–8.

Pearce, D.G. (1995a) *Tourism Today: A Geographical Analysis*. Longman, Harlow.

Pearce, D.G. (1995b) Planning for Tourism in the 1990s: An Integrated, Dynamic, Multiscale Approach. In: R.W. Butler and D.G. Pearce (eds), *Change in Tourism: People, Places, Processes*. Routledge, London, pp. 229–44.

Pearce, D.G. and Elliott, J.M.C. (1983) The Trip Index. *Journal of Travel Research*, **22**(1), 6–8.

Pearce, D.G. and Johnston, D.C. (1986) Travel within Tonga. *Journal of Travel Research*, **24**(3), 13–17.

Pearce, P.L. (1993) Fundamentals of Tourist Motivation. In: D.G. Pearce and R.W. Butler (eds), *Tourism Research: Critiques and Challenges*. Routledge, London, pp. 113–34.

Peterson, G.L. and Neumann, E.S. (1969) Modelling and Predicting Human Response to the Visual Recreation Environment. *Journal of Leisure Research*, **1**, 219–37.

Phongpaichit, P. (1981) Bangkok Masseuses: Holding up the Family Sky. *Southeast Asia Chronicle*, **78**, 15–23.

Pigram, J.J. (1977) Beach Resort Morphology. *Habitat International*, **2**, 525–41.

Plog, S.C. (1974) Why Destination Areas Rise and Fall in Popularity. *Cornell HRA Quarterly*, **14**(4), 55–8.

Plog, S.C. (1991) *Leisure Travel: Making it a Growth Market again!* John Wiley & Sons, New York.

Pollard, H.J. (1970) The West Indian Tourist Industry: Panacea for Small Island Development. *Swansea Geographer*, **8**, 15–21.

Popp, H. (1991) Auswirkungen des Fremdenverkehrs auf Raum und Gesellschaft in Marokko: Entwicklung – Strukturen – und Folgen. *Passauer Mittelmeerstudien*, **3**, 183–212.

Poser, H. (1939) *Geographische Studien über den Fremdenverkehr im Riesengebirge. Ein Beitrag zur geographischen Betrachtung des Fremdenverkehrs*. Abh. der Gesellschaft der Wissenschaften Göttingen 20.

Pratiwi, W. and Wilkinson, P.W. (1994) A Gender Analysis of the Impact of Tourism on a Traditional Fishing Village: Pangandaran, Java, Indonesia. Paper presented at the 90th AAG Conference 1994, San Francisco.

Pruitt, S. and LaFont, S. (1995) For Love and Money: Romance Tourism in Jamaica. *Annals of Tourism Research*, **22**, 422–40.

Przeclawski, K. (1993) Tourism as the Subject of Interdisciplinary Research. In: D.G. Pearce and R.W. Butler (eds), *Tourism Research: Critiques and Challenges*. Routledge, London, pp. 9–19.

Pura, C. and Owens, C. (1992) Economy Should Weather Storm from Political Strife, Analysts Say. *Asian Wall Street Journal*, June 22, p. 5.

Radetzki-Stenner, M. (1989) *Internationaler Tourismus und Entwicklungsländer. Die Auswirkungen des Einfachtourismus auf eine ländliche Region der indonesischen Insel Bali*, LIT, Münster.

Reed, R.R. (1979) The Colonial Genesis of Hill Stations: The Genting Exceptions. *Geographical Review*, **69**, 463–8.

Richter, L.K. (1992) Political Instability and Tourism in the Third World. In: D. Harrison (ed.), *Tourism and the Less Developed Countries*. Belhaven Press, London, pp. 35–46.

Richter, L.K. (1993) Tourism Policy-Making in South-East Asia. In: M. Hitchcock, V.T. King and M.J.G. Parnwell (eds), *Tourism in South-East Asia*. Routledge, London, pp. 179–99.

Richter, L.K. (1995) Gender and Race: Neglected Variables in Tourism

Research. In: R.W. Butler and D.G. Pearce (eds), *Change in Tourism: People, Places, Processes*. Routledge, London, pp. 71–91.

Rinschede, G. (1992) Forms of Religious Tourism. *Annals of Tourism Research*, **19**, 51–67.

Ritter, W. (1986) Hotel Location in Big Cities. In: F. Vetter (ed.), *Grossstadttourismus*. Reimer, Berlin, pp. 355–64.

Robinson, D.W. (1994) Strategies for Alternative Tourism: The Case of Tourism in Sagarmatha (Everest) National Park, Nepal. In: A.V. Seaton (ed.), *Tourism: The State of the Art*. John Wiley & Sons, Chichester, pp. 691–702.

Ross, G.F. (1993) Destination Evaluation and Vacation Preferences. *Annals of Tourism Research*, **20**, 477–89.

Ross, G.F. (1997) Destination Motivation among Backpacker Visitors to Northern Australia. *Pacific Tourism Review*, **1**(1).

Ruf, W.K. (1978) Tourismus und Unterentwicklung. *Zeitschrift für Kulturaustausch*, **28**(3), 108–14.

Ryan, C. (1993) Crime, Violence, Terrorism and Tourism: An Accidental or Intrinsic Relationship. *Tourism Management*, **14**, 173–83.

Salem, L.B. (1970) Aspects humain du développement du tourisme dans le Cap Bon. *Revue Tunisienne de Sciences Sociales*, **7**(20), 31–68.

Sands, S. (1966) Bahama's Prosperity Grows with Tourism Explosion. *The Commercial and Financial Chronicle*, **204**(6608), 788–9.

Schlentrich, U.A. and Ng, D. (1994) Hotel Development Strategies in Southeast Asia: The Battle for Market Dominance. In: A.V. Seaton (ed.), *Tourism: The State of the Art*, John Wiley & Sons, Chichester, pp. 402–14.

Senftleben, W. (1973) Some Aspects of the Indian Hill Stations: A Contribution Towards a Geography of Tourist Traffic. *Philippine Geographical Journal*, **17**(1), 21–9.

Sezer, H. and Harrison, A. (1994) Tourism in Greece and Turkey: An Economic View for Planners. In: A.V. Seaton *et al.* (eds), *Tourism: The State of the Art*. John Wiley & Sons, Chichester, pp. 74–84.

Shackley, M. (1995) Just Started and Now Finished: Tourism Development in Arunachal Pradesh. *Tourism Management*, **16**, 623–5.

Sherry, A. (1993) Building Boom Hits Vietnam. *South China Morning Post*, November 3, p. 5.

Simonis, U.E. (1991) Least Developed Countries – Newly Defined. *Intereconomics*, **26**, 230–5.

Simpson, E.S. (1994) *The Developing World: An Introduction*, Longman, Harlow.

Sinclair, M.T. (1991) The Tourism Industry and Foreign Exchange Leakages in a Developing Country: The Distribution of Earnings from Safari and Beach Tourism in Kenya. In: M.T. Sinclair and M.J. Stabler (eds), *The Tourism Industry: An International Analysis*. C.A.B. International, Oxon:, pp. 185–204.

Smith, R.A. (1991) Beach Resorts: A Model of Development Evolution. *Landscape and Urban Planning*, **21**, 189–210.

Smith, R.A. (1992) Review of Integrated Beach Resort Development in Southeast Asia. *Land Use Policy*, **9**, 209–17.

Smith, S.L.J. (1990) A Test of Plog's Allocentric/Psychocentric Model: Evidence from Seven Nations. *Journal of Travel Research*, **28**(4), 40–5.

Smith, S.L.J. (1995) *Tourism Analysis: A Handbook* (2nd edn). Longman, Harlow.

Smith, V.L. (1990) Geographical Implications of 'Drifter' Tourism, Boracay, Philippines. *Tourism Recreation Research*, **15**(1), 34–42.

Society of Incentive Travel Executives (1990) *The Incentive Travel Case Book*. Society of Incentive Travel Executives, New York.

Spencer, J.E. and Thomas, W.L. (1948) The Hill Stations and Summer Resorts of the Orient. *Geographical Review*, **38**, 637–51.

Stansfield, C.A. (1971) The Geography of Resorts: Problems and Potentials. *Professional Geographer*, **23**, 164–6.

Studienkreis für Tourismus [StfT] (various years) *Urlaubsreisen, Kurzfassung der Reiseanalyse*. StfT, Starnberg.

Stymeist, D.H. (1996) Transformation of Vilavilairevo in Tourism. *Annals of Tourism Research*, **23**, 1–18.

Swain, M.B. (1989) Developing Ethnic Tourism in Yunnan, China: Shilin Sani. *Tourism Recreation Research*, **14**(1), 33–40.

Taylor, V. (1975) The Recreational Business District: A Component of the East London Urban Morphology. *South African Geographer*, **5**, 139–44.

Teuscher, H. and Lang, H.R. (1982) Inland Tourism in Developing Countries – A possibility to reduce regional disparities. *Tourist Review*, **37**(2), 2–5.

Theuns, H.L. (1991) *Third World Tourism Research 1954–1984: A Guide to the Literature*. Peter Lang, Frankfurt/M.

Thiemann, H. (1989) Reisende Männer: Sextourismus als spezielle Form der ökologischen Zerstörung – Das Beispiel Thailand. In C. Euler (ed.), *Eingeborene – ausgebucht: ökologische Zerstörung durch Tourismus*. Focus Verlag, Giessen, pp. 91–103.

Thiessen, B. (1993) *Tourismus in der Dritten Welt*. Geographische Gesellschaft Trier, Trier.

Thompson, C., O'Hare, G. and Evans, K. (1995) Tourism in The Gambia: Problems and Proposals. *Tourism Management*, **16**, 571–81.

Thurot, J.M. (1973) *Le tourisme tropical balnéaire: Le model caraïbe et ses extensions*. Unpublished PhD dissertation, Aix-en-Provence.

Tlusty, V. (1980) Building Up Tourism in Developing Countries. *Tourist Review*, **35**(1), 10–13.

Tourism Authority of Thailand (1991) *Annual Report on Tourism in Thailand, 1990*. Tourism Authority Thailand, Bangkok.

Tourism Council of the South Pacific [TCSP] (1995) *Western Samoa Visitor Survey*. TCSP, Suva.

Trabold-Nübler, H. (1991) The Human Development Index – A New Development Indicator. *Intereconomics*, **26**, 236–43.

Um, S. and Crompton, J.L. (1990) Attitude Determinants in Tourism Destination Choice. *Annals of Tourism Research*, **17**, 432–48.

UNESCO (1976) The effects of tourism on socio-cultural values. *Annals of Tourism Research*, **4**, 74–105.

Ungefehr, F. (1988) *Tourism und Offshore-Banking auf den Bahamas. Internationale Dienstleistungen als dominanter Wirtschaftsfaktor in einem kleinen Entwicklungsland*. Peter Lang, Frankfurt/M.

Unwin, T. (1992) The Place of Geography. Longman, London.

Uthoff, D. (1991) Tourismus und Küstenveränderung auf Phuket/Südthailand. *Erdkundliches Wissen*, **105**, 237–49.

Vetter, F. (1986) *Grossstadttourismus*, Reimer, Berlin.

Vielhaber, C. (1986) Vom Fischerdorf zu einem Zentrum des Fernreise-tourismus. Das Beispiel Pattaya, Thailand. *Geographischer Jahresbericht aus Österreich*, **43**, 31–76.

Vorlaufer, K. (1979) Fremdenverkehrswirtschaftliche Entwicklung und Beschäftigung in der Dritten Welt. *Zeitschrift für Wirtschaftsgeographie*, **23**, 161–71.

Vorlaufer, K. (1980) Die räumliche Ordnung der Fremdenverkehrswirtschaft in Sri Lanka. Eine standort-theoretische und empirische Studie zur Entfaltung des Tourismus in der Dritten Welt. *Zeitschrift für Wirtschafts-geographie*, **24**, 165–75.

Vorlaufer, K. (1984) *Ferntourismus und Dritte Welt*. Diesterweg, Frankfurt/M.

Vorlaufer, K. (1993) Transnationale Reisekonzerne und die Globalisierung der Fremdenverkehrswirtschaft: Konzentrationsprozesse, Struktur- und Raummuster. *Erdkunde*, **47**, 267–81.

Voss, J. (1984) *Die Bedeutung des Tourismus für die wirtschaftliche Entwicklung. Ein Beitrag zur Integration von Tourismusforschung und Entwicklungspolitik*, PhD dissertation, University of Berlin.

Wahnschafft, R. (1982) Formal and informal tourism sectors. A case study in Pattaya, Thailand. *Annals of Tourism Research*, **9**, 429–51.

Wain, B. (1993) Paris Meeting Formalizes Vietnam's Rebirth. *Asian Wall Street Journal Weekly*, November 8, p. 14.

Wall, G. (1982) Cycles and Capacity: Incipient Theory of Conceptual Contradiction. *Tourism Management*, **3**, 188–92.

Wall, G. and Dibnah, S. (1992) The Changing Status of Tourism in Bali, Indonesia. *Progress in Tourism, Recreation and Hospitality Management*, **4**, 120–30.

Wang, Y. and Sheldon, P.J. (1995) The Sleeping Dragon Awakes: The Outbound Chinese Travel Market. *Journal of Travel & Tourism Marketing*, **4**(4), 41–54.

Weaver, D.B. (1988) The Evolution of a 'Plantation' Tourism Landscape on the Caribbean island of Antigua. *Tijdschrift voor Economische en Sociale Geografie*, **79**, 319–31.

Weaver, D.B. (1990) Grand Cayman Island and the Resort Cycle Concept. *Journal of Travel Research*, **29**(2), 9–15.

Weaver, D.B. (1993) Model of Urban Tourism for Small Caribbean Islands. *Geographical Review*, **83**, 134–40.

Weightman, B.A. (1987) Third World Tour Landscapes. *Annals of Tourism Research*, **14**, 227–39.

Widmer-Münch, R. (1990) *Der Tourismus in Fes und Marrakech. Strukturen und Prozesse in bipolaren Urbanräumen des islamischen Orients*. Basler Beiträge zur Geographie 39.

Wilkinson, P. (1987) Tourism in Small Island Nations: A Fragile Dependence. *Leisure Studies*, **6**, 127–46.

Wilkinson, P. (1989) Strategies for Tourism in Island Microstates. *Annals of Tourism Research*, **16**, 153–77.

Withington, W.A. (1961) Upland Resorts and Tourism in Indonesia. *Geographical Review*, **51**, 418–23.

Wolfe, R.I. (1952) Wasaga Beach: The Divorce from the Geographic Environment. *Canadian Geographer*, **2**, 57–66.

Wolfson, M. (1967) Government's Role in Tourism Development. *Development Digest*, **5**(2), 20–6.

Wong, P. P. (1986) Tourism Development and Resorts on the East Coast of Peninsular Malaysia. *Singapore Journal of Tropical Geography*, **7**, 152–62.

Wood, R.E. (1979) Tourism and Underdevelopment in Southeast Asia. *Journal of Contemporary Asia*, **9**, 274–87.

Wood, R.E. (1980) International Tourism and Cultural Change in Southeast Asia. *Economic Development and Cultural Change*, **28**, 561–81.

Woodside, A.G. and Sherrell, D. (1977) Traveler Evoked, Inept, and Inert Sets of Vacation Destinations. *Journal of Travel Research*, **16**, 14–18.

Woodside, A.G. and Lysonski, S. (1989) A General Model of Traveler Destination Choice. *Journal of Travel Research*, **27**(4), 8–14.

World Bank (1991). *World Development Report 1991: The Challenge of Development*. Oxford University Press, New York.

World Bank (1992) *Mauritius: expanding horizons: A World Bank country study*. World Bank, Washington.

World Bank (1994) *World Development Report 1994: Infrastructure for Development*. Oxford University Press, New York.

World Tourism Organization [WTO] (1991) *Tourist Arrivals Worldwide and in the Americas, 1950–1990*. WTO, Madrid.

World Tourism Organization (1994a) *Yearbook of Tourism Statistics* (46th edn). WTO, Madrid.

World Tourism Organization (1994b) *National and Regional Tourism Planning: Methodologies and Case Studies*. Routledge, London.

World Tourism Organization [WTO] (1995a) *Yearbook of Tourism Statistics* (47th edn). WTO, Madrid.

World Tourism Organization (1995b) *Compendium of Tourism Statistics 1989–1993* (15th edn). WTO, Madrid.

Yokeno, N. (1968) *La localisation de l'industrie touristique: application de l'analyse de Thünen-Weber*. Centre des Hautes Etudes Touristiques, Aix-en-Provence.

Zimmermann, E.W. (1933) *World resources and industries*. Harper and Brothers, New York.

Zimmermann, E.W. (1951) *World resources and industries* (2nd edn). Harper and Brothers, New York.

Zimmermann, G.R. (1990) Der Tourismus auf Bali in Indonesien. Zur Erklärung der Fremdenverkehrsstruktur in ihrer raum-zeitlichen Entwicklung. In: Institut für Tourismus, FU Berlin (ed.), *Tourismus in der Dritten Welt*. Verlag für Universitäre Kommunikation, Berlin, pp. 103–22.

Zinder, H. (1969) *The Future of Tourism in the Eastern Caribbean*. Zinder & Associates, Washington.

Index

Accommodation development 60
  see also Hotel location
Africa 9, 148–9
AIDS 140–1, 143, 10
  see also Social impacts
Airlines 19, 22–3, 133–4
  price structure 86
  routes 85–6
  see also Transportation network
Airport 50
  see also Infrastructure
Algeria 90, 150
Alternative tourism 13
  see also Tourist types
American Samoa 87
Antigua *95, 115*
Architecture 122–3
Argentina *11, 49, 89, 91, 110*
Aruba *49, 95*
Attractions 79, 82, 107–8
  see also Resources

Backpackers 42, 154–5
  see also Tourist types
Bahamas 8, *11, 49,* 50, 60, 95, *115*
Bahrain *11*
Balance of payments 16, 20,
  109–10, 148
  see also Economic impact
Bangladesh *95*
Bali 7, 20, 39, 59, 112, 119, 130–1
  see also Indonesia
Barbados *49*
Barbuda *95*
Bermuda *49,* 60, *115*
Bhutan 1, *95*
Bonaire *102*
Boycott 26
  see also Government involvement
Brazil 6, *11, 49,* 85, *91, 102, 110,*
  119
British Virgin Islands *49, 112*
Brunei 81
Business travel 135, 142
  see also Tourist types
Buying power 3

Cambodia 81
Canada 6
Capital City Index 48
  see also Indices, Spatial evolution
Caribbean 1, 8–11, 38, 48, *49,* 59,
  82, 148, 154
Carrying capacity 123–4
  see also Environmental impact
Central America 2, 6, 7, *49,* 149
  see also El Salvador, Guatemala,
  Latin America, Mexico,
  Panama
Central Business District (CBD)
  63–4, 72–8
  see also Resort development
Chile *11, 49, 91, 95, 110*
China 6, *11,* 27, 88, *89, 95, 110,*
  147, 150
Chinatown 72–8
  see also Resort development
Coastal tourism 54
  see also Tourism destination
  development
Cohort effects 98
Comoros *95*
Concentration Index 93–4
  see also Indices, Spatial
  evolution
Convention travel 136, 142, 153–4
  see also Tourist types
Cook Islands 87, *115*
Costa Rica *49, 95, 102*
Country Potential Generation Index
  94–5
  see also Indices
Crime 85, 118
  see also Social impacts
Cuba 8, 21, 27, *49,* 60, 86, 151
Cultural impacts 117, 119–20
  see also Impacts
Cyprus *11,* 26, *95, 115*

Data availability 6
Defert's Index 46–7
  see also Indices
Demonstration effect 117–18

  see also Economic impact, Social
  impact
Departure tax 86
  see also Government
  involvement
Dependency paradigm 13, 39–42
  see also Development paradigm,
  Sectoral paradigm
Destination
  attractiveness 107–9
  choice 83–4
  evaluation 66–9
  familiarity 104–5
  image formation 130
  life cycle 36–7, 56–70
  perception 84
Developing countries
  definition 4–5
  see also Least developed
  countries
Development
  concentration 49–50
  dispersal 49–50
  guidelines 50
  models 35
  paradigm 13, 35–42
  objectives 152
  plan 50
  policy 50, 56
  process 3
  stage 3
Diffusionist paradigm 36–9
  see also Development paradigm,
  Sectoral paradigm
Disposable income 147–8
Domestic tourism 82–3
Dominica *49*
Dominican Republic *11, 49,* 65,
  115, 119
Drifters 42
  see also Backpackers, Tourist
  types

East Asia/Pacific 8–9, 147
Economic
  development 16

Economic *continued*
  impact 16, 109–17
  integration 154
Economies of scale 50
Educational travel 80–2, 86
  see also Tourist types
Egypt 7, 11, 80, *110, 115*, 148, 150
El Salvador 6, *49*
Embargo 26, 86
  see also Government involvement
Employment 111–12, 114
  see also Economic impact
Enclavic structure 40–2
  see also Spatial evolution
Environmental impacts 120–4
  see also Impacts
Exchange rate 20–2
  see also Economic impact

Familiarization trip 145
Family life cycle 98–9, 148
Fiji 39, 87, *95*, 150
France outbound 89–90, *102*
Foreign exchange earnings 109–10,
  141
  see also Economic impact
Formal sector 43–6, 65–7
  see also Informal sector, Sectoral
    paradigm
Future development 146–56

Generation effects 98
German outbound travel 23, 80, 87,
  102–5
  see also Outbound travel
Ghana 27
Government
  incentives 18, 110–11
  involvement 17–23
  ventures 21
Guatemala *49, 112*
Gulf of Mexico 61
  see also Central America
Guyana *49*

Haiti *49*
Handicrafts 120
  see also Cultural impacts
Health
  issues 148–51
  tourism 82, 150–1
Hill resort 58–9, 106
  see also Resort development
Holiday entitlement 147–8
Hong Kong 5, *11*, 26–7, 88, *96*,
  100, *115*, 117
Hotel location 53–4, 72–8
  see also Resort development

Human Development Index 3
Human resources 33
  see also Economic impact

Image 84–5, 129–31
  see also Destination
    attractiveness, Destination
    image formation
Impacts 106–24, 153–6
  see also Cultural impact,
    Economic impact,
    Environmental impact, Social
    impact
Importance-performance analysis
  109
Import propensity 114
  see also Leakages
Incentive travel 135
  see also Tourist types
Income 110, 114–17, 141
  see also Economic impact
India *11*, 21, 23, 48, 92, *102, 110,
  149*, 150
Indices 46–9, 67–9, 93–7
Indonesia 7, *11*, 12, 20, 50, 80, 81,
  83, *89, 95, 102*, 147
  see also Bali
Inflation 17, 113
  see also Economic impact
Informal sector 3, 43–6, 65–7
  see also Formal sector, Sectoral
    paradigm
Infrastructure 20–1, 34, 49–50, 81,
  110–11, 133–4
Intranational demand 91–7
Investment policy 20–2, 34, 141,
  155
  see also Government incentives,
    Development policy
Iran *149*
Iraq *149*
Ireland 5, 26
Italy outbound 89–90

Jamaica *102, 112, 115*, 120
Japan outbound 87–8, *102*, 147
Jordan *96*
Journalist 135

Kenya 24, *95, 102, 112*, 119, 150
Kiribati *115*
Korea, Rep. of 11, 26, 88, *89, 110*,
  117, 119, 128, 131, 147, 153
Kuala Lumpur 64, 71–8
  see also Malaysia
Kuwait *96*

Landscape evaluation 107–9

  see also Resource evaluation,
    Destination attractiveness
Laos 1, 81
Latin America 6, 9–11, 48–9, 90
  see also Central America, South
    America
Leakages 91, 114–16, 152, 155
  see also Mulitplier effect, Import
    propensity
Least developed countries 4
  see also Developing countries
    definition
Lebanon *96*
Legal environment 128
Leisure time 128
Length of stay 95
Life expectancy 17
Literacy 17

Macau *11*, 27, 100
Malaysia *11*, 19, 21–2, 47, 59, 64,
  68–9, 71–8, 81, 87, *89*, 90–7,
  100, 106, *110*, 113, 147
Maldives *95, 102*
Market
  dependency 113
  mix 137
Marketing 140–5
  plan 138
  strategies 144–5
Martinique *49*
Mauritius 39, 52–5, *115*
Mexico 1, 5–7, *11*, 12, *49*, 61, 82,
  85, 89, *96, 110, 112*
Microstates 1, 17
Middle East 5, 9
Morocco 1, 7, 11, 12, 82, 86, 90, 95,
  102, 110
Motivation 79–80, 84
Multinational corporations 114
  see also Economic impact
Multiplier effect 39, 41, 114–16,
  152, 155
  see also Economic impact,
    Leakages
Myanmar 23, 81, 86

National tourism organization
  (NTO) 18–20, 101, 129–32
  see also Government
    involvement
Nepal *102*, 111, 113, 120, *149*
New Caledonia 23
Newly industrialized
  economies 5
  see also Developing countries
    definition
Outbound travel 88–90, 147

Outbound travel *continued*
  see also France outbound,
    German outbound, Italy
    outbound, Japan outbound, UK
    outbound
Ownership 32, 43–4, 114
  see also Economic impact

Package tour 80–2
  see also Tourist types
Pakistan *149*, 150
Panama *49*
Papua New Guinea *115*
Paraguay *49*
Peripheral areas 21
  see also Regional development
Period effects 98
Peru *49*, 80, *91*, *102*, *112*, 150
Philippines *11*, 19, 20, 23, *49*, 81,
  90, 119, 150, 153
Plantation model 38, 52–5
  see also Development model,
    Spatial evolution
Political
  environment 128
  stability 148–50
Population pressure 5, 17
Portugal 5
Promotion 81
Prostitution 118–19
Puerto Rico *11*, *49*, *110*, *112*
Purchasing power parity 3

Quality of life 4
Quality tourism 146, 151–5
Quasi states 26

Recreational Business District
  (RBD) 61, 63
  see also Resort development
Regional
  conflicts 149–50
  development 35–51, 91, 116,
    152
  disparities 3, 40
  impact 154
Religious travel 86
  see also Tourist types
Repeat visitation 104
Resort
  development 56–66
  typology 56, 69
Resources
  evaluation 106–9
  inventory 107
  limitation 151
Rural tourism 49–50
Russia 6

Safety 148–50
  see also Social impact
St. Lucia *49*
Sales
  department 136–7
  plan 137–8
Seaside resort 59–62
  see also Resort development
Seasonality 112–13
  see also Economic impact
Second homes 61
  see also Tourism destination
    development
Sectoral paradigm 13, 42–6
  see also Formal sector, Informal
    Sector
Seychelles *102*, *115*, 116
Sex tourism 18–19
  see also Social impact
Shopping 75–8
  see also Motivation
Short break 148
Singapore *11*, 19, 22, 81, 88, *89*, *96*,
  100, *110*, 114–15, 153
Social impacts 117–19
  see also Impacts
South America 2, 22, 49, 90–1,
  149
  see also Argentina, Brazil, Chile,
    Colombia, Latin America,
    Venezuela
South Asia 9, 58
  see also Bhutan, India, Maldives,
    Nepal, Pakistan, Sri Lanka
South East Asia 2, 21, 58–9, 64–5,
  81, 90, 92, 120
  see also Cambodia, Indonesia,
    Laos, Malaysia, Myanmar,
    Philippines, Singapore,
    Thailand, Vietnam
South Pacific 22
  see also Fiji, Microstates, Tahiti,
    Tonga, Vanuatu
Spatial evolution 44–6, 53–4, 60
  see also Destination life cycle,
    Resort development, Tourism
    destination development
Special interest tourism 135–6
  see also Tourist types
Sri Lanka *102*, *110*, *112*
Statistics 81, 100–1
Strip development 63
  see also Resort development

Tahiti 87
Tanzania 86
Taiwan *11*, 26, 88, *89*, *96*, *110*, 128
Tax reduction 21

  see also Government incentives
Technological environment 127–8
Thailand *11*, 19, 23, 50, 59, 62, 65,
  81, *89*, *95*, *102*, *110*, 117, 119,
  132, 140–5, 147, 153
The Gambia 112
Thünen-Weber model 63
  see also Spatial evolution,
    Tourism destination
    development
Tonga 87, *95*, *102*, 115
Tourism
  demand 79–101
  destination development 56–66
  development 52–4
  development plan 18–20
  enclaves 40
  history 7–8
  intensity 46–8
  marketing 18, 126–38, 140–5
  planning 107
  policy 50, 81
  research 12–13
  space model 37–8, 41, 45
Tourism Intensity Index 48
  see also Indices
Tourist
  definition 5–6
  expenditure 151–2
  flow 92–4
  flow bias 92
  psychographics 58, 97
  spending 116–17, 154
  types 97–8, 116, 151, 154
  typology 96–7
Tour operator 23–5, 134
Transnational structure 25
  see also Multinational
    corporations, Vertical
    integration
Transportation network 50, 62,
  85
Travel
  account 148
  agents 134
  barrier 85–6
  behaviour 147
  experience 98–9, 146
  inertia 104–5
  itinerary 86–8
  itinerary model 88
  life cycle 98–9, 146
  purpose 79
  writers 135
Travel Dispersal Index 95–7
Trekking 113
  see also Tourist types
Trendsetter 155

Trip Index 67–9
Tunisia 1, *11*, 23, 82, 90, *102*, *110*,
    112
Turkey *11*, 21, 83, 85, *96*, 103, *110*,
    112, *115*, 150

United Kingdom outbound *89*, 90,
    102
United States 6, *89*, *102*
U.S. Virgin Islands 150
Urban tourism 62–5
    see also Resort development
Uruguay 7–8, *49*, *91*

Vanuatu *115*

Vegetation 122
    see also Environmental impact
Venezuela *49*, *89*, *91*, *95*, *102*
Vertical integration 24, 114
Vietnam 1, 19, 27, 29–34, 81, 86
Violence 85
    see also Crime, Social impacts
Visa regulation 22–3
    see also Government
        involvement
Visiting friends and relatives (vfr)
    82
    see also Tourist types
Water
    conflict 122

usage and pollution 121
    see also Environmental impact
Western Samoa 87
West Indies 8
    see also Caribbean
Wholesalers 134
    see also Tour operator
Wildlife 122
    see also Environmental impact
World tourism
    arrivals 8–9
    receipts 8

Yield management 137